Y0-CBC-219

6/21

COVERED & KEPT

THE TEARING BETWEEN TWO WORLDS

THE KAREN JOHNSON STORY

AUTHOR KAREN R. JOHNSON

For there is nothing covered that will not be revealed; and hidden, that will not be known.

(Matthew 10:26)

PRESS

Copyright © 2011 by Karen Johnson

Covered & Kept
The Tearing Between Two Worlds
by Karen Johnson

Printed in the United States of America

ISBN 9781612155876

All rights reserved solely by the author. The author guaran-
tees all contents are original and do not infringe upon the legal
rights of any other person or work. No part of this book may be
reproduced in any form without the permission of the author.
The views expressed in this book are not necessarily those of
the publisher.

Unless otherwise indicated, Bible quotations are taken from
The New King James Version. Copyright © 1979, 1980, 1982 by
Thomas Nelson, Inc. Used by permission; and The Holy Bible,
King James Version, KJV.

www.xulonpress.com

Alicia—

I hope this book brings
you to a place where God
can say well done my
good and faithful servant!
"May your name be inscribed
in the book of life."

Psalms 91:4

Love
Kara Johnson

Dedication

To my Mom and best friend, Venetta Gardner, who has loved and nurtured me unconditionally through the good and the bad. She has cheered, consoled, and encouraged me to become strong and resilient in the face of adversity, making me the woman I am today.

I would also like to dedicate this book to my one and only precious son, Tristan, who has had a great attitude about me sharing our lives with the rest of the world and understands the significance of this project. I couldn't have asked for a better or more loving son. You have grown up with me and grown into a very ambitious, talented young man whom I love very dearly.

To my spiritual mom, Virginia, who discipled me, taught me about the love of Christ, and saw something in me to the extent that—years ago—she suggested I write a book about my life. I thought I wasn't worthy and doubted that anyone would care to read about my testimony.

To Esmie Branner and her husband Arthur who counseled us and discipled me. Your acts of kindness and mercy have spoken volumes to me especially in my darkest hours and have created a special bond between us.

To my precious siblings whom I love very much: Patricia, Cherryl, Ronnie and my twin sister Kathie. I want to say thank you for supporting me while allowing me to be Karen and coming along side me when I needed your strength and guidance especially in my darkest hour.

To my favorite Auntie, "Aunt Dean" who stepped in for me when my reputation and character was being assassinated and so lovingly helped out where ever needed during the most trying time in my life.

But most importantly, I dedicate this book to my Heavenly Father whom I love because He first loved me. He revealed Himself to me in a very powerful way when one Saturday night my "so called" perfect little world came crashing down. And when I didn't know if I could pick myself up, He fought my battles. When I had no strength and was gripped with fear, He gave me courage. And when the enemy was encamped all around me, He calmed and protected me. He blessed me with a newfound faith.

For I am persuaded, that neither death, nor life, nor angels, nor principalities, nor powers, nor things present, nor things to come, nor height, nor depth, nor any other creature, shall be able to separate us from the love of God, which is in Christ Jesus our Lord. (Romans 8:38, 39 KJV)

Acknowledgments

Covered & Kept was inspired over four and a half years ago, when God planted in my spirit the urge to create a book about my life's journey after experiencing one of the most ghastly trials ever waged against me. Two weeks after my husband's horrifying death, I was quickened by the Holy Spirit to step out in faith and pour my heart and energies into this book. Once the manuscript was finished I asked the Lord how I was going to afford to get the book published. The Holy Spirit impressed upon my heart to tell anyone who was within earshot about my predicament. One day while training, I mentioned to my girl friend Felicia my need for financial support. Without hesitation she suggested I seek donations by writing a letter to family and friends telling them about my inspired book. She offered to donate to the project herself. I owe my gratitude to all my family, friends and organizations whose financial support and belief in me has made the publishing of this book a reality.

Friends and Family:

    Tristan Gardner

    Venetta, Patricia, Ronald and Cherryl Gardner

    Brandon Foster

    Bob and Gloria Stiner

    Elder Leon Jones

    Mr. & Mrs. Michael Merriweather

    Felicia Byrd

    Howard Redmond

    Marion Jones

    Patsy Calloway

    John Savage

    Dee, Charles, Riley and Angela Thomas

    Della Moultry

    Mr. & Mrs. Ervin Hunt

    Jack Barnett

    Mr. & Mrs. Danyell and Mitchell Fusilier

    Lucille Washington

    Denise Richardson

    Mr. & Mrs. Randy Williams

    Otasowie Uyigue

    Mr. & Mrs. Damon Washington

    Mr. & Mrs. Byrd

    Tonji Smith

    Yvonne Hayden

    Pastor Ivan & Kathleen Williams

    Tyrone Anderson

Marcellus and Sylvia Combs

Ms. Karone Jackson

Pastor Reginald & Lashawn Horton

Dr. Richard Lynton

Andrew Rachal

Adrian Gardner

Sam Gulley

Organizations

Sacramento Southgate SDA

The Gospel Vine.com

Saint Paul Baptist Church

Young Ladies Ministry – "Another Level" – Capitol City

SDA Church

Mr. & Mrs. Gary Henson – Businesscoach.com

Mr. & Mrs. Tom Pooler – T.R.P. Construction

Allen Wayne Warren – New Faze Development

Keith Johnson – Praise Break

Leading The Way Men's Ministry

Jeff Clanagan – Code Black Entertainment

Ask and it will be given to you, seek, and you will find; knock, and it will be opened to you. For everyone who asks receives, and he who seeks finds, and to him who knocks it will be opened. (Matthew 7:7-8)

Table of Contents

Introduction

Why this book came about...

Today, I strongly believe we are living in the most solemn period of earth's history, at the end of time and Jesus is coming back soon. We are experiencing firsthand men committing some of the vilest crimes against each other. Wars, pestilence, famine, divorce, gluttony, intemperance and moral decay are raging all around us. The fate of many is being decided, and events of vital importance are taking place everywhere. The event that has been so long doubted by the multitudes is rapidly approaching and we must be ready to meet Jesus. (Ellen G. White, "The Great Controversy")

First, I applaud you who dare to read this riveting story, for you will be enthralled as it takes you on a roller-coaster ride, uncovering many of the deep dark secrets that people struggle with daily. It is only by God's grace that we can be transformed and saved.

Secondly, it is important to understand that there are two powers working in the world today—good and evil; however, it hasn't always been that way.

In the beginning, man was created in the perfect image of God and placed in the Garden of Eden. While in the Garden, man was without sin, privileged to talk with God and the holy angels face to face. It wasn't until, by disobedience, sin entered, severing this special relationship and making man susceptible to death and degradation. Man was no longer permitted to look upon the wonderful glory of God, or to live in paradise in His presence. Though man, in his sinful state, could no longer enjoy such a close bond with his maker, God still loved and chose to die on our behalf. God's nature is love; God's law is love. It has always been and it will always be!

For God so loved the world that He gave His only begotten Son, that whoever believes in Him should not perish but have everlasting life. (John 3:16)

Your journey unfolds as I attempt to help you understand how my early life, my deliverance and my walk as a Christian woman led me to the evening of March 25, 2006. I write this book, not for selfish gain, but because those who stood by me (my dear mother, sisters, pastor Ivan Williams, spiritual mom, and close friends) urged me to share how God's faithfulness sustained me as the war between good and evil unfolded in my life when death came knocking near my door. My purpose for sharing my story isn't to condemn anyone but to illustrate first hand how faithful and true God is. His word edifies, encourages, and points us to Jesus Christ, letting us know that—if we put our faith in Him, even though the storm is raging all around us—God will prevail because He is in control. He tells us that He will never leave us nor forsake us and this book attests to that.

In Matthew 24:24, the Bible makes it very clear that Satan's supreme goal is to deceive us, for it says that, if possible, even the elect will be deceived. I praise God that even during my wilderness experience; He provided the guidance I needed to reach the other side. God revealed the battle raging all around me and how even when I was in the fire (like the three Hebrew boys[1]), Christ was right there in the fire with me. The Holy Spirit brought conviction upon my heart to tell my story and help others who may feel they are battling alone in the wilderness. In the four and a half years I have been compiling this book, I have grown even closer to Jesus. Through my tears and dealing with my fears, I have learned to praise, study, worship, pray and meditate on Him and His word.

---

[1] See Daniel 3:16-26

Do you know Christ? Are you ready to walk with Him? If not, I hope this book will prick your heart to search the scriptures for **truth** and commit your life to stand on the rock of Jesus Christ.

And we know that all things work together for good to those who love God, to those who are the called according to His purpose. For whom he foreknew, He also predestined to be conformed to the image of His Son, that He might be the firstborn among many brethren. Moreover whom He predestined, these He also called; whom He called, these He also justified; and whom He justified, these He also glorified. (Romans 8:28-30)

It wasn't until I continued to meditate on this passage of scripture that things began to come into full focus to help me understand this "Great Controversy" between good and evil.

Chapter One

Divine Day

S tartled awake from a deep sleep, I rolled over and quickly answered the phone.

"Why didn't you call me? Why did you let me oversleep?" It was my husband, Jon.

Unaware of the time, I responded, "Because I'm so tired. I hardly got any sleep worrying about you and Tristan."

When I mentioned our 17-year-old son, Tristan, Jon asked if he had a good time at his senior prom. He chuckled at my affirming response and affectionately declared he would be home shortly.

Now opening my eyes, I realized it was nine a.m. Jon should have been home hours ago and getting ready for church like he promised. He heard the disappointment in my voice, so he apologetically assured me that he was indeed leaving the television station. Knowing the bay area traffic, my instincts told me he wouldn't make it home in time; and, once again, we would miss our time of worship together. I decided not to make a fuss and told him to drive home safely.

Wide awake now, I decided to stay home and engage myself in solitary worship. Two things I knew for certain. Jon was not going to make it home in time and Tristan was still asleep. I rolled out of bed, jumped into my tan sweat suit and house shoes and made my way down stairs to get a bite to eat. After my simple meal, I settled on the couch in the family room to read my Bible and watch my favorite Bible movie.

Between anxiously waiting for Jon and dozing through my movie, the day seemed to pass slowly. Each time I woke up, I glanced at the clock in the kitchen to check the time. Where was Jon? When I tried to call him, he was not available. He promised to be home by nine a.m. and now it was one o'clock in the afternoon. Just as I began to feel a little upset, the phone rang. Jon was in great spirits!

"What are you doing, Karen?" Jon asked in his country boy voice, the way he always talked to me when he was in a playful mood.

I told him that I was watching a Bible movie and waiting for him. Jon said he was almost home and asked me if I had fixed something to eat. I hadn't cooked but I didn't want to change his mood by telling him that. More importantly, I didn't want him to stop and purchase something to eat, so I assured him that food would be prepared by the time he got home.

Although we had missed our time together at Church, I didn't want to miss that special lunch we always had after Church. So I gathered up some energy, got off the couch and went into the kitchen.

Just as everything in the kitchen was ready, Jon walked through the door. I hadn't even heard the chirp of our security system, so I hadn't anticipated his silent approach. As usual, he tip-toed in and his tall brown frame closed in on me. As I looked at him, I thought, "You are so fine!" I felt so blessed to have Jon as my husband.

Inspecting my hair, Jon circled around me, then stepped away to observe from a distance—my first hair weave. Uneasy with the silence, I asked him if he liked it.

Nodding, he said, "I like it!"

Those words made my day! Mr. Johnson liked it and that compliment from him made me feel *so* good. I walked up to him and we embraced. Jon, the "man's man," loved to have his woman soft and affectionate toward him. Out of the two of us I was the more affectionate one. I like to hug and kiss, hold hands and spend quality time together. I would always try to avoid arguments realizing long ago that life was too short to waste it arguing. Due to our busy schedules and the nature of his work, I wanted to savor each moment of the little time we had together and keep the peace.

Up and dressed, Tristan could hardly wait to see his dad and tell him all about his senior prom. Jon greeted Tristan cheerfully as he came downstairs.

"Chocolate Man! How was your prom?"

Tristan smiled and gave his dad a few details of the evening before. After thanking him for making it possible, he ran back upstairs to his room. Jon was so proud of our quiet, introverted son as he overcame his shyness and mustered up enough courage to ask a girl out on a date…his first date ever. Seeing and hearing Jon and Tristan's exchange was male bonding at its finest. Everything seemed so perfect and for the first time in five and a half years, I felt that our blended family was finally on one accord.

Shortly after Jon finished his meal, I put his plate in the dishwasher and walked over to sit beside him on the couch. I was in need of some "us time" since I had not seen him in four days. A man of few words, Jon didn't like to banter. After our small talk, he began making suggestions about how we could spend our evening. He asked me to call my brother Ronnie to see if he would be available to visit, but Ronnie had already returned home to San Jose.

Jon then suggested we stay home, cook dinner and invite my niece, Ameerah, and her kids over for dinner. I liked the idea, but I knew that Ameerah and her boy friend Hassan would be having his family over for dinner and suggested that we stop by to see them instead. Not wanting to intrude on Ameerah's plans, Jon decided to call so he could speak with his favorite great niece, eight-year-old LaRay, and great nephew, five-year-old Evian. Ameerah answered Jon's call then put the kids on the phone. There were no long conversations; but before hanging up, Uncle Jon said, "I love you" to each of them. Hearing the exchange end with each child saying, "I love you, too, Uncle Jon," was so endearing to me.

After Jon had spoken with Evian and LaRay, he announced that he was going upstairs to take a nap. My intent was to join him, but because I wanted to finish watching my Bible movie, I stayed downstairs quickly drifting off to sleep. Awakened by the sound of my cell phone, I almost didn't answer it until I noticed it was Jon calling me from upstairs.

A big smile warmed me as I said, "Hello."

His sexy baritone voice on the other end asked me what I was doing and invited me to come upstairs to lay with him. Being separated from him for four days, my body desperately craved his attention and affection. I wanted very much to make love to my husband but because he made me wait, I decided to "return the favor." I laid on the couch a little while longer before turning off the TV and bounding up the stairs to join him.

The Breeze and Bright Light

Our bedroom has two sets of double doors for entry. The first set is off the hallway and the second is adjacent to our office. Making my way to our bedroom, I quietly tip-toed to the double doors off of the office and paused for a moment. The house was as still as the night. When I slowly opened the double doors and stepped forward, I felt almost paralyzed as a very strange feeling came over me. It was a calming feeling but for a brief moment it was uncomfortable, and eerie. A cool, fresh breeze gently flowed through and brushed my skin, as a ray of light engulfed the room.

On the one hand, it was romantic to see my sexy husband, lying there on his side facing the window and wearing only the bottoms of the silk pajamas I had given him for Father's Day. He was pretending to be asleep and resting peacefully. I stood by, savoring the moment. On the other hand, I felt uneasy as I watched him "in his element." During an earlier process of decorating our bedroom, he had fastened a canopy drape to our large, king-sized bed. Seeing him lying there under the drape accentuated and heightened the mood while the feeling of the fresh, spring breeze and the ray of light seemed divinely unreal.

Jon was a very busy man who didn't require a lot of sleep. Since he had taken the new freelance job at Channel 2 in

Oakland, he would often stay over in Oakland. On this day, not only was he home, but it seemed that he was "*perfectly* at home."

Returning to reality, I noticed how cold the room was. I've always been sensitive to the cold, but this coldness was chilling and it made me uneasy. Looking back I now believe it was a supernatural experience.

Feeling creepy about the ambiance and the uneasiness in my spirit, I abruptly broke the silence with, "Why do you have the window opened so wide? It's cold in here!"

Jon calmly responded, "Because it feels so good."

Hot-natured, Jon enjoyed the cold air that permeated our room. On the other hand, I like the heat so I quickly shed my sweats and nestled into bed beside him, snuggling close for his body heat. Our tender embracing evolved into silent love-making. Our movement ebbed and flowed into rhythm not to be spoiled by my thoughts. Afterwards, Jon rose up over me and tenderly gazed into my eyes, as if he was looking right through me, but he said nothing. How I wished I could read his mind. What was he thinking? Whether it was an odd moment of silent perfection or a perfect moment of odd silence, I dared not spoil it, so I simply gazed back into his eyes and smiled. Without breaking the silence, Jon rolled over to catch a few winks.

Lying next to him, I whispered, "Honey, I want you to be home more often. I'd like for us to get our weekly date nights back."

He politely agreed to both. Although I was happy with our exchange and his willingness to make some changes to spend more time with the family, I admit that I was quite surprised when he didn't put up a fuss. Often when I try to have a conversation about him being away too much, he gets angry and starts an argument. It was as if this man lying next to me was not my husband, Mr. Johnny Ray Johnson, but a stranger impersonating him. It was indeed peculiar, but nice.

Showered and dressed after our brief nap, Jon's attention was captured by something he saw outside.

"Wow, that tree has really grown," he mused as he stood at the window near his side of our bed.

Now, I was definitely convinced this man must be an imposter, because the remark struck me as being quite strange. Jon was always so busy, so matter of fact. It seemed that he never had time to "stop and smell the roses."

"You've only been gone four days; not four years," I wanted to say aloud, but held my tongue except to agree that, indeed, the tree had grown.

Suddenly, the mood was broken and Jon was in the office and on the phone again. Hoping to speak to my nephew's children, he punched in their cell number and Zuzana, my nephew's wife answered. She said she was on her way to work and told Jon the kids were at home. Jon and Zuzana made small-talk and then he put me on the phone and I did the same.

Getting back to our plans for the evening, Jon shared with me his idea to hang out with his friend, Dwayne, before going to work.

"I'm going with you," I said as I jumped into the shower, submitting to his direction to get dressed.

I didn't want our time together to end so soon. As the water showered over me, I could hear Jon making other phone calls. He left one message for his cousin, LaRay, and another for Dwayne, letting him know I would be joining them.

Sporting my new hairdo, I wondered what should I wear on this cool evening? I wanted to look nice for my husband on our date night, so I decided on my jean pantsuit (the one he bought me for Christmas), a green turtleneck shirt and boots. Excited and ready to go on our date night, I suggested we stop at some restaurant and grab a bite to eat before heading to Dwayne's house.

First Things First

Tristan and D'Artagnan, one of his good buddies, were also on their way out for a bite to eat, but Jon –being the jock and an all-around athlete—wanted to give Tristan some coaching tips for his upcoming track meet. He often encouraged Tristan and his brother, Tray—both of whom were slow starters and not very aggressive about life in general, to do their best in their studies, sporting events, and to just win at life. Jon asked Tristan to promise he would give his all at his upcoming track meet. Jon assured Tristan that he was very capable and just as deserving as the next person. Tristan listened and promised his dad he would try harder.

Just before the boys went on their way, I felt the nudging of the Holy Spirit to pray together as we closed this beautiful day out. But not wanting to make D'Artagnan uncomfortable and realizing the boys seemed anxious to get out, I hushed the wooing of the Holy Spirit speaking to me. My instinct told me Jon might overrule me anyway, saying I often prayed too long and tell me to let the boys go. Not wanting to create any tension in front of the boys, I didn't say a word as the boys left the house.

I lingered behind Jon as we went into the garage and after he opened the garage door, he headed for my car instead of his truck. I paused for a moment, surprised at his gentle request that I drive. On one hand I wanted him to drive because it was our "date night." Then I thought about the long drive he had ahead of him back to Oakland and that he would be driving his news van all morning, so I agreed to drive. We jumped into my car and headed off for a night of food, family, fun and friends.

As I began to drive, my mind raced, trying to select a cozy but not-too-expensive restaurant. After all, we were on a date; not just hanging out. I wanted a different experience, new scenery and a place where we could get in and out quickly. I wanted to choose a restaurant that my husband would enjoy; someplace other than his favorite fast food Chinese eatery. I was in the driver's seat, and he was letting me decide.

Leaving our neighborhood, I proceeded to Bruceville Road and turned on to Laguna Boulevard where most of the popular restaurants are located. At Laguna Boulevard and Bruceville Road, we stopped at the red light. While Jon said nothing, I looked to the right at Friday's and almost suggested we go there but knew it would be crowded. I started to suggest going to Chili's but then I saw our son and his friend sitting in the lobby. I told Jon if we went there, the boys would think we were spying on them. We chuckled in agreement and kept going.

As we turned the corner Jon adjusted himself in his seat and said, "This is going to be a great year!"

I smiled, telling Jon I was happy to hear his positive words. As I continued driving I thought of the challenging financial hardships we had endured with both of us being self-employed and building our businesses. Being a blended family had also proved challenging though tonight, I felt at peace with the world.

To my left was a new restaurant, but I noticed a lot of cars in the parking lot, and wondered about their selection of vegetarian food. Silently, I drove on towards Highway 99 and just before we reached the next light, I spotted what seemed to be just the right place for us. Nestled in the back corner of a strip mall was another new restaurant—a sports bar and grill called, "Mandango's." After seeing the restaurant my mind flashed back to a conversation I had with a friend who said it was the new up and coming family restaurant in Elk Grove. I asked my husband if he wanted to go.

He replied, "What is that?"

When I told him it was a new sports restaurant, Jon asked, "Have you eaten there?"

"No," I told him, "but I've heard a lot about it."

"That's fine," Jon agreed.

I turned into the parking lot and parked on the opposite side of the restaurant, in front of the Asian Market. We walked across the dark parking lot, still damp from the huge downpour of rain the night before. As we entered the restaurant, I felt like we shouldn't be there for some reason, remembering that this day had been filled with spiritual themes. I couldn't help but focus on the sudden uneasiness in my spirit. I wanted to turn around and leave. The contrast of the day was very obvious.

People were eating, drinking and watching the Sacramento Kings play on the big screen TVs that were positioned all around the crowded, noisy restaurant. The music seemed to be playing at full blast, making me want to get out and find someplace quiet so we could have our quality time together. I began to wish I had driven directly to Jon's favorite Chinese place instead of seeking some place new.

But before I could voice my concerns to Jon, his attention had been captured by the Sacramento Kings' game. This was their night and I didn't want to selfishly spoil this opportunity for him to see his favorite team play. As we ordered our meals and ate in near silence, Jon's fixation on the game was only interrupted by the obnoxious woman seated next to us who's uncontrolled laugher trumped everything else making it obvious she had far exceeded her drinking limits. How I wanted to grasp Jon's undivided attention without ruining our special time together.

We were about halfway through our meal, when we suddenly realized how late it was getting. We still needed to stop by my Mom's house on the way to Dwayne's.

Jon didn't want to be late for work so he said, "Looks like we're not going to have time to go over to your Mom's house."

Typically, we would have celebrated Mom's birthday four days ago on March 21, but hadn't been able to because of

Jon's busy schedule. Determined to keep my commitment to my Mom, I hurried to get our waitress's attention for our bill.

Paid up and ready to go, I stood to my feet but Jon remained seated... not saying anything, and not looking at the game. He seemed to be in a world of his own just staring into nothingness. I found it interesting that five minutes earlier, he had been so concerned about the shortage of time. Now, no longer in any hurry, he seemed to be in some sort of a trance, as if he had gone inside himself. It appeared like he was having a supernatural experience, a still moment of contemplation such as I had never seen before. Hesitant to interrupt the moment and feeling as though something supernatural was forbidding me to, I solemnly waited. Strange as it seemed, in the middle of a noisy restaurant, Jon was in the midst of a private, secluded moment that I just couldn't interrupt.

Life, without Meaning

While I waited for Jon to come back from the "land of Oz," a twenty-eight year old man from the next county over was coming back from a totally different kind of land. Aaron Dunn had just completed another pointless day haunted by the same stressors that had become a part of his everyday life for as far back as he could remember. He had awakened that morning thinking death was his only escape from a life that was not only terribly painful but also apparently without meaning or purpose.

Unless the Lord builds the house, they labor in vain who build it; Unless the LORD guards the city, the watchman stays awake in vain. (Psalms 127:1)

Aaron was born into a family where the dysfunctions where typical of neglectful abuse. Drugs, sex, violence and alcohol now consumed Aaron's life. He was young, only 28 years old but far from innocent. Exposure to hostility, danger and emotional pain from an early age, Aaron's angry violent out bursts ultimately led to four years of lock up in the California Youth Authorities Facility.

His Mother, Sandra, a very homely looking lady, also had a history based on abuse and neglect. Raised by a single mom, Sandra had married a man who continued the pattern of abuse she had become so accustomed to. She had three children who were extremely difficult to manage since her husband had taught the children to have no respect for their mother. Poor Sandra was a passive, beaten down woman who had no respect for herself and just couldn't seem to get her own life together. She had no support from her abusive violent, drug abusing husband in bringing any kind of structure or discipline into their home. Her only sense of escape and peace from this chaotic home life was to find a job and stay at work as long as possible. While Sandra worked 10 hours a day at the Local Salvation Army thrift shop to support their family, her husband stayed home, did his drugs and tormented the children.

Aaron's father was so abusive that when he was not beating his wife, he would beat the children. Even if he didn't beat the kids himself, he got his kicks watching Aaron punch out his little brother. On many occasions, he even ordered the boys outside to fight the neighborhood kids. When Aaron was about 12, his dad brought home a prostitute which pushed Sandra over the edge. She left her children with her drug addicted monster of a husband who would often tie off his arm with a belt and shoot up heroin in front of them. When Sandra left so did his source of income so Aaron's father sold every piece of furniture they had to support his drug habit.

Aaron's father was a hopeless addict with no future for himself or his family. He was a crazed, obsessive and impulsive man, who cheated on his wife consistently with other men, as well as other women. He would drink himself mean and nasty; he had no conscience or heart, and even smoked crack cocaine with his youngest son. It's scary to imagine all that went on in that household.

To think anyone could survive such a childhood and go on to live a normal life would be asking too much. Aaron's father was later sentenced to prison for stealing from his elderly mother.

With his father often in a drunken stupor, Aaron had to grow up fast and often took on the father figure role for his two younger siblings. He taught his baby sister how to tie her shoes when she was a little girl and even in older years continued being a father figure to her. When she grew up and had her own children, he would babysit his nieces and nephews while she worked.

Aaron's Uncle Ernie was very much a part of his life, especially after his father went to prison. Uncle Ernie was the biggest drug dealer in the Marysville area and lived a life of drug use and drug dealing. With the exception of a grandfather who took Aaron to church from time to time as a little boy, Aaron grew up with two terrible male role models; his father and Uncle Ernie. Growing up in this environment led Aaron down a path of immorality, crime, hopelessness, pain, and later, death.

Sarah

Aaron met, fell in love with and married a fellow drug user named Sarah. Even though she experimented with drugs, she decided they both needed to get off of drugs when she gave birth to their daughter, who was the pride of Aaron's life. Aaron's life now had meaning and purpose. Sarah was a positive influence at times in his life when he needed it the most. After becoming a father, Aaron desired to provide for his family the best way he knew how. Unlike his father who did nothing but use drugs and alcohol, Aaron decided to work. He took a job as an electrician that required working long hours and unfortunately took him on the road and away from his young impressionable wife. Away from his wife and living in one hotel after another, his loneliness brought back the old struggles. After two years of marital bliss, the demons he had been exposed to as a child resurfaced and he started drinking in bars and sleeping with other women.

Suddenly, life was not so good and his brief season of marital bliss began fading fast. The harsh circumstances of life were negatively affecting this short lived fairytale and their relationship was on a downward spiral that neither of them seemed to be able to stop. Aaron's meth use was getting ridiculous, he lost his electrician's job and began to sell drugs for his uncle Ernie as a way to live and provide for his family. His heavy use of drugs made his life very inconsistent. As the arguments and fights intensified, a wall of distrust began building between them, so much so that they decided to become swingers. Aaron and Sarah agreed they could each have legitimate "friends" of the opposite sex outside the marital boundaries as long as the other knew about it.

This seemed to help for a while until Aaron began to have outbursts of violence and rage caused by his drug use. Sarah began to feel it wasn't safe to have him around their daughter and started to make other plans for her life with their daughter.

At first, she would move out then back in to try and patch up what was left of their relationship. As Sarah began to realize her marriage was irreparable, she became a convincing liar and a cheat. She started to contact men outside the swingers' ring they had established and not tell Aaron. She couldn't seem to make up her mind if she wanted to stay with her hopeless, drug using, drug dealing husband and work on her marriage or kick him out to the curb and start a new life without him. In search of something better, she began having affairs with men she'd met on the internet. One of these men happened to be a policeman.

Aaron had not only grown up with an utter hatred for policemen, but it turned out his father-in-law was a 25-year police veteran who disliked and despised the fact Sarah had married Aaron against his wishes. There was no love lost between Aaron and Sarah's father; the two hated each other. When Aaron found out his wife was seeing a "PIG" it took his drug abuse to a new level. All he could think of was "DEATH TO THEM." As things took a turn for the worst, Sarah decided to leave Aaron for this hated "PIG" officer.

As Sarah prepared to move them out, Aaron's daughter came to him and asked, "Daddy, are you still going to be my daddy, cause mommy said you're not, and I would have a new Daddy?"

Aaron was livid as the apple of his eye and the only thing he had to live for was now being taken from him.

Two Men – Two World's Collide

Aaron was tired of life, worn out by life's blows, so he desperately clung to the only things he had left; his drugs, his satanic Bible, and a stolen shot gun. He looked at his tattoo of the grim reaper and took off like a zombie to reap his harvest of blood. The day had come, March 25th 2006. Aaron was prepared to face his enemies and annihilate them for good. All the emotional pain he suffered throughout his young life was loaded into a gun; not an ordinary gun but a 12- gauge shotgun. Aaron knew an explosion was imminent and was ready to kiss life goodbye forever. But before he did, there was one last mission, one last thing that needed to be done; he had to say good-bye to those people in his life whom he felt deserved what would happen next.

Two men, from two different worlds with two different purposes were about to meet; a meeting that would change both their life paths forever. One loved life and had so much to live for while the other hated life with nothing to live for. One had just decided to make major changes in his life and marriage and was on a mission to soar to new unlimited heights while the other had decided to end his quest for life forever. When these two men met and their two worlds collided, the explosion would change the circumstances of life for everyone connected with each of them.

This "Divine Day" would cause me to stop and reflect upon the condition of my own life and begin seeking my own purpose for being alive. Before I share with you the results of the collision of the two worlds described in this chapter, I'll give you some background on what brought me to this point in my life. Bear with me as I take you on this journey back through my early years. I have discovered that each step of my life and all I experienced along the way not only led me to this "Divine Day," but also equipped me to move forward afterwards.

Chapter Two

Little Becomes Much

As I've reflected on my life's successes and failures, I've come to realize in a very painful way that my life hasn't always been a bed of roses. As I've tried to figure out who I am and sought to understand the divine plan and purpose for my life, I see it hasn't been such a bad life either. From the time I was a little girl, I've felt God had placed deep within me the desire and ability to make a profound difference in the lives of others. I have also come to understand that the greatest obstacle preventing me from growing into and achieving that purpose was me.

Like Dorothy, in my all-time favorite childhood movie, "The Wizard of Oz," it was my own choices that caused me to veer off course and often left me feeling lost as I sought to follow the yellow brick road. Confused about which path to take, not knowing who to trust in this twisted, wicked game of life, I've often found myself gripped with fear and plagued by doubt as I desperately tried to find my way. You see, I have always had a very trusting spirit and have often been called naive by my siblings and those closest to me. Endowed with a trusting heart, I suffered a lot of heartache along the way until I realized I needed God's divine guidance. Without a relationship with God, my trusting heart interfered with the divine purpose and anointing He had placed on my life from birth.

I once read, "God gives you life. What you do with your life is your gift to God." It has taken me 46 years to understand this great calling on my life and accept the new journey God has put before me. I now see life as an awesome privilege and it has made me more determined to write this book and share my story with you.

Flash Back

My sister and I were the last born and the second set of twins out of the six children born to Venetta and Hershel Gardner. I was a proud "military brat," born in Taipei, Taiwan but raised in sunny San Jose, California. However, my roots were in the South. My father was born and raised in the small town of Selmer, Tennessee. A town even many Tennesseans have never heard of. My mother was born and raised in Dallas, Texas. Both of my parents came from large families.

My father fought in World War II and in the Korean War. In 1963, my family returned to the United States from Taiwan. My Dad was stationed in Southern California at George Air Force Base, where we lived in military housing until he retired, after serving his country for 21 years.

Growing up in a house full of children was fun, but very challenging. As the youngest, my twin and I had to learn to fight. My twin sister fought with her fist and I fought with my mouth. I was a coward in the neighborhood but stood up to my brothers and sisters knowing I had a safety net within the family unit. I spoke my mind when necessary and tattled on my siblings when they broke the rules. I guess, at times, my twin sister felt betrayed because I tattled on her whether she fought my battles for me or not. Young, naive and having a reverential fear of my parents, wrong was wrong and I was going to make it known.

What I loved about being a twin, though, was that I didn't have to earn the affection of my sister. I had a friend for life which, since we were both shy, worked to our advantage in the earlier stages of our development. However, as the family talebearer, my siblings resented me and when my parents weren't around I was ridiculed, made fun of, bullied, and even wrongly spanked by my older sister who babysat during my parents' absences. Sometimes my siblings made fun of me and twisted my middle name, "Renee," branding me "Nee Nee" after a girl with special needs who lived across the street.

My First Near-death Encounter

It's not typical for children to have memories going back to the age of three but I distinctly recall my first near-death encounter as if it happened only yesterday. At the time I didn't know death was knocking at my door but my sweet mother did; and to this day, she reminds me just how gravely ill I was.

We were living in military housing on George Air Force Base in Southern California on this windy, fall day in 1963. My twin sister, Kathie and I were playing our hearts out and exploring the yard when we discovered some delicious-looking round red berries. We started plucking them off the bush and eating them. They didn't really taste like fruit, but I dropped them in a cup of water and kept eating and drinking them, not knowing I was filling my belly with many little *poisonous* berries.

After playing outside all day, I went inside and approached my mother asking for a bite of her chicken. As she denied me a bite of her food, she became concerned with something about my neck and alerted my dad saying we needed to go to the hospital. The doctor ran a few tests, assured my parents that nothing was wrong with me, other than a fever due to the common cold. We returned home but as the hours of the night passed, my mother kept a close watch over me and noticed that my neck was getting tighter and tighter.

When I became listless and not my usual self, my father also grew very concerned and encouraged my mother to take me back to the hospital while he finished preparing for work. My mother tells the story how, on the second trip to the hospital, a young doctor attended to me and became concerned the minute he laid eyes on me.

He was familiar with my symptoms, immediately ran some tests and discovered I had a very severe case of spinal meningitis. I was immediately admitted into the hospital and remained there until my disease was cured. According to the doctor, my illness was so serious that, if I had not returned to the hospital, I would not have lived through the night.

Aren't you glad for the watchful care God places over His little children when they don't even know He's there?

For He shall give His angels charge over you to keep you in all your ways.

(Psalm 91:11)

The Gardner Family

I was six years old when my father retired and we moved to San Jose, California where I grew up in a traditional yet relatively sheltered home. I admired my father very much experiencing firsthand the love and care he had for his family. Although he stood five foot ten inches tall, in my eyes he was a giant, a "gentle giant." He was kind and patient and he made me feel like I was his only child.

Isn't that how God is? When you consider the greatness of this world and yet He makes you feel like His only child and the apple of His eye.

My father was a hard working African-American man and a great provider for his family. He kept a roof over our heads and food on the table by working full time at Moffett Field Air Force Base after his retirement from the military. I am proud to say he earned his AA Degree, his BA Degree and a Master's Degree, all while providing for his family. After Father retired a second time from civil service, he became a college professor at San Jose City College and San Jose State University, as well as the author of two books. Yes, my father was an intelligent and well-respected man who instilled in his children the importance of a college education.

My mother was your traditional stay-at-home mom during the developmental stages of our lives. She had a tenth-grade education, and nurtured us with sophistication and discipline. My mother was a great cook and we enjoyed her delicious meals. She ran a well organized home, teaching us the importance of cleanliness and gave us daily chores. Mother's famous motto was, "get a job and work for what you want." She encouraged her children to be educationally and practically well rounded. I loved to look into my mother's face. I always thought she was so pretty, classy and quite a dresser.

The Gardner's were a close-knit family growing up during the 60' and 70's. In the evenings we would sit around in the family room together and watch such television shows and movies as: "Laugh In, Christy Love, That Girl, The Wizard of Oz, Go Speed Racer, Under Dog, and Julia. These shows made a tremendous impression on me. I always saw myself as being a beautiful, successful, independent woman who would speak out against evil and fight for the underdog. It was so cool to see an African-American police woman starring in "Christy Love," and Diahann Carroll in *Julia.* Carroll played a widowed single mother named Julia Baker whose fighter pilot husband had been shot down in Vietnam. She worked as a nurse in a doctor's office while raising her son in a clean, responsible and loving environment.

As I grew into womanhood, there were more positive images on the television and movie screens that I could relate to while trying to decide on a career. I knew I wasn't going to be a homemaker, and nothing turned me off more than getting married at a young age and having babies. I really wanted to see the world, experience life and become an actress. I wanted to be educated like my father and had a strong desire to be successful; however learning didn't come easy for me. Many of my insecurities in elementary and middle school stemmed from a problem that I had with stuttering which discouraged me from the needed practice of reading aloud. My mom encouraged me in my school work. My father, though he was patient with me, was busy working and going to school and hardly had time to tutor me. Though I aspired to be an actress, I shied away from enrolling in theatre classes in high school and college. The challenges I had with comprehension and reading seemed to be barriers that limited my career choices.

From the outside looking in, the Gardner's were the picture-perfect, well cared for, active, middle class African-American family. Our house was on a corner lot and the back yard was really huge. My siblings, our friends and I played safely there for many years. My mother ran a "tight ship" and took pride in managing the money. We always wore nice, clean clothes, played with the newest toys, had family picnics and sometimes went to church on Sunday. My brothers played sports and the family always attended their games. During the summer months, we children attended vacation Bible school. My twin sister and I even went to summer camp for two consecutive years. My brothers had their own band, and, as a high school student, I became very involved in extracurricular activities.

When we moved to San Jose I met my first true childhood friend, Keri. I don't know what I loved about Keri but I remember she was nice and very tender towards me. Whenever I got a chance, I would run about three blocks up the street to her house to play with her. One day Keri became very ill and when she stopped going to school, our playtime became very limited. I didn't know that she was dying from a rare form of brain cancer but I remember when I would see her, she had a bandage around her head and we had to be gentle when we played. Then, one day Keri died. Being young and still innocent, I had much to learn about cancer and death.

Shortly after Keri's death, a new friend, Diane Hill, moved around the corner from our home. Diane became my best friend and we would play together in her room. It was the late 60's and Diane's mother was a single mom raising three girls. According to what I knew, it was very unusual to see a white woman raising kids on her own. Diane's father had died and I noticed that her house was not quite as nice as ours and she didn't wear fancy clothes; but she was nice and that's all that mattered to me. Diane moved away and we lost touch, but I still considered her my best friend. I was so excited when we met up again in high school; however, I found out very quickly that Diane was not the best friend that I once knew.

In middle school, the bigger girls bullied me around because I wasn't a fighter and because I won the affection of boys. Never wanting to compete in a popularity contest, I avoided confrontation at all cost. I began to make rules about who I was and who I was not. I didn't need to "kiss up" to anybody so they would be my friend. It has always been important to me to be able to be myself and have fun.

As I reflect on my experience with Diane, I remember her wanting to hang out with those she thought were popular, which wasn't me. She now seemed more my rival then my friend. I think this was the turning point for me in terms of distrusting women, in general, and becoming a loner. In spite of the loss of my two very special friendships, one by sudden death and one through betrayal, life for me was pretty grand from birth to the age of twelve. However, nothing in my life so far prepared me for what I would experience next.

At the age of 12, I watched my parents' marriage dissolve. Mom and Dad had grown apart and now divorce seemed imminent. I will never forget the day when Dad broke his silence and told me he was leaving us as he packed up his car and strapped down his things.

I had always felt I was Daddy's little girl so I asked, "Where are you going, Daddy?"

I thought about our family, our home—the place where we had enjoyed so many fond family gatherings. My sister Cherryl's wedding had been held in our spacious back yard.

But now home had become a place of deep sorrow and would never really feel like home ever again.

When Dad said he was moving to Tennessee, I cried as I asked him not to leave us and wondered audibly why he was moving so far away. Didn't he love us anymore? He teased me, keeping me in suspense for a little while, and then he finally said he was moving to an apartment less than a mile away. My sadness suddenly turned into gladness knowing that my Dad wouldn't be too far away.

The Gardner Family Grows Up and Out

Out of high school, my brothers followed in my father's footsteps by heading off to the military. My two sisters and I stayed with Mom and we got along well. The fact that Dad was living just up the street and at our disposal brought great comfort to me. On the weekends, my sisters and I gladly went over to Dad's place in a brand new apartment complex with a swimming pool, recreational center and quick bus access to the Mall. Dad's moving also played to our advantage because he was now living in the school district where we needed to live to attend one of the most popular high schools at the time in East San Jose, Silver Creek High.

The highlight of my freshmen year was when I joined the school's very popular marching band and participated as a rifle girl. I had never twirled a rifle before but quickly learned since it was the only position left in the color guard. My middle sister Pat was in the band and I had to follow in her footsteps. Being a part of this elite group of talented students really helped me feel good about myself and my sister and I were able to raise enough money to travel with the band to Washington, D.C. and march in the 1976 Bicentennial Parade. It was a wonderful experience that I still hold near and dear to my heart.

There was a lot of high-school sports talent in our school during my sophomore and junior years and I enjoyed being on the varsity cheerleading squad. We won most of our games having top-notch athletes on the boys' football and basketball teams. Cheering for the undefeated "Raiders" was easy and a lot of fun. While in high school, I never had a boyfriend even though the boys showed interest in me. I was invited to the junior prom during my freshmen year, but I was afraid to date or get involved in a serious relationship. I also realized that the students with boyfriends and girlfriends were usually not mature enough to handle themselves. I didn't want to be a part of the high school gossip, so I chose to hang out with other girls who shared the same sentiment. My main focus was on my studies; hence, I graduated halfway through my senior year.

After graduation I worked full time while attending college, and moved in with my sister Pat. We shared an apartment and supported each other in college. Pat was my best friend and running buddy but I admit we didn't always encourage each other to do the right thing or make the best decisions. Those years were filled with innocent and sometimes risky behaviors, balanced with laughter and fun.

One thing I wish I'd had more of growing up was my father's perspective on how to have healthy relationships with men. I can only recall once in my lifetime when Dad gave me a compliment regarding my beauty and that was about me having nice legs. I was shocked but happy since his compliments had always been geared towards "brain smarts" and education. I was young and very impressionable and I needed validation because I lacked confidence in myself. When it came to boys, the only advice Dad gave was, "Stay away!" I soon found out why.

Father's, I admonish you to speak positive affirming words to your daughters. Teach them early how to be treated like a lady and help them to understand their value and worth not just to you but to God.

In the years to come I experienced many rocky relationships, made many mistakes and began to learn from them. Some decisions left me with deep regrets and emotionally distraught as I journeyed from one relationship to another in search of the man I needed, never feeling that void fulfilled. I watched as people I knew tried to fill this void with drugs, alcohol, sex and wrong relationships. Today, I thank God for the void He has placed in all of us, but then I didn't realize it could only be filled by His presence in my life.

And my God shall supply all your need according to His riches in glory by Christ Jesus.

(Philippians 4:19)

My Turning Point

I am a firm believer that nothing—and I mean NOTHING, good, bad or ugly—in life happens by accident, but only by divine providence.

For the eyes of the LORD run to and fro throughout the whole earth, to show Himself strong on behalf of those whose heart is loyal to Him. (2 Chronicles 16:9)

What I mean is, there are times in life when things happen to us and we wonder where God is in the midst of life's chaos. He is there in all our good choices as well as in all the bad ones, but like a good parent, He stands by, watching and waiting for us to recognize our need for Him. As we turn toward Him, He then utilizes His great power to turn our bad choices into opportunities and our poor decisions into coachable moments for our growth and spiritual development.

When God made Adam and Eve, He had a close relationship with them. He walked with them and talked with them. Like Adam and Eve, we are spiritual beings and God has designed each of us with a plan and a purpose for our lives. Also like Adam and Eve, our choices may move us out of relationship with God though He never leaves us nor forsakes us. Though, even now, some 2000 years later, a fierce battle rages all around us for our very souls, our loving God is constantly wooing us back to Him. He allows us to choose as we exercise our free will and even when we make bad choices, by His sweet grace we will find Him ever there to welcome us back into His loving arms. I pray you do not let the hardness of your heart keep you from finding your way home into His loving arms.

The fear of the Lord is the beginning of wisdom.

(Proverbs 9:10)

The College Years

The college years were very challenging; I was very happy to graduate and reflect upon my learning experiences. My Mother and Father were extremely proud and seeing me

Covered & Kept

graduate and pursuing a brighter future was truly a dream come true for my Father. I learned to face the challenges and experiences one is exposed to when you fall into the category of a minority. During my junior college years I was told by a faculty member and counselor, that I was not college material. Those words fueled in me an unquenchable burning desire to succeed no matter what the cost.

There were many other discouraging moments and set-backs during my college years that made me think I was not going to make it. However, the drive in me for success was greater than the pull of defeat. My Father's voice of encourage-ment was a great asset to me. The very thought of telling my Father that I couldn't make it and seeing the disappointment on his face was a stronger detriment than anything I could have ever imagined. My Dad was the main financial supporter of my Junior and Senior years in college and, against all odds, I was the first of my siblings, to walk across that stage and receive my Bachelor's degree in Radio, Television and Film from Long Beach State University.

I am so thankful that I didn't let anyone steal my dream. Words are so powerful! They can be used to build up or to tear down. I'm so glad I chose not to let that counselor's words tear me down. Even when I've had to go it alone, I am determined not to be a quitter. When I put my mind to something, by God's grace I work until it's accomplished.

Blessed is the man who walks not in the counsel of the ungodly, nor stands in the path of sinners, nor sits in the seat of the scornful; But his delight is in the law of the Lord and in His law he meditates day and night. He shall be like a tree planted by the rivers of water, that brings forth its fruit in its season. Whose leaf also shall not wither; and whatever he does shall prosper.

(Psalms 1:1-3 New King James Version)

Chapter Three

Fate Would Have It

With college behind me, I had big dreams for myself and felt there was nothing that could stop me now! Living in Southern California with all the lights, camera and action, I began to pursue a career in the television industry. I got the first job that I applied for as the Public Access Coordinator for Inglewood Cable Television in Inglewood, California, home of the Los Angeles Lakers. The job didn't pay much, but I was fresh out of college with no real job experience in the industry and it was a great opportunity to learn and make mistakes. I could also meet new people, hone my skills and move up the corporate ladder. In my middle management job, I was given the opportunity to train, produce and direct cable programs as well as interview political figures, city officials, players from the Lakers and various celebrities. I managed a team of interns, worked long hours; sometimes seven days a week which was fine with me because I was driven and on a mission.

During this time in my life, I had no connection with Jesus. I wasn't attending church and was content with not going. I was away from home, gainfully employed, independent, empowered and in charge of my life. While I was growing up, church was optional. My maternal grandmother was a spirit-filled, saved, sanctified, mighty woman of God. Mom occasionally took us to church but I do not recall my Dad ever going with us. We would go to church when we visited Granny in Richmond, CA especially on such holidays as Easter and Mother's Day. For the most part, when we went to church, Mom sent us; so I didn't feel like I was doing anything out of harmony with God.

After two years of employment with Inglewood Cable my zeal for success with this company seemed to dwindle, I became disenchanted with the low pay and the high stress of working late nights. Leaving the building at 10:00 p.m., with no security or escort to my car began to take a toll on me physically. When I started experiencing panic attacks, I began to hate my job and started looking for alternatives. I wanted out! I began to work as a part-time secretary/receptionist for a dear friend named J.B. to pick up some extra money and to help him out. The office was directly across the street from the University of Southern California (USC), right where the 1984 Summer Olympic Games were being held. I will never forget what happened to me that summer while working for J.B. I was so thankful for the little exposure I had to the LORD when I found myself in amongst some "wolves."

Too Good To Be Great!

I began a friendship with a man who appeared to be pretty well off and generous with his money and his compliments. Dave asked me questions about what kind of car I wanted, where I would like to live, what kind of company I wanted to work for, etc. The more we talked, the more excited I became. He promised me a new car, a new job working for United Airlines and a penthouse apartment overlooking Marina Del Rey.

He took me to a high-rise penthouse apartment and told me that a famous singer had just moved out. He said that if I wanted it, the apartment could be all mine. Being the naïve, sheltered, 24 year old country girl from orchard town San Jose and desperate to get out of my stress filled job, I went along with the fantasy knowing deep in my heart it was probably too good to be true.

One warm summer's day as I was fast at work at my buddy J.B.'s office, Dave called and suggested I meet him for lunch. I went downstairs to a café just across the street from the stadium. The place was crowded because of the Olympics so

I was sitting outdoors waiting when Dave walked up behind me and tried to grab a kiss. Startled, I moved away from him. Even when I realized who it was, I rejected his playful act of affection having no romantic desire to be with him. In response to my reaction, he went off on me for rejecting him when he was promising to "give me the world." I politely waited as he went on and on, but when he was through, I gave him my "two cents," reminding him I had not asked him to do those things for me. I told him that being able to look myself in the mirror was more important than all the material wealth he was offering. When I was finished, I got up and walked away.

A couple of nights later, Dave called while I was working at Inglewood Cable. He was very composed and just wanted me to hear him out. He said he was calling to commend me for standing up for my values. He went on to say he admired and respected me because many women in Los Angeles would have jumped at the opportunities and compromised their integrity and character. He wished me well and I never heard from Dave again. I have pondered over that situation many times and, although I was not walking with God at the time, He gave me the discernment to see something wasn't right about this man's spirit. It felt like if I continued in this man's company I would be selling my soul to the devil. I don't know what might have happened to me, but I believe he was setting me up to be a "call girl."

I've learned that when you don't know who you are, when you are empty and striving for material wealth or you are disenchanted with life, be very careful. It is during these times you could sell your soul to the devil, all while thinking God is blessing you. Satan has a way of making things look glamorous as he tries to lure you into seduction. He will often tempt you with the very things you may be striving for.

Sin comes three ways: lust of the flesh, lust of the eyes and the pride of life. That is how Satan came at Eve in the Garden of Eden. In Genesis 3:6, the Bible plainly states that when Eve saw that the tree's forbidden fruit was good for food (lust of flesh), that it was pleasant to the eyes (lust of the eyes), and a tree desirable to make one wise (the pride of life), she took of its fruit and ate. She also gave to her husband who was with her, and he ate. From there, sin entered the world and now we have to do battle against these three temptations but God has promised to give us what we need to gain the victory!

He Woos Us

It was while I was working at Inglewood Cable, striving to make connections and make a name for myself, that an elderly little man named Joe Letcher put in my hand a small, autographed book called, "Steps to Christ." Although I didn't read it at the time, that little book traveled with me from apartment to apartment until the appointed time. Fifteen years later, my mind flashed back to that little man trying to introduce me to Christ. I see now that God was wooing me even though I was running from Him as I tried to find my own way. He was there all the time trying to show me the right path. Even when I rejected God, He didn't stop wooing me. I just recently learned from a group of widows at my church that Joe has since died, but I am certain he would have been happy to know that I am counted worthy in God's Kingdom.

Through the LORD'S mercies we are not consumed, because His compassions fail not. They are new every morning; great is Your faithfulness. (Lamentations 3:22-23)

Two Years Too Long

When I heard that another cable company was looking for someone with my experience, I jumped at the opportunity, applied for and got the job. It was in Palos Verdes, California with Times Mirror Dimension Cable Services. Mom would say, "Haste makes waste;" and, boy was this quick move a big mistake! Although I was blessed to be making more money and working in a very upscale community, I felt I was missing out on the diversity that I had become accustomed to. I could not relate to the people, nor could they relate to me. I went from living a fun fulfilled but broke life to more money and a miserable life. What that taught me was money does not equal happiness.

My new job responsibilities were pretty much the same. However, while working with this company I interacted with many people with hidden agendas and proved to be cut-throat, manipulative and backstabbing. After two years, I knew I needed a change. My work experiences had given me a small taste of what the television industry was like but in the process I lost myself while trying to protect my job and my integrity. Being unfulfilled and looking for a way out left me vulnerable and in no position to intelligently reason my way to further success.

It was during this time that I was being considered for a very high-profile position in the City of Los Angeles. The person chosen would build and run one of the largest cable television stations in the city. I was invited to a job interview and lunch at an expensive restaurant in Palos Verdes. Excited about this wonderful opportunity, I shared my views and put my best foot forward thinking this was my way out.

I was devastated when I was not chosen for the job. Apparently my secret struggles of failure and my inability to finesse my way through the interview revealed a lack of confidence. I had also made a few enemies along the way whose negative input helped sway the final choice away from me. Looking back, I realize the job was not mine because the LORD wanted to save me from another wrong choice. I now believe that had I been chosen for the job, I would have sunk even deeper into a life of sin.

Then It Happened

It was during the 80's that Ed, a trusted friend, introduced me to a business opportunity with "Cernitine America," a wellness network marketing company in Southern California. Ed was already successful, one of only a hand full of African American men working in Hollywood as a First Assistant Director. He had gained fame when he worked with Aaron Spelling and Norman Lear on the successful night-time soap opera drama, "Dynasty." My thoughts were that if this "big shot" believed in the Cernitine America product and was a distributor with the company, why not try it. Since my investment was minimal and it seemed I had very little to lose, I decided to try my hand at this golden network marketing opportunity.

At the age of 27, I realized I had an entrepreneurial spirit. I longed to run my own successful business where I could make unlimited income, help improve people's lives and retire from the "rat race" forever by the age of 35. Cernitine America offered me an opportunity to take the first steps in that direction as an independent distributor of their products. One Saturday in 1987, a team of us decided to assemble ourselves together and head to San Francisco for a big wellness/health convention being held at the Moscone Center. I will never forget the weekend that changed my life forever.

We had a large, impressive booth on one of the main arteries of the facility, with good exposure, and heavy foot traffic. I stood with my clipboard in hand, fingernails nicely manicured, wearing vanilla tights, a yellow Cernitine America sweatshirt with a belt around my waist that showed all my curves and a pair of black pumps. I was an aerobics instructor so my body was tight and fit and my long, flowing hair was in a beautiful braid weave. As I greeted people walking by trying to interest them in our products and services, I noticed two men approaching me. One of them kept going, but the other stopped and struck up a conversation with me. He was tall, dark, handsome, outgoing and flirtatious. Standing about six-feet tall, he was ripped and had one of the most beautiful smiles I had ever seen.

Grabbing my hand, he looked at my ring finger and exclaimed, "You mean to tell me a woman like you is not married?"

I knew it was a pick-up line, but because he was extremely handsome I didn't care. I laughed and started to flirt right back.

His name was Kevin and within a matter of minutes, he convinced me to leave my booth and walk outside to see his exhibit. He had a huge truck, converted into a mobile gym. As a body builder and personal trainer, Kevin took this very impressive traveling gym to his clients and trained them. Being an aerobics instructor and into fitness, I was most impressed. The gym was assembled with free-weight equipment, a pull-up bar and even a sauna.

Athletes were my weakness. In college, with an exception or two, I only dated football players because they were popular, fun and had such great bodies. When I met Kevin, I was attracted to his winning smile, his charismatic aura, his fine physique and the brains I thought he had. I fell for him "hook, line and sinker."

When the convention in San Francisco ended, it had been my plan to have a little visit with Mom in San Jose before returning to Los Angeles. Kevin had other ideas. He invited me to see his office in San Bruno, a small city near the San Francisco International Airport. After grabbing a bite to eat and getting more acquainted with each other, we realized how the time had flown. Kevin didn't want to drive to Oakland and I didn't want to drive to San Jose, so as risky as it was I spent the night with him at his office. Kevin's behavior was that of a perfect gentleman and I instantly trusted him.

I returned to my home in Carson but work suddenly bored me out of my mind. My thoughts were only of Kevin and how I imagined a life with him would be; full of fun, adventure, twists and turns. Kevin and I kept in touch by phone on a daily basis. Captivated by his charm and great sense of humor, I was "under his spell." He told me how much he missed me and how much he wanted me to come and live with him. Kevin was living on a boat docked at the Oakland Marina, but he promised that if I would come to live with him he would move the boat to Sausalito. His plan was for us to live on his boat while we served the very affluent residents of Sausalito as personal trainers.

Tired of answering to other people and sick of the politics that came with my job, I desperately yearned for a change. I was excited that all of Kevin's dreams and plans were now including me! The more we talked, the more we both dreamed about being together. Soon the phone calls were not enough and Kevin made plans to visit me at my home in Carson. Being together again was so unbelievably wonderful and exciting that I knew I *had* to be with this man so I told my sister Pat that I was moving to the Bay Area. I gave my two weeks' notice at work and called Mom to inform her of my decision to go and live with Kevin.

Born and raised in San Francisco, Kevin was not your run-of-the-mill black man. He was most certainly one of a kind. He loved the water and he loved his home town. Kevin had a beautiful green parrot named "Polly" that sat perched on his shoulder as an attention getter while he went about his day.

Kevin was definitely a free spirit and loved adventure. I thought he was a religious man and one to be admired. I had never dated a man who professed to love the Lord the way he did. Kevin even spoke of having had dreams of becoming a monk and going to Tibet for a year to pray.

The Truth of the Matter

Frankly, I was in denial about what was really going on with me and my handsome "prince charming." As I was leaving the wellness convention in San Francisco with him, I do remember thinking to myself that I didn't know this man at all. But I was a risk taker and he seemed harmless so I quickly dismissed those thoughts. I used absolutely no reasoning or logic as I involved myself with this man, choosing to believe whatever he said. I didn't realize that what I believed was being "madly in love" was actually being "madly in lust."

Although I considered it an exciting adventure at the time, my decision to leave my home and job to live with Kevin made no sense. It went against everything I believed in and knew to be right. Up until that time, I had never had a desire to live with a man other than the one I hoped to one day marry. The thought of "shacking up" with a man was very demoralizing to me, but somehow when Kevin made the proposition, I readily accepted it. All I knew was I *had to be with him.*

I remember on his first visit to see me, Kevin told me that he was sterile and that I didn't need to use any form of birth control because he would not be able to father any children. Not wanting to get pregnant, I probed into the sterility issue; but he assured me I had nothing to worry about. I couldn't understand why he would lie about such a thing so I stopped using my contraceptives.

When I met Kevin, I was not actively involved in church; but I still had a good understanding of right and wrong. It wasn't long into our relationship that I realized what Kevin said and what he did just did *not* add up. We were sexually active yet he told Mom, my aunt, uncle and other family members that both of us were celibate. He shunned responsibility and conned people out of whatever he could, be it money, a place to stay, clothes, jewelry, cars, or property. Not only did he con women; he conned men, as well. And, for some reason, I went along with his foolishness.

Shocked and totally disappointed by my unwise decision and indiscretion, Mom desperately pleaded with me not to uproot from my home and job in Southern California until I knew for sure that things were going to work out with Kevin. I did accept some of her wise counsel and packed up only as much as I could take in my car before heading north, to live with Kevin on a trial basis.

New Year's Eve 1988

Our plans to ring in the New Year together involved me driving to Mom's house in San Jose and then driving on up to Oakland to meet him. Kevin told me he was returning from Las Vegas and that as soon as he got in, he would call me. As the evening hours approached with no word from Kevin, I didn't think too much about it until he neither answered nor returned my phone calls. With each passing hour, Mom began to get suspicious but she held off saying anything until she could no longer contain herself.

I did not want to believe Mom's words, "He has another woman!"

My first thought was she said it because she didn't approve of Kevin and she didn't want me to be with him. However, the later it got, the angrier I became and my curiosity began to get the best of me. Finally, I asked Mom what she thought I should do. She told me to go to sleep and just before dawn to get into my car and drive to Oakland. Mom believed that if I went early in the morning I would catch Kevin with the other woman.

I finally fell asleep on the couch but as soon as there was the slightest hint of daylight, I headed for Oakland. Determined to get to the bottom of this, I couldn't get there fast enough. I pulled up on the dirt road and saw an unfamiliar car parked outside Kevin's place. The first thing that popped into my mind was what my mom had said. I knocked on the door, but there was no answer. I knew they were there, so I persisted. Finally, a woman flung the door open. I told her who I was and all about my move from Los Angeles to be with Kevin. We started comparing notes. Both of us were livid! Tammy packed her things and before leaving together we decided to leave Kevin a little memento. We flattened all the tires on his precious truck! Kevin was nothing more than a two-timing con-artist, full of pipe dreams.

Now what was I going to do? I had no job and living back at home with Mom in San Jose was not part of my plans for success! As I sat there trying to figure out what my next move would be, the telephone rang. It was Kevin. Nervous about flattening the tires on his truck, I silently listened to what he had to say. Like the con-artist that he was, Kevin was good at apologizing. He convinced me he would never be with Tammy again and, despite what had happened New Year's Eve, I really did not want things to be over between us. I knew Mom would be angry with me, but I accepted his apology and decided to go and stay with him as planned.

Brisk Day in the Bay

It was a beautiful, warm day. The sky was a pristine blue and the wind was very calm and mild. As I looked out into the bay waters, I saw boats every where; big boats, little boats, speed boats and sail boats. It seemed that any boat imaginable was on the water that day; and, like us, people were soaking up the sun and having fun.

Mike, a long-time friend of Kevin's, was at the helm, steering the boat while Kevin and I were taking it all in. Because the day was so perfect, I couldn't resist this once-in-a-lifetime opportunity to put on my little bikini and sunbathe while we sailed to Sausalito. The swimsuit I was wearing was a very sexy, two-piece, black metallic, with a high cut around the thighs.

Kevin and Mike watched me sunbathing as we cruised the Bay. I was basking in the moment as my skin glowed from the warmth of the sun. I was in heaven! This was my first experience at sailing. Finally, I thought, my dreams were coming true. Without a care in the world, I laid there in the sun until, suddenly, a voice told to me to go inside. I paid no attention and continued to lie out in the sun. Then, the voice returned saying, "Go inside!" Again, I hesitated until the third and final warning. This time I immediately obeyed, rose up and entered the cabin just in time as some choppy waves suddenly tipped the boat over on its side. Alarmed, the three of us braced ourselves and rode it out until the choppy waters subsided. As the boat tipped a second time, all I could think of was had I not paid attention to the warning, the sudden tip would have tossed me overboard like a rag doll into the choppy ice cold water. Whether I would have survived or not only God knows. However, I trembled in fear as I thanked the Lord for protecting me. Needless to say, I stayed in the cabin for the remainder of the cruise.

Finally, we made it to Sausalito where Kevin's truck was parked. We anchored in the water and took a small boat to shore. From there, we jumped into the truck and drove Mike to his home in Oakland. Still a little shaken, I said little on the way to Mike's. Kevin, however, remained true to form. Part of what made life with Kevin so adventurous was that he was the type of man who rarely had a game plan. He would often "fly by the seat of his pants," laughing and cracking jokes along the way. He had us all laughing by the time we reached Mike's. He was just so charming that everyone, women and men alike, seemed to love being in his company.

However, an adventurous spirit left unchecked can some-times lead to adversity. Shortly after Kevin and I got back together, he started having a wave of bad luck. One day, his big beautiful mobile gym went flying off the freeway, hit a huge retaining wall and smashed into pieces turning our plan to make money into a pile of junk. I desperately needed to prove to my mother and sister that I was not wrong about my deci-sion to leave my career, home, and security to be with this man. I had a lot invested in this new life and I was determined to make things work, in spite of the lies and this sudden turn of events. Never a quitter, I wasn't ready to throw in the towel.

A Series of Unfortunate Events

I had been under the impression that once we got the boat to Sausalito, Kevin would rent space and dock the boat at the marina. His plan, however, was to keep it out in the water and live like a pirate.

I wasn't happy with this decision, but once again, I just went along with the game plan. Sometimes we stayed on the boat, other times we stayed with Mike. Then, there were times when I would go to Mom's to shower and sleep in a real bed.

It was during one of my visits with Mom that I received a phone call from Kevin telling me his boat had sunk when the automatic pump failed. Kevin said he thought we could salvage some of our belongings if he had a pump to extract the water from the boat. Wanting to help, I rented the pump on my credit card and we drove out to see what we could salvage. When we got to shore, we realized that someone had stolen our paddle boat. Kevin borrowed someone else's small paddleboat to transport us to his 42-foot cabin cruiser. When we reached it, the boat was full of water, but the tide was low. In his eagerness to get his boat pumped out and hoping it would miraculously float once emptied, we quickly went to work pumping the water out of the cabin.

As the day drew to a close, I was good and ready to go when I looked up and noticed that the paddleboat had just seen its last glimpse of light and slowly dipped below the water's surface. Petrified, I gasped in fear, quickly letting Kevin know that our only means of transportation to shore had just sunk out of sight. Knowing we had made another serious judgment error, I begged Kevin to find a way to get us to shore as the rising tide began to again fill the cabin cruiser with water. All around us was nothing but cold, dark water. Time was of the essence, we needed to act fast. Should we swim or wait for someone to save us? But who knew we were out here? Should we try to wait it out on the boat until morning? What, oh what, should we do?

From Sea to Shore

As angry as I was with Kevin, I was even angrier with myself for allowing myself to be in such a precarious predicament with him. Scared and getting angrier by the minute, I waited for one of Kevin's harebrained ideas to get us off the boat. All we could see around us was darkness and impending danger. Oh, how I yearned to be docked safely in the harbor as I gazed at the lights and calmness of the marina. It represented peace and safety if we could only get there. As I watched the boats docked in the marina where we should have been, I couldn't help but think what my parents would think of me for being so stupid.

We were probably a quarter of a mile out from shore; so close, yet so far away. With the tide steadily rising we were running out of options. With no other way back, Kevin suggested we swim back to shore before the tide rose any higher. When he asked me if I could swim, I told him I was an "okay swimmer," and if this was the only option to get us back to safety, then I would prepare myself for a swim.

Not wanting any harm to come to me, Kevin decided to test the waters before putting me out there. He slowly lowered himself off the back end of the boat and into the water. Freezing cold, he quickly jumped back into the boat. Shivering and laughing he said, "We would freeze to death before we'd make it to shore!"

Safe Passage

Suddenly, Kevin came up with a brilliant idea. He went inside the cabin and came back carrying the bathtub. Doubtful but desperate, I hoped he was right and the tub would stay afloat long enough to carry us to safety. Almost as if time stood still, I held my breath as he dropped the tub into the cold, dark waters. Like oil floats on water, the tub miraculously stayed afloat. I leaped for joy as I watched our only means of transportation to safety resting on the waters, waiting to provide safe passage to the other side. Kevin hopped in first while I watched; holding my breath, afraid it would start sinking. It stayed afloat with him in it so he helped me in and I nestled down inside the tub. The tide had risen but the waters were calm as God lead us safely to shore in our little "row tub."

I didn't know how to pray then, but when I think back on that incident, Psalm 23:1-2 comes to mind:

The Lord is my shepherd; I shall not want. He makes me to lie down in green pastures; He leads me beside the still waters.

Although we were cold, wet and shaking from the whole ordeal, we were happy and thankful to be on the shore. We knew we couldn't drive from Sausalito to San Jose in soaking wet clothes; so we quickly disrobed and ran naked through the dark to my car. Once in the car, I turned on the heater and we drove to Mom's house in San Jose. I parked and we ran nude from the car to her apartment in hopes that no one would see us. Knowing that my Mom was not at home I quickly washed and dried our clothes.

Looking back on the many ordeals that God allowed me to experience with my mystery man, he never harmed a hair on my head. Even though he used me for his personal gain, my Lord always knew all about both Kevin…and me. God was beginning to get my attention even then.

Great is the Lord, and greatly to be praised; And His greatness is unsearchable. I will meditate on the glorious splendor of Your majesty, And on Your wondrous works. Men shall speak of the might of your awesome acts, and I will declare your greatness. They shall utter the memory of your great goodness, and shall sing of your righteousness. The Lord is gracious and full of compassion, slow to anger and great in mercy. The Lord is good to all, and His tender mercies are over all His works. (Psalm 145: 3,5-9)

Trying to hang with Kevin was beginning to be a bit much for me. It was not what I had signed up for. I knew that, eventually, I would have to figure out what to do with my life. My behavior was not what my family expected from me; maybe from my twin sister, but not from me. I had been known to be the responsible one who "played it safe." Here I was 27 years old and carrying on like a 16-year-old. By this time, my Mom had grown really tired of Kevin as well. Not only did she want the $600 back he had conned her out of, she wanted me to leave him and move back to Los Angeles. When I shared my many close encounters with my favorite cousin, Sam, he would shake his head and tell me I was crazy. He could not imagine any woman putting up with what I had taken from Kevin.

God Had a Plan

Between running back and forth to Mom's house, hanging out with Kevin and being sexually active, I missed my menstrual cycle. Too soon to get alarmed or to let Kevin know, I decided to take a home pregnancy test and to my surprise it was positive. Not wanting to alarm Kevin, I decided to wait a few days before taking a second test, but rehearsed what I would say to him if the second results confirmed the first test. I questioned how it could be possible since he had told me he was sterile and I been faithful in my relationship with him. I was numb on the outside, but inwardly happy. I wanted his baby and I wanted Kevin to want it, too. However, his response did not line up with my secret hopes. The only thing he wanted to hear was that I would be getting an abortion.

To some extent I felt stupid; but for the most part I felt *chosen*. Even though I had lost a lot and the direction of my life had changed drastically, I felt it was a privilege to be carrying another life within me. It further amazed me that Kevin had been dating two women; neither of us used birth control believing he was sterile, and yet I was the one who was pregnant. Driving down Capitol Expressway on my way to Mom's house, my mind began to wander as I contemplated breaking the news of my pregnancy to Mom. I had to do something and soon! Each day that I delayed making a decision was another day that the baby was growing inside of me. I was a bundle of conflicting emotions!

God had been protecting me all along and now He knew I was going to need some extra help from one of His guardian angels in order to make the right decision. As I sat at a red light waiting for it to turn green, I glanced over my left shoulder and caught a glimpse of a Planned Parenthood Clinic. When did they put that there? I had driven up and down this street many times and never noticed it, but on this day it stuck out like a sore thumb. In an instant, I decided I needed a professional opinion and that maybe I wasn't really pregnant after all. So, I made a U-turn and pulled into the driveway of the Parenthood Clinic.

I walked up to the front counter and requested to take my third pregnancy test. Oddly enough, the front lobby was empty and I didn't have to wait to be served. After the test, I patiently waited for the results and prepared myself for the worst. Finally, a mature Latino woman walked slowly over to me as if in deep thought.

In a slow calm, low tone the woman sat down next to me, took my hand and said, "You're pregnant. What are you going to do?"

Of course, I wasn't surprised by the test results, but I was shocked by her question. I paused for a moment; then, matter-of-factly told her I was going to have an abortion. She immediately began to plead with me not to abort my baby. I told her I wasn't married and could not raise a baby on my own. I told her the father claimed to be a Christian; yet he wanted me to have an abortion and I didn't understand why.

"Because he *isn't* a Christian," she said as she went on to ask me about my level of education and my occupation.

When I told her my age and that I was a college graduate, she pressed me even harder to have my baby. Still confused and not convinced to have my child, I noticed tears rolling down her cheeks.

Firmly holding my hand she said, "Babies are a gift from God; please don't abort your baby."

I was numb. As I sat there, she pressed me again, "Please, promise me you won't get rid of your baby."

In silence, I sat there filled with shame as my mind flashed back to another time I had been down this lonely road. Yes, I had an abortion before but that time no one had shown the care and compassion this woman crying next to me was showing. I cringed as I realized I was preparing to do it again, take another life but this time it wasn't because I didn't want my baby or the responsibility of being a mother. This time, my baby's father didn't want me to have him.

Suddenly, out of nowhere, my confusion disappeared and I began to believe what this passionate mature woman was saying. Yes, I thought, I could take care of my baby. I was educated and independent. It no longer mattered if I lost Kevin! I suddenly didn't care about what people might say or think about me, another single black woman raising a child without the father. Deep in my heart, I knew I was doing the right thing. The spell Kevin had cast over me had been broken, my mind was made up. I had a complete paradigm shift as this dedicated Christian woman prayed and wept for my unborn child. I turned to the woman in a moment of clarity and told her I would not be aborting my baby and would keep it.

Relieved by my response, the woman smiled and assured me that everything would be alright. I never saw or talked to that dear lady ever again, but I am so thankful God put her there for me. God had plans for my life and they included this life that was growing inside of me. I was determined to be responsible, step up to the plate and raise my child even if it entailed doing it alone. This very important decision put me on a new path but somehow I knew it was the right path for me and for my baby.

Chapter Four

A New Path

I was certain that Kevin would be angry at my decision to have our baby and Mom wouldn't be any better; but for the first time since I discovered I was pregnant, I was no longer confused. I knew what to do. I would leave Kevin, return to Los Angeles and prepare to have my baby. Before going to bed that night, I knelt by my bed and told God I was going to keep my word and have the baby. I prayed, expressing my need for Him to do His part—to take care of us and help me raise my child.

I'll never forget the day I broke the news to Mom. It was a Saturday morning, I had stayed the night at my mothers' and was awakened by a telephone conversation Mom was having with my deceased brother's girlfriend. Kara had hoped to someday marry my brother Donny and have children with him, but fate had something else in store for her. She had just broken the news to Mom about being pregnant with her boyfriend's child and becoming a single mom. Mom knew that Kara really wanted children with my brother when he was alive and expressed her happiness as she affirmed Kara with positive words. As I listened to all the encouragement Mom offered Kara on the phone, I began to build my own defense. When Mom said goodbye to Kara, I went into her room and sat on her bed to break my news.

When I told her I had something important to tell her, she asked me in a very loving tone, "What is it?"

I had expected a response similar to what I heard between her and Kara but when I broke the news about my pregnancy, Mom's entire countenance changed and she hit the roof!

"How is it that you were so encouraging to Kara, Mom?" I cried, "There is no difference in our situations. Kara isn't married either."

Mom made a few excuses and demanded that I have an abortion. Firmly, I told her that abortion was out of the question and that I *would* be having my baby.

After a thoughtful moment, Mom said, "You can take care of a baby, but you can't take care of a no good man."

I agreed with her and told her I wouldn't be with Kevin anymore. I knew keeping the baby would be the final straw for him. I also knew it was time for me to begin a new path and Kevin was not going with me. When Kevin came to see if I had done what he had asked, Mom was waiting for him. She had come to terms with my decision to keep the baby, as long as I left Kevin.

Still angry with Kevin, she confronted him about doing the right thing by taking care of his child. In an arrogant tone, he told Mom that any child of his would be taken care of and would want for nothing. However, his actions spoke louder than his words.

Los Angeles Here we Come

Most of my possessions had been destroyed on the boat, so I packed the few articles of clothing I had left and moved back to Los Angeles to await the birth of my child. My pregnancy was easy. For the first time in my life, I ate whatever I wanted without reservation or worry about gaining weight. After all, I was *eating for two*. My best friend Shari and her boyfriend did a lot of nice things with me to help me feel really good about myself.

From time to time, Kevin would call me to try and talk me into having an abortion; but with each passing day, my decision became even more resolute. I was not turning back. I had made a promise to God and the lady at the abortion clinic *and* I was determined to keep it. I also realized I really wanted my baby. Kevin was frustrated, so he pulled out all stops to get me to have an abortion. In his final, desperate attempt to get me to abort, Kevin called me one night to tell me he had AIDS. He also told me that if I had the baby I would be passing the disease on to my child. Part of me knew he was lying again, but I knew he lived in San Francisco and had a gay friend I didn't know very well. The possibility crossed my mind that he could have been bisexual and might indeed have AIDS. When I asked Kevin how he knew he had AIDS, he said he had sores on his body.

Immediately after hanging up the phone, I ran into my sister's bedroom crying, "Kevin says he has AIDS."

"That boy doesn't have AIDS! He's lying," my sister retorted and added that I was stupid for falling for Kevin's lies.

Pat assured me he was just saying he had AIDS to get me to have an abortion. I calmed down and decided not to talk with Kevin while I was pregnant because I didn't want to pass any undue stress on to my baby.

God Keeps His Promise

As I prepared for a life as a single mom, I signed on with a temporary agency to do some administrative work and earn the money I would need to support the two of us. I did not like the assignment or the hard taskmaster of a manager I was hired to work for but it wasn't very far from my home and I was bringing home a paycheck.

On one particular day, I had decided to go home for lunch and was rushing back to work when I got stuck at a red light. Anxious to get back to the office on time so I wouldn't get fired, I impatiently waited for the light to turn green. However, when the light did turn green, I felt a sudden calmness rush over me and I just sat there as if the light was still red. Even though the light was now green and I was supposed to be in a hurry, I kept my foot on the brake. Suddenly, out of nowhere, a car raced right past me through the intersection, running the red light. I sat there in a state of shock thanking the Lord for saving my life again; and this time, my baby's life, too. You see, not even the fear of being fired could foil God's magnificent plans for my baby and me. God kept His promise to take care of us!

Coming to Him as to a living stone, rejected indeed by men, but chosen by God and precious. (1 Peter 2:4)

As the summer drew to a close, I was huge, miserable and so ready to have my baby. It was becoming very difficult to get in and out of my small, two-seater Pontiac Fiero and my stomach was literally sitting on the steering wheel. One day an older lady walked up to my car in anger telling me how dangerous it was to be driving with my stomach on the steering wheel like that. Offended with her approach, I agreed with her and finally sold my Fiero to a friend and bought a used clunker of a car that was spacious but wasn't very dependable and had no air conditioning. I didn't keep the car long and swore I would never carry a baby again during the summer months.

When my healthy, bouncing baby boy was born on August 27, 1988, I weighed in at a whopping 188 pounds. In just nine months, I had gone from 128 to 188 pounds. It was an easy pregnancy but a hard labor; and no matter what the doctor did to induce labor, I only dilated three centimeters. Tristan was finally born by Cesarean Section because the doctor lost his heart beat twice during labor.

In a letter dated October 7, 1988, I announced the blessed news of my beautiful baby boy's birth to his father:

Dear Kevin:

I have contemplated for weeks on whether I should write this letter. For starters, you fathered a healthy baby boy. His name is Tristan Colin Gardner. He was born at 7:05 a.m., Saturday, August 27, 1988, at California Medical Center. He weighted 7 pounds 13 ounces and measured 20-½ inches long.

My real purpose for writing you is two-fold: to give you the opportunity to acknowledge Tristan as your child and to express how much I need financial help to raise him. He is here on this earth and there is nothing you can do to erase that fact. (God knows you tried!) You can continue to deny him if you want, but you know within your heart that TCG is yours.

Kevin, do you remember telling my mom that you were a man and that, if I had your child, you would take care of him? You also said that no child of yours would have to worry because you would see to it that he was taken care of. Well, be that man and take care of your responsibility.

I think $400 a month would be sufficient. Diapers, formula and clothing, as you well know, are very expensive; not to mention my need for reliable daycare, which is $65-75 dollars per week.

Sadly for Kevin, he chose to deny his son and not to be a part of his life. Kevin did, however, see Tristan twice; but he never paid child support. In spite of his decision to be a deadbeat dad, the LORD kept His promises to me.

My Gift from God

The Lord continued to bless and keep me. I was fortunate to be able to stay off work with my baby for ten months. During that time, I had so much fun loving and bonding with my baby boy. I had always wanted my first-born to be a boy and God granted me my wish. I nursed Tristan for ten months and carried him on my chest in a pouch. Mom often told me I carried him around like he was a doll. We were inseparable. He was a gift from God—all mine, to raise and parent as I saw fit.

When Tristan was just a few months old, I presented him back to the LORD in a ceremony of dedication. When Tristan was just four months old, the Lord blessed us with a trip to visit friends and family from California to New York, to New Jersey, to Oklahoma and back to Los Angeles. It was my baby's first Christmas and we spent it in Oklahoma with my oldest sister Cherryl, my brother-in-law Al and other family members.

When I started back to work, I was blessed to find both a good paying job and childcare just blocks from our home. God was so good to us! I strove to be the best mom I could be. Motherhood slowed me down quite a bit but I welcomed the change. My sister Pat and I continued to live together until Tristan was about a year old. We were both single mothers and the house was becoming too small for the four of us. Pat moved into a two-bedroom apartment in Gardena and I moved into a one-bedroom apartment in the same complex to keep my costs down.

I was enjoying bonding with and raising my son on my own, even though I received no child support or welfare. I always hoped my son's father would come around and play an active role in our son's life; but only on the condition that he would love him and be a dependable father to our little boy.

If Kevin could not be dependable, I did not want him in Tristan's life; therefore, I decided to give my last name to my son. The Gardner men—from my father and brother to my uncles—took good care of their kids, and I wanted my son to stay connected with the Gardner legacy. I didn't want to give him the last name of a man who didn't want me to have his child.

Going to work for the City of Carson's Parks and Recreation Department, was the best thing I could have done at that time. The money was good and I was able to work out and work off the 60 pounds I had gained with Tristan. With my weight down, teaching aerobic classes again afforded me extra spending money. More importantly, though, it helped me to regain my confidence and my competitive edge.

Moving On

Since being with Kevin, I hadn't had a boyfriend, nor had I desired one. Then a young Christian couple moved into a downstairs apartment near mine. I noted that they seemed to be happy and we spoke when we saw each other. One day, when their good friend, Cliff, was visiting, he noticed me and inquired about me.

Just over six feet tall, with a light complexion and a nice smile, Cliff carried himself like a male model (not particularly "my type"). He worked as a bank teller at the Security Pacific Bank across the street from my apartment complex. One day while my sister was visiting with me, Cliff brought me a bouquet of beautiful red roses. When Pat saw him, she commented on how handsome he was and suggested I give him a chance. I was very impressionable and valued my sister's opinion, so I decided to go against my intuition and give him a chance.

Cliff was very gentle and attentive to my son. Although he was a young man, he was good at fixing cars. He was neat, clean and very charming. We began spending a lot of time together and things were going good. Within a matter of weeks, he had proposed to me. I was flattered because this was my first official marriage proposal and it came at a time in my life when I was ready to receive it. In times past, my previous boyfriends and I discussed marriage or hinted around but there was never anything forthright. I was also flattered because Cliff was five years my junior. He had a son of his own but was eager to be a dad to my Tristan. Cliff said all the right things. I especially thought it would be nice to raise my son with a good father figure, so I accepted Cliff's marriage proposal.

After losing his job, Cliff began to spend more and more time at my house. With each visit, I noticed more and more articles of his clothing showing up in my closet. I would bring it to his attention, but he would shrug it off like it was no big deal. Determined to make up for the loss of his job, he began to help with more things around my apartment and with Tristan. I was *not* looking for a househusband. I wanted a man who could love and provide for my son and me; a man I could partner with and build a beautiful future together. We realized we both wanted to follow God and began going to church together.

Soon my home with Tristan was Cliff's home, too. Setting a wedding date and making plans to get married became more intense. Cliff wanted to go down to the courthouse to stand before a judge and get married, then have our wedding at a later date. Being strong-willed, I let him know that this "courthouse marriage" idea was out of the question. I had *other* plans for my wedding day. At 31 and after waiting this long to get married, I was not going to suddenly rush into marriage.

In my heart of hearts, everything had to be just right and I was still getting to know Cliff. For my special, dream wedding day, I had envisioned a beautiful, "Garden-of-Eden" style wedding, where my Daddy would give me away and my family would be a big part of this very special day.

However, with each passing day Cliff was becoming more of a liability than an asset, and I was becoming more and more suspicious of him. As Cliff became comfortable with me, he began to share his shady past. By the time I found out he was fired from the bank due to illegal activity, I had already begun to seriously question his character. The pieces of the puzzle were coming together. He didn't have an honorable relationship with his mother and—instead of taking responsibility for his actions when things went wrong—he always blamed others. Supposedly, he had a huge amount of money saved up and stashed at his mother's house; yet, he was always broke.

I didn't want to believe that all of the ugly things I was learning about Cliff were true. He seemed so sweet that I just didn't want to think he could have possibly been involved in the things he so vividly described. As time passed, however, something started happening to me. I began to question his integrity and my future with a man like him. I knew that I didn't want to be married to a crook; nor did I want my son to have a loser for a dad. Besides, I was not desperate! I had known and dated educated, professional and successful men. I did not have to stoop that low!

Since we had begun attending church together, I tried to convince myself that the behaviors and incidents that Cliff shared with me were *all* in his past. I did not want to know that Cliff, like Kevin, was not truly converted as he pretended to be. The reality was that I had allowed myself to be suckered in and taken by his good looks, nice smile, charm and a false illusion. Now, I was knee-deep in the relationship and I didn't know how to get out. This time, though, I had much more at stake: my precious, little, two-year-old son Tristan.

Cliff was already attached to me like a leech, and what I said and did from that point forward was critical to our survival. Cliff began to frighten me! I began to notice that his mind was unstable. He had health issues and was emotionally unbalanced. I believe he was looking for a mother figure, but I knew that I wasn't "the one." He was "in darkness" and he began to speak a lot about violence and death.

Without marketable skills, Cliff needed to go back to school to earn a college degree; so I tried to steer him in that direction. I knew that his having more education and becoming marketable would be the only way we would have a viable future together. I knew I wanted and needed a man who was smart, educated and professional...like my Dad. However, the more I persisted, the more excuses Cliff made.

Backdrop

Cliff landed a job at a refinery in Carson, not far from my apartment. He was gainfully employed but not satisfied. The hours were long; the work was laborious; and the job politics were increasing his stress level. I was dissatisfied, too, because he was in a dead-end job that would not provide the financial security I knew I needed and his job at the refinery did not fit my idea of the occupation a husband of mine should have.

During this time, the Rodney King trial had been going on and there was unrest in Los Angeles. Cliff and I debated back and forth about the fate of the city if the jury rendered an unfavorable verdict. Cliff felt if the police officers got off there would be a riot like none other in Los Angeles. I disagreed. I told him he was being militant and nothing of the sort would happen. We were under a lot of stress as we tried to get to know each other, blend a family and earn a living. In short, we were from different sides of the tracks and I *wasn't feeling* his side. There were also the many personal issues Cliff was dealing with regarding his health, his mother and his son.

One night Cliff was lying face down on the couch in the living room while I was standing in front of the wall heater trying to get warm. I had just come home from teaching an aerobics class and I was cold from my sweat. Cliff hadn't been home from work very long when he and I became embroiled in another one of our discussions about black verses white and the black man's plight in society. Hotheaded and opinionated I had very little patience or compassion. It was my way or the highway! I was a single mother, raising a son and had very little patience with men, especially after what I had gone through with my baby's father. As soon as Cliff gave his view in the discussion of work and education, I shot him down and gave him no consideration for his side of the argument. I told him that what he was saying was nonsense and went on to explain why.

At that point, my mild-mannered, sweet-talking Cliff calmly said, "Karen, I'm not in the mood."

I thought to myself, "I heard you out, so you are going to hear me out!" I persisted.

Again, Cliff calmly said, "Karen, I *don't* want to talk about this."

"You can't tell me you can't get a job and go to college! My Father fed eight mouths, worked a full-time job and got his master's degree. And he did it during the late 60's and early 70's when it was very difficult for a black man to get an education, let alone provide for a family."

Unable to stop once I got started, I went on to tell Cliff that if my Daddy could obtain a master's degree back then, anybody could. As I finished my tirade I told him that he was just making excuses and needed to man up.

The Clutch of Death!

When I told him that he was just making excuses, Cliff went into a violent rage like I had never seen before. He was like "The Hulk!" He transformed into the monster he had candidly told me about but that I refused to believe. The brutal, uncontrollable rage was loosed! Cliff forcefully smashed his fist into my glass coffee table then he leaped off the couch and lashed out at me. Grabbing me by my neck, he lifted me off the floor and held me in mid air like a chicken. As he slung me against the wall, I begged and pleaded for him to let me go. He held me, cursed me and told me he would kill me.

With all the breath and strength I had, I pleaded and tried to break free; but his grip was too strong. Still holding me by my neck, the Cliff-turned-monster slammed me like a rag doll into another wall. As he tightened his death grip on my neck, he angrily continued to curse and threaten to kill me. I could feel the life beginning to leave my body. I was beginning to lose consciousness. I had no doubt that I would die that night.

I hoped that Tristan was still sleeping in the next room and had not heard us. Oh, how I desperately wished he were big and strong enough to save me from the clutches of this savage beast. The third time Cliff slammed me onto the couch; he loosened his grip on my neck enough so I could finally breathe. Cliff held me down, strangling me with one hand, while taunting me with a jagged piece of glass with the other hand. Crying, begging and pleading for my life, I laid there at his mercy. Then, in an instant, he let me go, got up and left. Shocked by the sudden change, I ran in the bedroom and grabbed my baby. Thankfully, Tristan was still sound asleep. Traumatized, but too afraid to call the police, I gathered up some clothes, grabbed my baby, jumped in my car and raced to spend the night with my girlfriend, Shari. At daybreak, I took my baby and we headed for Sacramento, where I could feel safe.

Cliff later told me it was a picture of Jesus hanging over my couch that convicted him. He went on to say that while he was taunting me he glanced up and the picture caught his eye. He realized he had been tormenting me in the presence of Jesus. In an instant, a calming spirit came over him and he loosed me from his grip. Cliff acted as if he was demon possessed!

There are times we may have to contend with evil forces but God has given us the weapons we need to overcome them.

Finally, my brethren, be strong in the Lord, and in the power of his might. Put on the whole armour of God, that

you may be able to stand against the wiles of the devil. For
we wrestle not against flesh and blood, but against princi-
palities, against powers, against the rulers of the darkness
of this world, against spiritual wickedness in high places.

(Ephesians 6:10-12)

The Voice of Reason

In fear of my life, I decided to move to Sacramento. With
no future job prospects, I searched for a place to live and
found favor with the manager of the first apartment complex
I visited. For some reason, Brenda took a liking to me and
approved me for a beautiful, upscale two-bedroom apartment
on the lake in Sacramento's Pocket area. Although I knew my
decision to relocate meant leaving a good job with benefits
and starting over from scratch, I did not care. I felt certain I
would lose my life if I went back. I also knew that, if I took this
leap of faith, the LORD would provide. I felt completely justified in my decision. I wasn't worried about whether I would be
able to find a job, make new friends and find good, Christian
childcare for my son, as long as we were safely away from
Cliff.

When I felt I was able to talk with Mom about what happened, she listened intently as I told her everything. But
when I finished, she candidly told me to go back home to Los

Angeles. I could not believe what I was hearing. I told her if I went back Cliff would surely kill me. She said Cliff wasn't crazy enough to kill me, and if I were going to leave Los Angeles, I needed to do it the *right* way. She said I needed to go back, give two weeks' notice at work, properly inform my apartment manager, etc. I was so traumatized that I didn't care about any of that.

I told Mom that Cliff could have my apartment, furniture and everything. I didn't care! I just wanted to be as far away from him as possible. Mom persisted and assured me I had nothing to worry about. Hesitant, I took my mother's advice and returned to my home in Carson. I was afraid to see Cliff. How could I stay under the same roof with him? I knew if I went home, he would be there.

Heeding the coaching from my mother, I knew I needed to return home with a more gentle spirit. Cliff didn't have to worry about me arguing with him anymore, since Pandora's Box had been opened and the true Cliff had been unleashed. Determined to make it through my two weeks after giving notice on my job, I tried to be as nice to Cliff as I knew how. Mom said to deal with him "with a long-handled spoon." I had to keep him calm and let him know that I was in his corner. Mom had also said I should tell him how much I loved him.

On my return, Cliff had been very apologetic and I accepted his apology; but when he became upset, I did exactly what

Mom said to do. I spoke calmly and I did not argue with him. I was agreeable and did my best to keep him calm. I was learning that what the word of God says in Proverbs 15:1 is so true. "A soft answer turns away wrath, but grievous words stir up anger." I was learning to listen to the voice of reason and God was making His way into my life though I was not aware of it at the time.

Cliff's mom, a highly educated, professional woman, wanted the best for her son. She tried to get him to leave California and go to North Carolina. She wanted him to get away from his environment, go to college and make a fresh start. I loved that idea and encouraged him, as well. I told him I was moving to Sacramento but that I would marry him after he graduated from college. To keep the peace, I continually reassured him of my love for him. Eventually, we talked about the night of that violent attack. Cliff denied any intention of killing me. He said that he just wanted to *put fear in me*. That he did! Not wanting to upset him, I went along with him, and things went well for a few days. Then, one night his demon re-emerged and I was tested again.

Fast Asleep

To the best of my recollection, it was a weeknight. Tristan and I had retired early because I had to rise early for work the next morning. Although we lived in a one-bedroom apartment, my bedroom was large enough to fit a twin bed in it along with my queen-sized bed. Tristan had his own bed, but I would often put him in bed with me when Cliff wasn't around.

In a deep sleep, Tristan was stretched out next to me and together we slumbered and slept peacefully. Without my knowledge, Cliff slipped into my room and sat on the edge of Tristan's bed, his twisted mind contemplated taking my life as he watched us sleep.

Suddenly, I was awakened by his presence and saw Cliff sitting very still in the dark, staring at me in utter silence. Spooked, I could clearly see his image in the light of the small nightlight next to my bed. Now completely conscious, I cautiously rose up to talk to him. He was leaning forward with his arms resting on his thighs and his hands hanging between his legs. I couldn't tell whether he had anything in his hands or not but I knew his behavior was very odd. When I suddenly sat straight up I could see he held a butcher's knife.

I was frightened to death but as calmly as I could, I asked Cliff what he was doing with the knife. He slowly moved from Tristan's bed and sat next to me on my bed. He put the knife to my neck and told me he was going to kill me that night. With my little angel sleeping next to me, Cliff taunted and tormented me with the knife, but as frightened as I was I remembered Mom's instructions.

Calmly I said, "Cliff, I love you." I begged him not to harm me and promised we would be together after he finished college. Once again God kept me from the clutches of death and covered me with His protection. As that demon was loosed, Cliff let me go. He went into the bathroom, collapsed on the floor and wept. He told me he had a bleeding ulcer but he didn't want to go to the hospital, he just wanted to be held and cuddled.

No Turning Back

I can remember there was a time I swore by Los Angeles. I did not want to live in any other place. I loved the weather, the beaches, fulfilling my dreams and exploring numerous opportunities. I had made many friends and had a lot of fabulous memories until my life became entangled with Cliff. I never had any plans to move away from Los Angeles, but now in grave danger and still feeling unfulfilled and empty I had come to the place that it was time to leave "the city of angels" and could hardly wait to start all over again. In fact, I counted down the days until my move to Sacramento.

When I put in my two weeks' notice my immediate supervisor and the General Manager were deeply saddened by the news of my relocation. They respected my decision, and in fact admired my tenacity because I was a single mom and I didn't have a job waiting for me in Sacramento. They appreciated my professionalism, hard work ethic and level of commitment to my job. They threw me a very nice going away party and my General Manager even told me he would hold my job open for one year and welcome me back if Sacramento didn't worked out. Looking back, I am so glad I listened to my mother and did the right thing by giving my two week's notice and leaving my job, apartment complex and friends in good standing.

However, as long I was still in Los Angeles, I still was not out of the woods. There was no doubt about it; Cliff was unstable and emotionally unbalanced! There were times when I felt the only reason Cliff didn't go completely off the deep end was his deep love for his own child with another woman. I believe Cliff felt that his little boy was all he had to live for. Cliff knew that our relationship was over and often expressed his doubt that I would wait for him until he graduated from college. I kept saying the words; assuring him I would and even gave him my new telephone number in Sacramento so we could stay in touch. I didn't want him to think I was leaving him forever and out of desperation kill me and himself. God kept me and steered me to Sacramento where I could safely make a new life for Tristan and myself.

When I got to Sacramento, God continued to bless me though I didn't realize it at the time. I found the Sacramento people to be friendly and my new apartment complex manager, Brenda, became my first new friend. Brenda was also instrumental in helping me find a job. After I was settled in, I went to work, attended to my son and from time to time I would go out while my sister and her kids watched Tristan. I met and made new male friends, but nothing serious. I had lived at the Landing on the lake in South Sacramento for a year and then decided to downsize to start saving money for a home. Brenda was not happy about my decision, but I had to do what was best for Tristan and me.

God Speaks

I was a very protective mom and didn't let Tristan go outside to play alone. Most of the time, he played in our little apartment. One Saturday morning as I was doing my weekend chores, four-year old Tristan was bouncing around in the living room playing and watching cartoons.

He suddenly stopped what he was doing, looked up at me and spouted out in a jolly tone, "I want to go to church."

I was surprised by his outburst but when Tristan went right back to playing and watching his cartoons, I went on about my business not giving it much thought. When it happened again a few weeks later, I pondered what he said wondering where he had heard about church but didn't respond or act on his strange request. I was too busy working and "doing my thing" and church was not a priority! I was totally focused on working and mothering my son. After some time had passed, Tristan and I were in my bedroom when he said it for the third time.

"Mommy, let's go to church," he said in a very fun, loving tone just as he might say, "I want to go to Disneyland."

I don't know why, but this time it stopped me dead in my tracks and I got it! I knew the Lord had just spoken directly to me through my child and this time I knew I had to give my little boy's request serious attention.

From that day forward, I began my quest to find a church home. I began to ask others about their church homes and accepted several invitations to attend with them. Sunday after Sunday Tristan and I attended church after church; a Baptist Church, then the Church of God in Christ and several non-denominational churches as well. None of the churches compelled me to join and, although I returned to one, I had no interest in becoming a member.

One day when I took Tristan to the barbershop for a haircut, I asked the barber if he could recommend a church in the area. It turned out that the person whose hair he was cutting was a pastor. We all began to talk and I got a good feeling about this pastor. He was young, his church was small but growing and he appeared to be a forward thinker. The next Sunday, I went to that church and joined. I don't believe my meeting this pastor was happenstance. It was by divine providence for I was diligently searching and that church changed my life forever.

Now that I was in church, my life was beginning to come into harmony. I loved nothing more then being a mom to my child and spending quality time with him when I was not working. I was content being single and for the first time my spirit was at peace. I liked my new-found faith! In the meantime, my mother moved to Sacramento from Richmond, California and joined the same church. We enjoyed our worship experiences together. I got more involved in the church's activities and got Tristan involved, too. There were a lot of boys his age so he enjoyed church.

I met Tim at church and once again silenced the Holy Spirit and a good friendship developed. He was good company and it was important to me that he was a man who "truly loved the Lord and demonstrated that." He was from a respectable family and I dearly loved his sweet mother. It remained my heart's desire that the man in my life would sincerely love my son as much as he loved me. Tristan and I were a "package deal," so Tim, Tristan and I spent time together. As our platonic relationship grew, I discovered Tim was not completely sold on "the ready-made family." He had no experience with nurturing kids, and his personal needs left very little time for a woman with a child. It was during this time of awkwardness and uncertainties with Tim that I bumped into a tall handsome man named Jon.

As time went on, my pastor felt like God was calling the congregation to move to another location and the members embraced his vision. Time marched on and the church began to grow. The pastor came to the congregation a second time. We loved our pastor and wanted to support his vision, so the church was uprooted and moved again to a better location. About that time, some negative things transpired and even before my dating relationship ended with Tim, God began paving the way for me to move from this church family and worshipping with my mother to a new church home.

It was tough, though. I still had a lot to learn about my walk with Christ. During this time my Christian experience was just about church activities and "attending church." I didn't know about the sanctification process and what it meant to have a personal relationship with Christ. Sadly, I was in the church but ignorantly lost though I could sense this chapter of my church experience was beginning to close and a new one was about to open. Had I taken my eyes off Jesus, I don't know what turns my life might have taken.

But we all, with unveiled face, beholding as in a mirror the glory of the Lord, are being transformed into the same image from glory to glory, just as by the Spirit of the Lord.

(2 Corinthians 3:18)

It is only by beholding Jesus that we are changed into His likeness. His perfect life will then be assimilated into ours as we daily seek to know His will and surrender our lives to His control. This change is made possible as we study His word and come to Him in prayer.

Chapter Five

A Determined Destiny

My desire to walk closer with the Lord and come to know Christ and worship at a place where my son and I could feel at home in the truth of God meant so much to me. I remained prayerful as I sought God's direction for our lives.

First Impressions

It was 1996 when I met Jon, strictly by accident—or so I thought. At that time, he was a cameraman for KXTL Fox 40 News, Sacramento. I was an entrepreneur running a networking business and an aerobics instructor. As a single mom, I was determined to remain self-employed to maintain a flexible work schedule so I could spend quality time with my son when he was not in school.

On one sunny day, I had decided to take some fliers to a nearby Sacramento school to promote a new aerobics class I was teaching at the Salvation Army. I was driving around the Oak Park Neighborhood in search of a place to promote my class when I spotted an elementary school. The parking lot was filled with cars, so I thought it would be a great place to promote my new class. I pulled into the lot, but because it was full, I parked illegally in a red zone, behind a white van.

A gentleman rushed over and in a hyper but friendly tone of voice said, "Excuse me! But you can't park here!"

I thought to myself, "Who are you to tell me where I can park?" But I restrained myself and merely asked, "Why?"

"Because you will get towed away!" he answered.

Our attention was diverted to a mutual acquaintance that was leaving the event. It turns out this gentleman I had just met had videotaped the event that had just been held here at the school. The three of us talked and I learned the gentleman's name was Jon Johnson. During that time, I often found myself shifting gears from aerobics instructor to a recruiter for my network marketing business. The conversation with Jon went well, so we exchanged business cards and went our separate ways.

After a few days passed, I decided to give Mr. Johnson a call. He was very polite and willing to hear my presentation, so we met over lunch at Panda Express, one of his favorite fast-food restaurants.

Shortly after I finished my presentation, Jon made it very obvious that he was not the least bit interested in what I was trying to sell but he was interested in me! He invited me to his home after our meeting which I immediately declined. Trying to prove he was a perfect gentleman, Jon asked if we could meet at the pool where his kids would be swimming. I put two and two together; Jon was a single dad who spent time with his kids. Though I was impressed and he immediately scored major points, I still declined his invitation.

My Surprise

It was approximately 5:50 a.m. when I pulled into the parking lot at the Riverside Athletic Club. I jumped out of my car with only a few minutes to spare before my 6:00 a.m. class. Scurrying into the aerobics room, my Golden Girls were waiting and ready to move to the nostalgic tunes of the Big Band music I played for the senior's class. I had just walked over to the stereo to start the music when I saw a tall, African American gentleman aiming a television camera down at me from the second story. To my surprise it was Jon again and he was taping my class.

In spite of feeling totally unprepared to be videotaped, I smiled at Jon, sucked it up and started my class. The ladies had such great attitudes and loved being videotaped! Personally, I would have appreciated prior notice, but chose to "go with the flow." After taping for a little while, Jon left the room and I was able to calm down. When my class was over, Jon and his reporter were standing in the lobby area as if they were waiting for me. This was my second surprise encounter with the mysterious Mr. Jon Johnson but I was already involved in a relationship, so we exchanged a few words and went our separate ways. Jon's conversation was always so pleasant. He was soft-spoken, very easy going, a good listener and non-threatening.

Being a single mom and always "on the go," I embraced and welcomed challenges as I strived to make ends meet. While Tristan was at a private Christian preschool, I worked my networking business and taught aerobics classes. I had several contracts and taught approximately 12 to 13 classes a week at various health clubs around town, including the Salvation Army, Step One, Riverside Athletic club and the City of Sacramento Parks and Recreation.

On one particularly busy day, I had to make a quick stop at the Salvation Army to pick up some fliers. As I made my way to the office to talk with the director, I was surprised to see Jon and his reporter walking toward me. After greeting each other, he shared he had just finished doing a story on some of the players from the Sacramento Kings. We talked for a few minutes and again went our separate ways. Astonished by the unlikelihood of running into each other a third time, I began to ponder the various times we had "bumped into" each other. Was it fate or did God have something to do with our paths crossing?

I was more than just curious having learned to seek God before assuming every man that came into my life was a potential "Mr. Right." One Christian writer advises we double up on our prayers when we are praying for God to provide a lifelong partner. I knew I needed someone special and I knew God would not let me down if I allowed Him to work His purposes in me first. I knew God had some serious work to do in me even before I met my life's mate. I was still a babe in the Lord with only "a mustard seed size faith," but the scriptures say that's all I needed to accomplish great things.[2] Though my faith was small, I had enough to trust God to one day bless me with the right man.

My relationship with Tim began a downward spiral, as I found him to be prideful and self-centered. A previously failed marriage had left him vulnerable and needing constant attention. Although I kept hoping our relationship would take a more positive turn, the more I got to know him, the more I was

---

[2] Matthew 17:20

convinced that we were a mismatch. I felt the relationship was beginning to take its toll on all of us. I had to come to grips with the fact that Tim was not the man for me or the father figure for my child. After dating Tim for about a year, we agreed that what we both wanted and needed in a relationship were very different and decided to part on friendly terms.

Right around the time of my break up with Tim, I decided to take on a part-time job with a Wireless cell phone company to generate more income. One particularly quiet day, I decided to close shop and take a 30-minute lunch break. I didn't want to venture far from my job, so I decided to go to the nearby fast food restaurant. After a quick burger and fries, I headed out the door just as Jon and a friend were entering. I was pleasantly surprised but since we were both in a hurry we briefly exchanged greetings before going our separate ways. This was our *fourth* chance encounter and I was convinced that our meetings were not by accident, but by divine providence. God now had my full attention.

Even though I wasn't seeing Jon, we talked on the phone from time to time for about a year. During my times of frustration with Tim, Jon seemed to instinctively know when to call and what to say. It seemed like whenever Tim and I would have a major disagreement; Jon would call and patiently allowed me to vent my frustrations. I loved the "patient quality" that I found in Jon but I made it very clear to him that I was a

Christian woman not interested in just dating. I was interested in a *husband*, not a long term boyfriend.

Official Date

After my breakup with Tim, things became really uncomfortable in my church. I knew it was time to leave but where would we go? I decided to wait on the Lord, be still and prayerful and let Him speak to me about where I was to go from there. In this quiet time with the Lord, I believe He was encouraging me to make Him the main man in my life and to realize no other man could satisfy my needs like Jesus could. As I studied His Word, I read the story of the Samaritan woman who came to fetch water, and met a Jewish man there who asked her for a drink of water.

Thinking it was an unusual request; she gave Him some water and entered into one of the most important conversations of her life.[3]

In the course of her conversation with Jesus, He told her He would give her living water to drink but first she needed to go and get her husband. She told him she had no husband. Jesus looked at her and His eyes pierced into her soul as if He were reading her heart and mind. Then He began to tell her about herself, how she had had five husbands and the one

---

[3] See John 4:1-26

she was with at the moment was not married to her. Realizing He knew all about her, she listened carefully as Jesus told her He was the Messiah and what He had to give her would satisfy all her needs.

Jesus answered and said to her, "Who ever drinks of this water will thirst again; but whoever drinks of the water that I shall give him will never thirst. But the water that I shall give him will become in him a fountain of water springing up into everlasting life."

(John 4:13-14 NAS)

I began to realize that having a man in my life was nothing compared to having God in my life. I had already learned the hard way that men can fail to keep their promises and will cheat, lie, betray and even desert me when I needed them most. But now I was learning that Jesus is always trustworthy, faithful, and hears me when I call. He understands my frustration and my pain because the Bible says He suffered just as we do.[4] He is not suspicious or overbearing, and He has promised to be a father to every child. With His promises in my heart, I decided to focus my attentions on raising my son and building my business as I waited for Him to lead me to the man and the church He wanted for me and my son.

---

[4] See Isaiah 53:3-5

I told myself I would wait as long as it takes but soon I began to have a longing for companionship. I was bored with the monotony of life when, out of the blue Jon called and asked me out. I had been toying with the idea that our so called chance meetings might have been divine appointments so when Jon called, I committed to a dinner date. Our first official date was at the quaint, Black-owned *Jazzmen's Art of Pasta Restaurant* in Old Sacramento. I can still remember it as if it was only yesterday.

It was a rainy dreary December day. I wanted to look nice for my date so I asked my niece, Ameerah, to braid my hair. She labored all day with the braiding of my hair but when she was finally finished, I was not at all pleased with the results. The weather was bad, it was definitely a bad hair day and I really wanted to just cancel my date with Jon. I couldn't find his phone number and definitely not wanting to stand him up, I quickly changed into my tan, silk Ann Taylor pantsuit, put on my makeup, jumped into my white BMW and scurried toward Old Sacramento, hoping Jon would still be there.

By the time I arrived at the restaurant it had started to rain again. I worried if I would find a parking space but to my surprise there was one right in front of the building. In spite of my easy access into the restaurant, I was not able to make it inside without getting my hair wet in the rain.

Once in the restaurant, I panned from left to right before spotting Jon sitting near the center of the dining room all by himself. Mortified by my hair, I wanted to turn around and go back home. Instead, I took a deep breath and made my way to the table where Jon was seated.

He smiled politely, but his words were few; my big hair had thrown him for a loop. Very self-conscious, I dominated the entire conversation, hoping to divert his attention away from my hair. After a very uncomfortable dinner, Jon abruptly announced that he had to go. When I asked him why, he gave me one of the lamest excuses I have ever heard—he needed to pick up a Christmas tree for his children. He walked me to my car and our first official date was over.

Once settled into my car, I couldn't wait to call Mom and tell her all about my worst date ever! I explained that our time together was no more than 45 minutes, that Jon barely talked and I doubted that I would ever hear from him again. I decided I would not call him; he would have to call me.

All Not Lost

Jon did call again and we chuckled about our first date. He told me that had our first official time together been a blind date, he never would have called me again but since he knew I was capable of making my hair look nice and I wasn't usually a chatter box, he decided to ask me out again. Thankfully, our second date was really quite romantic and very lovely. We continued to talk by phone and went out on a few more dates before we decided to establish a committed relationship with each other.

Jon and I had busy schedules but we saw each other when time permitted. He was still working as a cameraman for Fox 40 News and the Sacramento Kings. I had just taken on a full-time job in outside sales, which left very little time for Tristan let a lone a romantic relationship. Most the time spent with Jon was on weekends. While Jon and I dated, I often invited him to attend church with me but he always turned me down. I was still attending the same Church where I had met Tim but as I mentioned before, I knew the time had come for me to move on. I was inwardly hoping and praying that God would give me a deeper experience in Him and the messages I was hearing seemed watered down and not challenging enough. On top of that, I had to deal with my ex-boyfriend flaunting his new girlfriend who was at least 10 years his junior.

The Human Struggle

I was now a new employee of Pacific Bell Wireless, and had to go to Pleasanton, California for two weeks of training. On one or two occasions, Jon drove down to visit me.

I struggled with my relationship with God and Jon in the area of purity. I wanted to live in obedience to God's Word and stay away from lust and sex outside of marriage. Jon admired my sincere interest in serving God. We agreed to be loyal and committed to each other and to explore the possibility of marriage in the near future. But Jon was not a Christian. I began to understand why the Bible tells us to not be unequally yoked with an unbeliever.[5] It's hard enough for two believers in a relationship to stay pure but when only one is trying, the desire to please the other sexually can become overwhelming.

The sexual drive is a powerful thing and unless it is brought under the power of the Holy Spirit, one can only go so far playing with temptation. I'm not sure how long Jon and I dated before I gave in to the sexual act. At first I had a hard time dealing with the guilt, but as things progressed it became easier and easier to justify what I was doing. What I thought was bad suddenly didn't seem quite so bad and with time, it even felt normal. As we got deeper involved sexually, Jon became everything I needed and God subtlety took second place in my life. I gave into sexual lust and would do whatever it took to keep Jon in my life. I was being driven by lust not love which led me astray and into sin.

---

[5] See 2 Corinthians 6:14

While I still thought God was first in my life, my judgment was misconstrued and my reasoning abilities were seriously limited. I could not see the obvious flaws in Jon's character until a few months later I began to stumble upon some inconsistencies in Jon's behavior.

From Meager Beginnings

Jon and I had very special moments together especially when he began to share where he came from and who his parents were. I felt these were important for me to know if I were to choose him as my life's partner. I wanted to know how he treated his mother so I could get an understanding of how he would most likely treat me as his wife.

Jon was born to a large sharecropper family in Arkansas and was always referred to by his family as Johnny Ray. Johnny Ray learned at a very young age the importance of hard work, education and perseverance. As a young child, he experienced separation and loss when his mother sneaked away with his sisters to California under the cover of night, leaving little Johnny Ray and his brothers for their father to nurture and "raise."

While growing up in the Deep South, Johnny was no stranger to racism. He encountered the Ku Klux Klan (KKK) firsthand when the owner of a little convenient store he frequented as a little kid, would taunt his family by night with racial threats and cross burnings in the front yard. Though the man was cloaked with a mask Jon said he recognized his voice. Especially endowed with a heart of gold, Johnny did not learn to hate people as a result of these racist incidents. If anything, those encounters developed in him the keen aware-ness of how to deal with all kinds of people, as well as the ability to love *all* people and deal with adversity.

Johnny Ray had a very close relationship with and greatly admired his father. A hard working, strict Christian man, Mr. James Johnson protected his boys and provided for them to the best of his ability. Johnny's early years were occupied with picking cotton on the plantation with his Dad and brothers often in the sweltering heat and for very little or no wages. Although most people would find a life of toil to be depressing, Johnny's hard work ethic had been cultivated. Johnny loved sharing stories about his childhood experiences. He was proud of his father's love and loyalty as a single parent, providing for the best years of his life.

One story that Johnny would share is how he walked for miles on the dirt roads to and from church, Sunday after Sunday. Johnny would often be angry that his dad chose him over his brothers to make the weekly journey. Once at church, Johnny had to sing while his Dad proudly accompanied him on the piano. Though Johnny had a beautiful voice, he had an aversion to singing in public and sometimes broke down in tears when his Dad made him sing.

An inward thinker, soft-spoken and very kind-hearted, Johnny Ray always expressed a great admiration for his Dad even when he did not agree with his methods of discipline or his ideas on how to be a good Christian man. Johnny said his father would take his little lunch money and give it to the "less-fortunate" kids. As much as Johnny Ray hated some of his father's practices, those experiences taught him to appreciate what he had. Johnny's humble beginnings explain why he was happy with the simple things of life.

I asked Jon to share a fond memory of his mother knowing he had been deeply affected by his mother's desertion and the lack of maternal love every child yearns for. Jon said he remembers when he was about four years old, his mother was bathing his sisters in a big steel tub and the lights suddenly went out. While his mother continued to bathe her girls in the dark, Johnny sneaked into the water and his mom began to bathe him. He longingly recalls the tender touch of his mother's hands which ended when the lights came on and she realized she was bathing Johnny. Startled, she quickly took her hands off him.

Sadness swept over me as I wondered how a mother could shun loving her child. Although there was no reason to believe Jon's father did not do his best to love and care for his sons, little Johnny's life was incomplete. As often happens when a child is abandoned by a parent, he doubted his mother's love for him and believed he was the cause of his parents' breakup.

After his father's sudden death, 15-year-old Johnny scrounged up enough money to catch a bus and headed west to Oakland, California hoping to be reunited with his mother and sisters. It did not take long for Johnny to discover that living with his mother was not going to work out.

Johnny began dating and eventually living with a woman twice his age. With no closure between him and his mother, Johnny was left to "figure things out," and he developed a very unhealthy attitude towards women. Growing up in the streets of Oakland around pimps, prostitutes and drug dealers, Johnny learned what *not* to do and miraculously "kept his nose clean."

As he entered adulthood, the only male role model Johnny had was a pimp who took interest in his well-being and encouraged him to stay in school. He allowed Johnny to make a little money by watching over his prostitutes. Johnny decided his ticket out of the ghetto was to get an education and excel in sports. While going to school, pursuing sports and trying to make a name for himself, Johnny changed his name from Johnny Ray to Jon.

I realized Jon was truly a troubled man, with a deep and painful history. His attitude toward women was not healthy and

I could see why. His Mother abandoned him for no apparent reason and even when she was apart of his life she gave him no nurturing love. I began to realize Jon was a survivor but he didn't have a healthy respect for women. Jon wanted women who would appease him and supply the great need he had for love, nurture and compassion. He desired the physical touch of a woman as well as emotional satisfaction.

I also knew Jon was a good man with a sweet compassionate heart. I saw Jon as a diamond in the rough, an unpolished stone that needed God to supply the love that had been missing in his life. But since a child's first image of God is found in the way he sees his parents, Jon had a distorted view of his Heavenly Father. As Jon looked at his mother, he saw a God who was not very kind or compassionate. Jon did receive a glimpse of God's heart through his Dad who did his best to raise his sons in love and reverence for the Lord.

Jon knew the depth of his need but did not know how to express it. He had in him a God-given gift of unconditional love especially toward children. I believe he saw himself in every child that was not loved or who had careless abusive parents. Jon always wanted to make others, especially children feel better. Yet at the same time he didn't know how to make himself feel better or how the wounded child within him could receive the healing he so desperately needed. As a result he pacified himself by moving from relationship to relationship, often entertaining many women simultaneously. It was really bizarre how I found out he was dating a reporter at his job, while in a "committed relationship" with me.

From Better to Worse

One hot summer's day, I had taken Tristan and Jon's two children to a movie when one of the children asked to go to the restroom. When I stepped outside with them, I saw Jon's reporter friend, Daisy.

We greeted one another and when Daisy realized that I was there at the movies with Jon's kids, she knew he had been lying to her about his involvement with me. I could not believe what I was hearing! Jon had told Daisy we had broken up. Knowing that I might not believe her, Daisy opened her purse and pulled out cards from Jon that expressed his love for her. I was absolutely livid!

Unable to reach Jon by phone, we jumped into our cars and headed straight to his condo. Not wanting to make a scene in front of his house, Jon took his kids inside and left us standing at his door. Daisy was in tears and wanted to flatten all the tires on Jon's vehicle. To avoid repeating the immature act I had engaged in eight years earlier with Tristan's father, I went home and vowed never to be with Jon again. Later, when Jon came to my house and asked for forgiveness, I told him it was over between us. I meant what I said realizing he was no different from the other cheaters I'd had in my life.

Break-through

After my breakup with Jon, I received the big break-through that changed the course of my life forever. While working in the Activation Department for Pacific Bell Wireless, I applied for a promotion and was selected for the Account Executive position. In this exciting but demanding new position, I would be selling cellular phones business to business. I was required to make a monthly quota so I was always in search for business referrals. Going over my list of possible contacts, I decided to ask the youth pastor at my church for some referrals. He didn't have many but he did give me the name and phone number of his best friend, Michael.

I met with Michael and in the course of my presentation, we started talking about God. In a very lively tone, he told me that I had not been to a Bible study until I had been to one of his. I was starving spiritually and asked Michael when the next Bible study would be held. He told me he wasn't able to do one right now because his mother was seriously ill and on her death bed. Realizing that this was not a good time for Michael, I agreed to meet with him another time to discuss both my business and my need for a Bible study.

Several weeks later I called to see how Michael was doing and he told me his mother had passed away. I offered my condolences and then we set up an appointment to meet. He decided to purchase a phone from me and said his sister needed a phone as well. When I pressed him to purchase two phones he consented on the condition I would allow him to do a Bible study for me. I agreed.

A few weeks passed before I thought again about Michael and his Bible study. Until one day, I was driving north on Interstate 5 with the drop-top down on my convertible and my music playing loud. It was a beautiful warm day and I should have been enjoying the drive but I suddenly realized how empty my life was. My heart was aching for change, for truth and for a new revelation from on high. I needed my spiritual and emotional tank refilled. I was missing Jon and feeling that God was not hearing my prayers. My thoughts turned to Michael and his Bible study offer so I called him.

As soon as he answered his phone I asked, "When I can have my Bible study?"

Michael questioned my sincerity about wanting this study, but as I explained my need for a spiritual refill we arranged to meet that night. I invited my mom and my nephews to join Tristan and me.

Michael began by asking us if we all loved the Lord. Without question, each of us responded in the affirmative. Pleased with our responses, Michael prayed and attempted to launch right into the study when Mom interrupted him.

"Michael, how should we worship?"

Michael chuckled and said, "Mom, I don't want to answer that question right now."

Mom insisted, "I really want to know."

Not wanting to get off track with what he had planned for the Bible study, Michael suggested he answer her question another time. But as she persisted, I became curious and wanted to know as well.

Michael explained, "If I tell you some of it, I have to tell you the whole thing."

We persisted until Michael gave in and started out by telling us the true day of worship is the Sabbath which is Saturday not Sunday.

Shocked, I interrupted him asking, "But I thought the Sabbath was Sunday?"

Michael opened his Bible and read Exodus 20:8-11 to us.

Remember the Sabbath day, to keep it holy. Six days you shall labor and do all your work, but the seventh day is the Sabbath of the LORD your God. In it you shall do no work: you, nor your son, nor your daughter, nor your male servant, nor your female servant, nor your cattle, nor your stranger who is within your gates. For in six days the LORD made the heavens and the earth, the sea, and all that is in them, and rested the seventh day. Therefore the LORD blessed the Sabbath day and hallowed it.

Then Michael asked me to get a calendar and a dictionary and to look up the meaning of the word "Sabbath." When I found its meaning and read the historical events that took place in order for the Sabbath day to be changed, I realized it was man who changed the day from Saturday to Sunday and not God. Michael explained that if God didn't change it then it really hadn't been changed.

My covenant I will not break, nor alter the word that has gone out of My lips.

(Psalm 89:34)

"That's why I began by asking if you all loved the Lord. If we truly love God," he patiently explained, "then we would want to be obedient to Him and follow as He leads and not after the traditions and laws of men that rise up against God's law for John 14:15 says, 'If you love Me keep My commandments.'"

When I received this new revelation a wave of conviction swept over me. This made such logical sense to me there was nothing to argue about, my mind was made up. I thanked God for giving me the answer I had been searching for. My

18-year-old nephew DeAndre also accepted this line of reasoning. Both of us were eager to hear more. Mom, however, rejected the new revelation and didn't want to hear any more about it. DeAndre told his grandma that we had invited the Holy Spirit to teach us and suggested we be careful not to close down what the Holy Spirit was trying to teach us. He said the study should continue so we could hear more and Michael went on to teach us about the Sabbath.

The presence of the Lord was there and we knew God was filling us with new grace and power. It was an awesome moment of God revealing His truth and we each had to decide for ourselves to accept it or harden our hearts from it and carry on in our ignorance, pretending that we never heard it. Even though all of us in that room may not have fully understood everything that was taught, I realized God was making Himself available to answer our quest for His truth.

Michael's study was so enlightening for me. I had never had anybody teach me about the Bible the way he did, and I insisted on another study. Being impressed to put us in the care of someone who was much more knowledgeable than he, Michael lead me to his spiritual mom, Virginia, who agreed to continue the studies with us.

Excited about my new revelation from God, I called my dear friend Arthur T. to confirm what we had just been taught about the Sabbath. After all, he had advised me to pray, watch and wait for God to lead me to a new church. He told me that if knowledge and understanding were what I was seeking, I was in the best place I could possibly be.

Then he confirmed the Lord's Holy Sabbath day and gave me his blessing. With a cheerful heart, I knew this was my answer to months of prayer and eagerly looked forward to more such in-depth Bible studies.

Jon's Second Appeal

It had been at least a month since Jon and I had broken up when he called, wanting to get back together. Convinced that we were destined to be together, I decided to give him another chance on the condition that he would attend Bible studies with me and participate in what I was learning. Jon agreed and we began our new journey of studying and learning the Bible together. I was growing closer to God and no longer wanted to sin against my body, but I didn't want to lose Jon either. I knew that sex was his weakness and if I denied him, he might go elsewhere. I was "stuck between a rock and a hard place," as I continued to straddle the fence between my new found revelation and desiring the things of the world.

Jon and I decided we needed some time away and took a week-long, luxury vacation to Montego Bay, Jamaica, where we lodged at the Breezes Hotel. This was my first trip to the

Caribbean and it was more than I could have ever imagined. From the island's breathtaking beauty and clear blue sky to its pristine beaches and carefree atmosphere, it was a perfect romantic getaway. We spent our days leisurely eating, lounging, taking lots of photos and dancing. Being That I'm an outdoors person, I love being close to nature and enjoyed the mountains and the water.

One day, I decided it might be fun to go snorkeling and talked Jon into trying it out. We walked down to the beach, rented our gear and I quickly suited up ready to test the picturesque waters. When I looked around for Jon, I noticed he seemed to be just going through the motions of putting on his gear. Wondering what the problem was, I pressed him for an explanation. I couldn't refrain from laughing when "my country boy from Arkansas" embarrassingly confessed that he did *not* know how to swim. Although I persisted that he come into the shallow water with me, he did not budge until I finally persuaded him to submerge his body just long enough for me to take a couple pictures of him looking like a starfish.

All too soon our vacation was over and we had to go back to reality. We still faced many challenges struggling to deal with our old ways. Though we maintained our Bible studies with Virginia we did not seem to be able to change our circumstances. Jon finally admitted he'd only agreed to study the Bible with me to shut me up but he did establish a strong bond with our dear teacher, Virginia and embraced the Sabbath. Lovingly, she met a need in Jon caused by his mother's absence from his life. He soon began calling Virginia, "Mom."

I realized I loved Jon but I wondered how long I could put up with his behaviors. Even though I understood why Jon cheated, it was still very hard to accept. It wasn't easy but I decided to hang in there in the strength of God and to go forward with this man I felt God had brought into my life. I felt strongly to look beyond Jon's faults and see his need for real love. I knew I could not do it in my own strength but the promise in Philippians 4:13 continually encouraged me. "I can do all things through Christ who strengthens me."[6] I just wanted to see Jon come to know God as his Father and find in Him the shelter and the unconditional love only God can give. I knew what God was doing for me and I wanted the same for Jon.

Ask, and it will be given to you, seek and you will find; knock, and it will be opened to you.

(Matthew 7:7)

---

[6] KJV

Chapter Six

Signs, Wonders and a Wedding

One afternoon after a routine dental appointment, I decided to drop by Jon's house to see if he was home. He lived close by and I had a flexible work schedule at the time. As I approached Jon's home, I noticed a young, attractive woman driving up to the gate in a car that looked just like Jon's. I waited at a distance to see if she was going to park in Jon's stall and sure enough she did. Not wanting to jump to conclusions, I moved closer to the house but maintained my composure as I waited to see if she would go inside Jon's condo. When she did, I hopped out of my car and scurried to the door. When I rang the doorbell, the mystery woman opened the door wearing a nurse's smock. I politely introduced myself as Karen, Jon's girlfriend, and she introduced herself as Diana, his wife. Shocked but needing some answers, I accepted her invitation to come in.

I suddenly realized that since Jon and I had reunited, he always came to *my* house. As I stepped inside, a creepy feeling came over me. Whenever I had previously been there, Jon's place had always been freshly scented and very tidy. But this time there were dirty dishes in the kitchen sink and on the counter tops. Things were strewn all over the living room which was far different then the character I had come to know. As she openly began to talk about herself, she told me how much she loved smoking weed and that her habit took priority over everything, including Jon. I could hardly believe what I was hearing. She didn't seem to be Jon's type and when I asked her where her wedding ring was she said she didn't have one. She took me into Jon's untidy bedroom, opened the closet and showed me a few articles of her clothing. Somehow, I still was not convinced she was his wife; maybe an old girlfriend or a fling but not his wife! I stared at her in utter disbelief!

Determined to confront Jon and hear his side of the story, "his alleged wife" and I devised a plan. I told her Jon owed me money and I would call and ask him to bring it to me at the Safeway Store. We agreed on the time and location then went our separate ways. Jon and I met up at the store as planned. While we were talking, Diana arrived and we confronted him together. I asked him who this woman was to him and he confessed that she was indeed his wife. Jon and I were the same age but his wife was at least 10 years younger. As I processed it all; her marijuana smoking and her Daisy Duke shorts, I knew I had been "played for a fool" again. I took my money, bowed out gracefully and went my way, determined not to ever let Jon back into my life again!

Mr. Johnson was a "smooth operator" and he continued to pursue me. I must admit that Jon was a true challenge for me. I loved him and desired to have him. Jon knew about the size of my ego and that I was quite a competitor who detested losing. When I allowed him to plead his case, he knew all the right things to say. He began by telling me he didn't have a traditional marriage, that he wasn't living with his wife and that he did not even love her. Jon shared that his wife had three sons and needed to show Social Services that she could provide a stable home for them. He claimed he had only married her to give the appearance of stability so they wouldn't take her kids away from her. He said they were going through a divorce and if I would just be patient with him, the whole process would soon be over.

I gave in to Jon, but I knew it would take a lot for me to trust him again. I really wanted to settle down and believed it should be with Jon, so we continued to date while he was going through his divorce process. We had our ups and downs as I struggled with trusting him, but we continued. Our boys were the same age and got along really well. They were growing close and we enjoyed events as a family, especially during the summer season. We also continued to have our Bible studies. I prayed that, through learning God's Word, Jon would fall in love with Jesus, be truly converted and follow Christ completely. I desired for us to be a godly family someday.

When I asked Jon what it was about me that he liked, he said it was the fact that I was striving to be a Godly woman. I didn't just talk about church, but I was actually *in* church. He also complimented me on being a good mother to my son. Unlike me, Jon didn't have a close and loving relationship with his family. He would talk with his siblings from time to time and told me they had grown further apart over the years. He had no connection with his mother and often spoke of how badly she had treated him. I found myself trying so hard to make up for his lack of maternal love that I over looked the red flags and the many inconsistencies in his life. I just wanted him to find Christ and I sincerely believed that I was the bridge to that connection.

How naive and foolish I was as I think back to how I tried to devise my own plan to accomplish what I wanted and tried to get God to agree with me. I should have stayed away from Jon during this time and allowed God to do the major surgery Jon needed on his wounded heart. I've since learned that God works more efficiently and quickly when we stay out of the way and trust Him. Hindsight is always twenty/twenty but it just makes me love God more when I think of my own ignorance and blind determination to have things my way. He knew what I needed even though I couldn't see that at the time. I just needed to walk with Him and remain upright and let God do things His way and in His timing without trying to help God bring about my desired solutions.

"For My thoughts are not your thoughts, nor are your ways My ways," declares the Lord. "For as the heavens are higher than the earth, so are My ways higher than your ways and My thoughts than your thoughts."

(Isaiah 55:8-9 NAS)

Yet Another Sign

Even with his many years of photojournalist experience at Fox 40 News, Jon knew it would be difficult to provide for a family and continue to live on his meager salary. He decided to leave Fox 40 to pursue work as a freelance photojournalist. Having many connections in Sacramento and the San Francisco Bay Area, Jon landed a favorable position in San Francisco with a station that quadrupled his earnings, provided a company vehicle, company credit card, high-rise apartment overlooking the city, and a healthy expense account. I wasn't too keen on the idea of him living away and seeing him only on the weekends but we settled into a routine that seemed to work at the time. One evening, Jon asked me to put the boys in the car and take a ride to the Bay to hang out with him. He wanted us to see where he was living and to let the boys hang out in the city for a day. He wanted to put my mind at ease and we all had a nice time together.

My own new sales job also came with a nice pay increase and the desire to buy a brand new house began to fill my thoughts. Many of my colleagues were buying new homes and I felt my son and I were just as deserving as the next family. I didn't want Tristan to grow up in an apartment. My sales position yielded me a nice, stable income. I worked hard to meet my sales quota every month and continued to save money. With my goal to buy a house in front of me, I became more aggressive in my prospecting. I made sure to ask for referrals from each sales call that I made.

One day, I received a referral to call a man named Allen, a young up-and-coming land developer in Sacramento. When I met him, there was an instant connection between us. As we talked, it seemed as if I had known him all my life. I really wanted the sale but I quickly discovered that our network was too new and that it was also inferior to his present carrier (our competitor). I needed the sale, but I had to maintain my integrity. So I walked away from the deal but gained a friend for life and more referrals.

One of the referrals I received from Allen led me to a person who knew Jon. Typically, I went to the customer but for some odd reason this man came to my apartment to work out some final details. In the course of our conversation, I told him my boyfriend worked as a cameraman in San Francisco. He shared with me that his sister was dating a "bigwig" cameraman who also worked in the Bay Area. When I showed him some pictures of my Jamaica trip with Jon, he suddenly became angry saying that was the *same man* his sister was dating. It's amazing how many signs God was giving me, yet I just continued to forgive and forget hoping that one day Jon would change.

Jon and I continued to date and attend our weekly Bible studies when he was available. I really desired to give my heart completely to the Lord, not holding anything back. I was tired of defiling my body and not living a true Christian life.

Because Jon knew my heart's desire, he didn't pressure me to have sex because he knew that's what his heart's desire should be, too. However, I knew that Jon continually dealt with much sexual temptation, thus, I straddled the fence and our lives became more and more entwined. He knew I wasn't going to play house, and it was "do or die" so we began to talk more and more about getting married.

Jon still owned his condo but desired a house where his kids could have their own bedrooms. He liked Elk Grove and was looking for a home in that area. I had been looking in my sales territory of Roseville but Jon made it very clear he was not moving to Roseville, so I surrendered and we began our search together for a home in Elk Grove.

House hunting together was extremely challenging. We saw many nice homes but could not agree. I fell in love with the lake front homes in Laguna West, however, Jon wanted to live in the more mature areas of Elk Grove with shade trees, easy school access and wild life. I loved the water and wanted to live on the lake in Laguna West and reasoned that by putting our money together we were more than qualified for a beautiful, single-story home on the lake. He did not see it my way and did not even entertain my logic. We continued to search for a house, but with no success.

In the meantime, things were stirring up on my job. Management was changing hands and with that came a new boss with whom I began to have conflicts. Anxious to get into a home before I lost or quit my job, I went ahead and qualified for a loan on my own while Jon took his sweet time looking for just the right house. Mom was also eager for me to make my first new home purchase, so she willingly accompanied me on many house-hunting tours. Stumbling upon a cute, little single-story home in Elk Grove, I put a deposit down and told Jon my plans.

Realizing I meant business, he accompanied me to see my new residence. Upon seeing it he immediately objected! He did not like the location, the size or the builder. He said if he were going to live with me, it would not be in that house. I withdrew my deposit and we started our house hunting afresh. Eventually, we found a house that we both liked in the Laguna Creek area and moved ahead with the purchase. Still not married, the house was purchased in my name only. I planned to live in my new home with my son until Jon and I became husband and wife.

By November 1998, it had been eight months of consistently going to church and studying with Virginia. I was ready to commit my life to Christ, completely. Jon, on the other hand, was "not quite there." I was moved by the Holy Spirit one Sabbath day at the Black Convocation that it was time for me to go all the way and get baptized. I went ahead without Jon, and eagerly called him afterward to share my news. Disappointed, he asked me why I had not waited for him.

Thrilled to hear his desire to get baptized, I arranged to get re-baptized, but this time with Jon and Tristan together as a family at Sacramento Central Seventh Day Adventist Church. I believed that having a new life in Christ would make life easier. At that time I also thought it would be best if we stopped having premarital sex until our wedding day.

The Flesh and God's Will

My spirit was willing but my flesh was weak. I struggled to do God's will and wait until we were married but slipped up from time to time. Totally disappointed in myself, feeling like a hypocrite and a failure, I was baptized a third time. This time Jon mocked and called me "Mother Theresa" as he and Tristan looked on. I wanted to get it right! I wanted to be pure! Finally, one day Virginia came to me and asked me why I was getting re-baptized. She explained to me that I did not need to get baptized every time I sinned. She taught me communion was instituted by God as a way of renewing us, giving us hope to keep going and a mini cleansing to give a fresh new beginning when condemnation and guilt threatened to overwhelm us.

In Him we have redemption through His blood, the forgiveness of sins, according to the riches of the Grace.

(Ephesians 1:7)

By March 1999, the new house in Elk Grove was ready for us to move in. I made it very clear we would not live together until after our marriage ceremony. When I moved into the new home it was with big hopes that within a few months we would be married and the two of us would become one. Jon agreed and though he moved out of his condo and moved his furniture into the new house, he lived with a friend.

Though I went ahead with our wedding preparations, Jon seemed to be stalling. As the time drew closer, I became concerned as Jon was not as excited as I was; in fact he seemed to be getting cold feet. Then he told me we had to hold off because he was having problems with his divorce. In spite of the fact that this had supposedly been an arranged marriage to help her out with Social Services, it appeared his wife was delaying matters and holding things up. He was very adamant about not moving ahead until matters of the divorce were completely settled. Of course I had to agree.

While on hold, I took things in stride and continued to decorate my new home; but looking back I believe God was still trying to get my attention. As with so many times in the past, there were many, many flagrant fouls that I chose to ignore. Driven to have this man, I became more and more anxious to move full steam ahead. Guilt over our sexual transgressions and convinced marriage would make things right with God, I was afraid to investigate the legitimacy of Jon's stories and turned a blind eye to the things God was showing me. I didn't realize how true Proverbs 14:12 would prove to be in my life. "There is a way which seemeth right unto a man, but the end thereof are the ways of death."[7]

---

[7] KJV

When Jon finally gave me the green light, I didn't waste any time moving ahead with plans for our wedding day. Tristan was almost 11 years old, he needed a father in his life and I had no time to waste! I was getting older and knew it was time to settle down. I focused on the positive and made myself believe once we were married everything would be alright.

During the summer of 1999, my older brother, Ronnie, came from San Jose to visit us in our new home. Surprised by the size, location and amenities, he urged our 77-year-old father to come and see it, too. Dad's health was rapidly deteriorating, but he came and expressed his pride in my home purchase. It was a new house on a corner lot, across the street from a nature trail and a wild life sanctuary. My Dad recalled that the first house he bought in San Jose was on a corner lot and the home he was residing in now was on a corner as well. Having met Jon on a previous occasion, Dad knew that we were dating but I don't think he knew how serious we were. Knowing Jon was about to ask my father for his blessing to take my hand in marriage, I got up from the table and exited the kitchen where they were sitting and went upstairs.

When Jon popped the question, Dad paused, then looked up at him and asked, "Really?"

When Jon responded in the affirmative, Dad dropped his head and slowly returned to eating his salad, while Jon anxiously waited for my Dad's affirming yes. Finally, Dad broke the silence and gave Jon his blessing. The fact that, in spite of his nervousness, Jon honored my wishes by asking my Dad's blessing made me see he was willing to work to make the marriage right. I deemed this an act of love, which helped me overcome those nagging doubts about his secret life and confirmed Jon's dedication and fidelity to me. I also thought Jon's baptism before the Church was a sign that he was ready to put his secret life behind him and strive to follow Christ as a devoted husband to me and committed father to my son.

With my Dad's blessing, we moved forward with our plans to become a real family. I just knew things would work out since we had so much in common. We were the same age, had both been single parents and our boys were the same age with birthdays only nine days apart. We had the same majors and graduated from college the same year. Jon and I were both outgoing and loved people. We had come through a lot and both knew we wanted to spend the rest of our lives together. We also knew there would be the challenges most blended families experienced but we were willing to give it our all. I had to contend with all my doubts resulting from Jon's relationships with other women, but like a steam engine I steadily pressed forward with a determination to have our wedding; refusing to allow anything or anyone to get in my way.

Still Stabbing in the Dark

Our wedding plans were coming right along, the date was set for Sunday, September 3, 2000, in Ride, California. I was so happy, as all my dreams seemed to be coming true. I would have the beautiful garden wedding I had dreamt of for so long and though my Father's recurring bouts with pneumonia and emphysema had confined him to a wheel chair, he would "give me away" to my husband on our wedding day.

As all brides do, I wanted to have everything right before our special day including premarital counseling. I had just turned 40 and had waited a long time to be a bride so I looked forward to our premarital counseling sessions hoping that I would get more insight into the man I was about to marry. We needed counsel on how to blend two distinctly different families together as we all grew spiritually and emotionally. With the odds against us, I sincerely wanted to start off on the right path. I was willing to put the past behind us and start anew.

Since Jon and I were baptized together as a couple, I wanted the pastor at Central Church to take us through our premarital counseling sessions. In order to do that, we needed to complete a questionnaire before we could proceed with our counseling which we gladly did. However, after reviewing our questionnaires, my pastor came to me and told me he could not counsel us. His news came as a blow to me and when I asked him why, he gave me no further explanation.

Determined to get premarital counseling, I asked a pastor from another church who consented and we geared up again for our counseling sessions. However, when that pastor found out Jon was a producer-cameraman, he could not stay focused on the counseling we were there to do. The pastor was so interested in getting his own television program that he didn't want to talk about anything else. Too often Jon and I left our counseling sessions without any sense of accomplishment or guidance.

Determined to get counseling before marriage, I sought out yet another pastor who agreed to counsel us as well as preside over our wedding. The sessions went smoothly and Jon was pleased. I really desired to delve deeper, but Jon and the pastor were more comfortable with "keeping things on the surface." Session after session I walked away with "warm fuzzies" though I never felt like we were getting into the areas we really needed. I definitely was not gaining the insight I needed regarding the mystery man I was about to spend the rest of my life with within the covenant of marriage.

Should I Really?

As the day I would say "I do" drew near, there were more tests and trials that threatened my resolve to overlook Jon's obvious character flaws. One of the things I loved about Jon though was his willingness to help kids in any way he knew how. Jon's love and concern for children brought out the best in him and helping them seemed to give him great joy. He videotaped them at play, gave them candy, showed them favoritism at the Sacramento Kings' games by getting autographs from their favorite Kings players, and allowing them to come down on the floor with him after the games.

However, his passion to mentor fatherless boys led to a call from a woman emphatically telling me Jon had been mentoring her son and also having an affair with her. Even though Jon had mentioned the name of the woman's son to me several times, I was now very suspicious.

She was determined to convince me that Jon was much more than just a mentor to her teenage son. When I asked Jon about her, he completely denied her accounts of their relationship.

Furious, I tried desperately to convince the woman to meet with Jon and me so we could get down to the bottom of the matter; but she refused. Although Jon acknowledged that the woman had interest in him, he was adamant and said she was not "his type." He said she was crazy and they were just friends. I tried my best to get more information from her, but she would begin to tell me things and then suddenly hang up. Jon continued to deny anything more than a friendship existed between them.

When I asked him how she happened upon my telephone number, Jon said he must have called me from her home telephone while he was there mentoring her son. Within the course of a few months, Jon had my phone number changed twice in an effort to keep any further such calls from reaching me. I was incensed at the number changes, but Jon manufactured so many intricate lies that I began to think I was crazy.

With the big day just two weeks away, I was confused and unable to trust my own judgment. I was beginning to question whether I should go through with this wedding. I called my dear Mom for advice. Though she was not surprised or fooled the least bit by Jon's charades, she knew I wanted to marry him more than anything, so she gave me her blessing. She did, however, warn me to proceed with caution. You see, I would be the only one of her remaining four daughters to marry; hence, she was really looking forward to wedding day. So, I went ahead with my wedding plans.

My Gut Said, "No"

Again and again Jon was able to smooth things over with me. My head would say, "No!" but my heart kept whispering, "Yes!" The more my heart said "Yes," the more my head would rationalize that I had come too far to turn back. Like me, Mom was counting on Jon to let go of his foolishness once we got married. I comforted myself with the thought that Jon would not want to marry me if he didn't love me. I was convinced that he could have any woman he wanted, yet he had chosen to marry me.

Jon was very attractive, a nice guy, funny, and talented with an easygoing, down to earth beautiful spirit about him. I was willing to take the bad with the good because I had convinced myself that his good far outweighed his bad. Even though I knew that a solid marriage could not be built on lies, I stood on the promise that, with God all things are possible.[8] I allowed my heart to persuade my head that it was worth the gamble and that Jon would put all of his obnoxious behaviors behind him once he said "I do." I was going ahead with my plans, for "better or for worse."

---

[8] See Matthew 10:27

Labor Day Weekend

Our wedding day was intentionally planned around the Labor Day weekend because we wanted "to kill two birds with one stone." The life-long legacy celebration of the Bold's Family reunion was scheduled for the same weekend. We have a strong family that loves the Lord and loves each other. We were also gathering together to honor those who had "fallen asleep until the resurrection." The living generations needed to gather and celebrate the inheritance that our grandparents handed down to us. Since we also wanted certain family members to participate in our wedding, we needed to make it economical for them to attend both events.

The Labor Day Weekend finally arrived! Family members had flown into town for the celebration of these two awesome events. Those who were staying in my home (including Jon's kids) were settled in, and from that point on, it was just a matter of time. Saturday would be the last opportunity for Jon and me to enjoy each other as boyfriend and girlfriend. It was great to see everyone at the Family Reunion as we enjoyed mingling with my many cousins and the rest of my extended family. It was truly a blessing to see how the family had grown. All of my relatives seemed to love and embrace Jon as a soon to be official member of the family. My family all wanted to see me happily married and to know that my son Tristan would now have a father in his life.

My millennium marriage to Jon would be the joining of two lives together in one of God's most sacred institutions. I wanted with all my heart to believe that God had indeed put us together. Since I had not received any more disturbing phone calls, everything seemed nearly perfect. I was looking forward to going from a single mom to Mrs. Johnson and Tristan would finally have a dad. I have to admit that I was still nervous and somewhat anxious that in less than 24 hours my life would be changed forever. I knew our marriage would take a lot of work but was not afraid of the challenge and the new commitment marriage would bring.

On the flip side, I knew the freedom and independence that I had enjoyed all of my adult life would now be intertwined with my soul mate. Now 40, I knew in my heart I was ready for my new life. As a saved Christian woman, I was making this covenant to Christ first and Jon second, therefore I knew, beyond a shadow of a doubt, I could and would be faithful to this man until the end. I had convinced myself that Johnny Ray Johnson was the man God had created for me and was ready to be "Mrs. Johnson." There would be no turning back.

The Family reunion was over. The stage was set. The special day that Jon and I had been looking forward to, finally arrived. In spite of a few delays, phase two of our weekend was upon us. Jon had some last minute loose ends to tie up with videographers, photographers, and sound equipment, and then stopped by to pick up Tray and Tristan. The men and boys lodged together at the motel, while my bride's maids all stayed at my house.

The suspicion and grief in my spirit seemed to overwhelm me when I began to wonder if Jon might have other plans once he got the boys settled in. Would he go out and party then not make it to our wedding the next day? I found myself begging Jon to stay with me, but he insisted that he would be staying in with our boys. He encouraged me to get some rest and went on his way. As I prepared for bed, I could feel the stress coming on and a wave of nervousness and fear engulfed me.

I already knew that my biggest wedding-day enemy would be lack of rest. Being a beautiful bride was my first priority so I needed to sleep. As I lay in my bed, doubt began to permeate my spirit. Exhausted from the day's festivities, I began to regret having our wedding so close to the family reunion. I desperately wanted to sleep but I could not. Aware that lack of rest would produce a headache and dark circles under my eyes, I became distressed about trying to fall asleep. Distracted and nervous about every little thing, I worried about the weather. We had planned for my dream garden wedding, but it had rained the night before. Then I began to think of all I had to do the next day and wondered how would I accomplish it all?

To make matters worse, my two sisters (in a festive mood) were downstairs in the kitchen talking and laughing loudly while they put the finishing touches on things in preparation for my big day. As they laughed and conversed their voices carried upstairs into my bedroom as if they were sitting at the foot of my bed. Desperate for sleep I asked them several times to lower their voices, but my pleas made no difference, in fact to my weary brain, it seemed they became even louder. Finally, out of desperation, I summoned my sister Pat and asked her to please quiet them down. For a moment things calmed down and I almost drifted off to sleep until their shrill voices once again pierced the darkness of my room. Praying they would get tired and go to bed, I had all I could do to hold back the tears. I did not want dark puffy eyes on my wedding day!

Long Awaited Event

My weary eyes popped open at approximately six a.m. and to my amazement my prayers for warm weather and sunshine had been answered. In spite of my lack of sleep, I rejoiced in the beautiful, sun-shinny day God had prepared for my dream garden wedding. Heading to the beauty salon to begin my transformation, I tried to muster up the energy I would need for the long day I knew awaited me. I was a long-time client of my hair stylist, therefore she didn't mind meeting me on her off day to create a classy up-do hairstyle for my wedding day. As Leah passionately worked on my hair; I began sharing my worries about having dark puffy circles under my eyes after not getting near enough sleep.

I had been counting on my oldest sister to apply my makeup when I got home, but not in a good mood and knowing she also had to get ready, I readily accepted my stylist's offer to do it for me. When my hair was done, she made a quick trip to her home to pick up her makeup before hurrying to my house.

Things were off schedule all morning and though I never intended to be late for my own wedding, by the time the wedding party was whisked away in a chauffeured limousine, we were indeed late. By the time photos were taken of the bridal party, the wedding started an hour late.

Grouchy from lack of sleep and irritated that we were running behind schedule, I was having trouble calming myself down. But as the doors to the hotel ballroom opened, I stood amazed at how lovely the room had become. Then it hit me, this was real. Suddenly, my elegant fairy tale wedding came alive right before my very eyes. Soon I would be Mrs. Karen R. Johnson. I felt like Cinderella on her way to meet her prince. When my eyes beheld my handsome groom, I knew he was my soul mate and the one for whom I had waited for so long. At that moment the thought hit me, we were destined to be together!

Most of the 80 guests who joined us on our special day were members of my family. I had hoped that Jon's mother would attend to witness her son's marriage vows and participate in our joyful event but she did not come. Jon's aunt attended in her stead. In hopeful anticipation, our guests sat in their seats waiting for the ceremony to begin. Jon had arrived quite some time earlier to set up equipment and assist in making sure our garden venue was perfectly wired for sound.

Although weak and fragile, my father made the road trip from San Jose to Sacramento for my special day. Seated front and centered, he waited and watched his baby girl walk down the aisle on the arm of my handsome brother. Dad wanted to let the officiating minister and all of our guests witness his blessing on Jon and me. I had long dreamed of the day when my father would give me away to the man with whom I intended to spend the rest of my life. I thanked God for that privilege of having my father there. As it turned out, it was a good thing I had insisted on getting married when I did or my father might not have been able to attend.

"Bone of My Bone, Flesh of My Flesh," was the sermon our dear friend, Pastor Branner preached on our very special day. Pastor Branner went on to describe God's plan and purpose for marriage and for our lives as a couple. He established that marriage came from when God formed Adam and Eve and placed them in the Garden of Eden. It was a garden where that first wedding ceremony was performed and a garden was where I had always wanted to be married. Pastor Art went on to describe the man's role in the family and the woman's role as his help meet, bringing clarity to marriage and aiming to get us off on the right track.

The ambiance was incredible. Even though it was hot, there was a lovely cool breeze in the shaded area where we spoke our vows amidst the beauty of the garden and the faces of our loved ones. With the loving support of family, life with Jon as a couple in Holy matrimony would now begin.

Not a Moment to Spare— the Conflict Begins

Alone at last! The reception was over. All the gifts, our children, the cleanup…everything was being taken care of by family and friends. I had nothing to worry about. I could finally exhale and spend quality time with the handsome man I had just married. I was Mrs. Johnson now, and for the first time I had no guilt, no shame, no hypocrisy attached to experiencing intimacy with this man, "my man!" As tired as I was, I could hardly wait to make sweet, passionate love, the right way, God's way, under the umbrella of marriage.

Marriage is honorable among all, and the bed undefiled.

(Hebrews 13:4)

What a Night!

Who can find a virtuous wife? For her worth is far above rubies. The heart of her husband safely trusts her; so he will have no lack of gain. She does him good and not evil all the days of her life. (Proverbs 31:10-12)

After we said goodbye to guests and family, Jon and I made our way upstairs to our invitingly beautiful, vintage suite, overlooking the delta. Perched like a jewel on the Sacramento River, our wedding suite was quite lovely. I plopped down on the bed to catch my breath planning to freshen up and slip into my sexy honeymoon lingerie.

Suddenly, Jon broke through my blissful thoughts announcing, "Honey, I have to go to Arco to take the equipment back."

I know my mouth dropped open as my heart sank. I could not believe my ears had heard him correctly, so I asked him to clarify what he had said. When he repeated his disturbing mission, I felt like someone had socked me in the stomach. Feeling my blood pressure rise and tears threaten to spill all over my beautiful wedding gown, I insisted that he stay with me. We had *just* gotten married! This was our honeymoon night!

Not only had Jon cancelled our honeymoon to Hawaii, spent the money we had saved for our time away and delayed our post-wedding trip to Tahoe for two weeks because he had to go to Australia, he was leaving me on our wedding night to drop off some audio equipment. I just couldn't believe it! No way did I want to fight on our wedding night, but I needed to know why Jon had not made other arrangements. His boss had attended our wedding. Why couldn't *he* have taken the equipment back? I was confused, as Jon left me alone on our wedding night to return the equipment. He promised to return with something to eat, kissed me and then he left. Tired and frustrated, I took advantage of the opportunity to take a quick nap.

It was the wee hours of the morning when Jon returned with the food he promised. I awakened hungry still wearing my sexy lingerie. We ate and then spent the rest of the night making passionate love...consummating our marriage. Delirious and satisfied, I laid happily in my husband's arms, before falling fast asleep until daybreak.

Chapter Seven

Affliction—Becoming One

All humanity is now involved in the great controversy between Christ and Satan regarding the vindication of the character of God, His law and His sovereignty over the universe. This conflict originated in Heaven when a created being, endowed with freedom of choice, and self-exaltation became Satan. He was God's adversary and led a portion of the angels into rebellion. He introduced the spirit of rebellion into this world when he led Adam and Eve into sin. This human sin resulted in the distortion of the image of God in humanity, the disordering of the created world, and its eventual devastation at the time of the worldwide universal conflict out of which the God of love will ultimately be vindicated. To assist his people in this controversy, Christ sent the Holy Spirit and the loyal

angels to guide, protect and sustain them in the way of salvation. (Ellen G. White, "The Great Controversy")

Day After - Wedding Day

M y folks were still in town for the Labor Day weekend so Jon and I left our quaint vintage wedding suite and went home early for breakfast and to see them off. Hungry, we all jumped into our cars and caravanned to Lyon's Restaurant in Elk Grove. Because our group was large, we waited a little longer than usual to be seated. We were laughing, talking and enjoying each other when Jon's cell phone began to ring. Enraptured by the love around us he silently ignored his phone and continued to entertain our guests.

While making our choices from the menu, Jon's phone continued to ring until he announced, "I'm not going to answer it!"

Deep in marital bliss, I was pleased that my new husband was more interested in spending quality time with me and family than in taking business calls. My sister, Pat, however, was leery about the numerous calls coming in on Jon's phone. She made a sly comment about it but Jon ignored it and we all went right on laughing and talking. Trying not to be distracted by his ringing phone, Jon carried on, keeping the family entertained, as he often did. Finally, breakfast was over and we all hurried back to the house so that Jon and I could open our wedding gifts.

As we said our last goodbyes I was looking forward to an afternoon alone at home with my new husband. Eager to pick up where we had left off back at our hotel suite, Jon turned to me and dropped another bombshell. He had to run an errand and wasn't sure what time he would be back. Thinking it was rather odd that he had to leave with such urgency, I thought about questioning him but, still basking in "marital bliss," I didn't want to spoil the moment.

Home alone and expecting my new husband to call any minute to update me on his "away status," I anxiously answered my cell phone when it rang. To my surprise, the caller was a woman yelling uncontrollably about Jon being her man. It was Lisa, the sister of the man I sold the cell phone to two years ago who discovered my boyfriend was the big shot cameraman she was dating were one and the same. Lisa told me that she and Jon were *still* dating. Angry that he was now married to me, she went on to tell me that he had slept with another woman the night before our wedding.

Devastated and disgusted, I listened to Lisa's account of the chain of events that took place between my husband and another woman the night before we got married. As I listened, I began to put two and two together. Lisa and I were both hurting. She knew she could not have Jon and she didn't want me to have him either. I tried to maintain my composure as I listened to her blow-by-blow account of how she found out about Jon's *other* affair. I wanted to explode! Not only had Jon left me alone on our wedding night with the lame excuse of dropping off audio equipment but he was still seeing other women right up until he said, "I do." I could not get off the phone with Lisa fast enough! I needed to get down to the bottom of things!

As a new and excited bride, I should have been immediately whisked away by my doting husband to enjoy a romantic honeymoon. Instead, I was left at home alone dealing with a contentious woman while Jon was supposedly running errands before he "trotted off" to Sydney, Australia, to film the Olympics. (I found out later that he had actually gone to Arizona to be with Victoria just days after our wedding.) So many lies! I didn't know who to trust or where to turn for help. My husband had slept with a woman named Trina the night before our wedding and was apparently still carrying on affairs with several other women. What a very sad time this was for me!

My family and friends had just joyfully witnessed my exchange of wedding vows with Jon. I had hoped this would be my one and only marriage, but here I was a bride of less than 12 hours finding out that my husband had already been unfaithful to me. In fact he had *continued* to be unfaithful to me! My natural instinct was to leave him, without delay, but then I faced the reality of being unemployed and steeped in debt from our wedding and the purchase of our new home. Doubt, fear and darkness engulfed me as I sat alone trying to figure out what to do and how to handle my precarious predicament.

My mind was racing and I did not want to make the wrong move. Who was this woman calling my phone number, anyway? How could I know that she hadn't just made up the story about Jon's infidelity to come between him and me? Then, I remembered the portion of our vows that said, "What God has joined together, let no man put asunder."

I wanted to keep a cool head and hear Jon's side of the story before I made any sudden moves. Eager to speak with Jon after hanging up the phone from Lisa, I called his cell phone.

It just couldn't be true that Jon's phone had been disconnected. It was still the Labor Day Holiday Weekend! Surely, I had misdialed a number! I tried a second time but the message was the same as the first. I felt as though I were drowning as waves of anger and hurt washed over me! Deep in my heart, I knew that there was some truth to what Lisa had told me.

Almost Paralyzed

As scenes of my beautiful wedding danced in my head, I tried to convince myself that everything Lisa told me was a lie and that she was just trying to hurt me because she was hurt. Dazed, I felt like I had been thrust into the middle of a horror movie instead of a happily-ever-after Cinderella story. It just couldn't be true that these things were really happening to me. Oh, how I wanted Jon to be truly committed and ready to turn over a new leaf as we began our new life together. I needed to talk to Jon but I couldn't reach him and had no idea when that might be.

I was desperate to talk to someone who could help me sort out my raging emotions, but who? I couldn't discuss my anguish with my immediate family and close friends! Finally, I decided to call our best man, Stanley. Angry and embarrassed by the turn of events, I began spilling my guts as soon as Stan answered his phone. I couldn't stop crying. Stan seemed shocked by my news, but managed to maintain his composure and focused on calming me down.

My Oath before God

As my tears turned to anger, I announced to Stanley that I would be calling the pastor who had performed our wedding ceremony and have our marriage annulled. He pleaded with me not to do either. He knew something about Jon's weakness for multiple women and shared how he had advised him, as a married man, to let go of the other women and "all that foolishness." Although Stanley patiently tried to reassure me that Jon did indeed love me very much, I was certain that my next move was to call the pastor and kick Jon out of the house before he had completely moved in.

Stanley then spoke the words that changed my mind, "Karen, you agreed in the wedding vows that you just took, to stay with your husband...for better or for worse."

I could not believe Stanley was throwing that in my face, but I listened. He reminded me of the covenant oath I had taken before God and witnesses, and that I needed to stand strong and stay with my husband. Because of my love for God and the covenant oath I made to Jesus, I slowly calmed down and decided against calling the pastor. That was my defining moment, for I purposed in my heart to stay and fight for my one-day-old marriage. The reality was that the honeymoon was indeed over before it ever got started.

Needless to say, the first couple of weeks of my marriage were very tumultuous. I was extremely angry that I could not be a happy, normal bride. On top of the situation with Jon, I was unemployed. Just weeks before our wedding, my account executive position at a new telecommunications company was suddenly terminated. I had not been able to appreciate the many challenges of my work situation, so at the time I had counted my job loss as a "blessing in disguise." I tried to fill my days with job hunting, attending to my son and house-keeping, but I was deeply saddened that Jon had sabotaged everything I thought we had done to prepare to live our lives "as one."

Home from Australia?

Now that Jon was finally home from Australia, it was time for our long-awaited honeymoon. As we left for our three-day trip to Tahoe, Jon seemed normal, as if everything was good. Although I did not share my thoughts and feelings with him, I sensed he knew something was not quite right as he watched me "go through the motions." He tried to cheer me up by promising to buy me expensive jewelry, but jewelry no longer interested me.

No matter how hard I tried not to be disappointed, the fact of the matter was that I knew things were not right. I knew that the only way our marriage would survive would be for Jon to embrace Jesus and become truly converted; he needed to make a 180-degree turnaround. I knew in my heart I could not do this on my own. Only God could do this, and God works through human instruments so I made myself available to Him and waited for Christ to bring about the saving of Jon's soul.

I knew that the other women in Jon's life were leading him on a path to nowhere, though he couldn't see that. I also knew that because of my connection to God, I could lead him to a place where he could receive complete healing and experience the nurturing spirit of God; a place where he would live eternally and be forever grateful. True love is not building each other up for earthly gain which eventually perishes. True love requires sacrifice and the building up of each other for eternity, where all things last forever. Not everyone can do this, but I felt deep in my spirit that Jon was who God wanted me to be with and that it was important I allow God to work through me in Jon's life.

Not Home

For more than a week after our return home from Tahoe, not only did Jon not make love to me, he did not even come to bed with me. He finally admitted that his difficulty with being intimate with me was based on what he did with Trina the night before our wedding. It was *my* belief that he couldn't sleep with me because he was either *still* sleeping with Trina or with someone else.

As the month of September moved along, things got progressively worse. Jon had stayed away from home for ten consecutive days accusing me of nagging him. What was I to do? His behavior was much more like a playboy than a happily married man. Feeling imprisoned inside my own marriage and not wanting to break the terrible news to my family, I decided to take action and call our spiritual mom, Virginia to tell her that her spiritual son was not being a Godly man or a faithful husband. I also decided it was time to call Stanley again for more advice.

Harsh Lessons of Life

Learning to forgive, love, live with, trust, understand, respect and cherish the man I married was definitely an uphill battle for me. It became extremely evident that I had married a man whose character was marred by deep, dark secrets, lies and disloyalty. What was my role now? I prayed to God for guidance. Blindly, I had been an enabler and had ignored the red flags that were now haunting me. I had to come to terms with the realization that the only thing that I had toward keeping my marriage together was the blessed hope I had in Christ. God had given me His word as a comfort and strength. I now leaned heavily upon and cherished the promise given in Romans 15:4; "For whatever things were written before were written for our learning, that we through the patience and comfort of the scriptures might have hope." I needed and wanted that hope. It's funny how trials either lead us further away from God or draw us closer to Him.

Though committed, my marriage was in constant turmoil and I was lonely more often than happy, but I never renounced my faith. I continued to seek answers and pray for new revelations from on high regarding my husband's intentions and whereabouts. Trusting the creator of marriage, I placed mine in God's hands. I knew that I needed to fully surrender to God and make him my pillow during the lonely nights ahead. In Christ we can bear all things, and be all things. I held to another promise I found in Galatians 2:20 that says, "I am crucified with Christ; it is no longer I who live, but Christ lives in me; and the life which I now live in the flesh I live by faith in the Son of God, who loved me and gave Himself for me."

If it wasn't for God and the promises in His word, I could not have done it. It was in Christ I found my self-worth, knowing I was special and loved by Him. I found the peace and stability I was not getting with Jon within my relationship with Christ. I had everything I needed and then some. I just needed to hold on to Him and rest in His profound love.

Christ has urged His people to pray without ceasing. This does not mean that we should always be upon our knees, but that prayer is to be as the breath of the soul. Our silent requests, wherever we may be, are to be ascending unto God, and Jesus our advocate pleads in our behalf, bearing up with the incense of His righteousness our requests to the Father. (Ellen G. White, "That I May Know Him," 78)

On August 21, 2001, I wrote this journal entry as I prayed for God's guidance in my marriage. "Ask him to reveal anything you need to start or stop doing. Perhaps he is waiting on you." I had chosen to marry Jon in spite of all that I knew about him. My heart had been inflamed with a burning desire to be with him, but now the trials were like an out of control wild fire in danger of destroying my love for him. I held to the promise in James 1:2-4 which says, "My brethren count it all joy when you fall into various trials, knowing that the testing of your faith produces patience. But let patience have its perfect work that you may be perfect and complete, lacking nothing."

As much as I wanted to throw away the man and the marriage, it was apparent I would have been allowing the enemy of my soul to destroy the family I had worked so hard to salvage. Jon and I and our children had become a family and the evil one makes no investment in families. I found I needed to focus on what God was trying to teach me about my own character, instead of dwelling on the injustices that others had done against me. I discovered there is always something to learn within the context of every trial.

Insightful Journey

During the process of learning how to make my marriage work, I took an insightful journey into knowing and understanding who I was. As I made discoveries about my temperament, my strengths and my weaknesses, I developed a deeper and closer walk with God.

Many nights I laid in our king-size bed alone; no one to talk to, no one to hold me as hot tears ran down my cheeks and soaked my pillow. I cannot count the nights I fell asleep wondering where Jon was and with whom. When he was angry, Jon would often keep his cell phone turned off or he just wouldn't answer my calls. All I could do was wait for him to cool down and return home. Too many times, I sadly and silently watched as he would come home, shower, get a change of clothes and take off again. During these times, I learned how to be still and not allow the anger to push me into returning evil for evil.

Through the trials of my marriage, I began to understand the powerful love of God. I also began to understand how God hates the sin but loves the sinner. It is also true that God hates divorce.[9] Anyone whose marriage is in jeopardy should be reminded of the oath that has been taken before God like Stanley did for me. I resolved in my heart that my covenant of marriage was made first with Jesus and then with my husband. No matter how unfaithful my husband was, I would not defile my temple by committing adultery just to try to even the score and get back at him. I could not break the heart of Jesus. Although the carnal man might say I was justified, it was important to me to be able to look at myself in the mirror with respect, love and dignity.

Anyone who hears my story may label me as "stupid," "gullible" or "naive." To questions of, "How could she marry a man like that and think he would be loyal to her?" or "After all, wasn't he cheating on you while you were dating?" my response is, "Don't tell my story until you've read my book." At one time or another, everyone wonders why another person handles a situation in a certain manner. The reality is that we really don't know what we'll do until we've walked in that person's shoes.

In fact, there are many stories in the Bible about people embroiled in adulterous affairs. Chapters five through seven of Proverbs warn against the immoral woman whose character is not only shallow but evil. Her lips are enticing as honey and smoother than olive oil. She is an adulterous wife whose rest-

---

[9] See Malachi 2:16

less unstable feet do not stay at home. King David and King Solomon had many wives and concubines but that doesn't make it right.

For me, through stories like these and my own personal experiences, God has been perfecting my character. God's perfect will is that we each mature in Him and that process is full of choices. God has a divine perfect will and a permissive will for each of our lives. I believe my marriage to Jon was God's permissive will, not His divine will for my life. God *allowed* me to choose this path but though it was not His perfect will, He was there to help me handle the consequences of my choices.

Teach Me, O Lord, How to Build!

It is true that our approaches to life were vastly different, but Jon and I shared many good times together as a family: holidays, family gatherings, vacations, camping trips, Sacramento Kings' games, and attending our children's various sporting events. The majority of our struggles centered on him being secretive, unfaithful and my inability to trust him when he was away from home. As we strove to blend our families together, issues sometimes arose that involved our children.

Jon's children, Tangela and Tray, lived with their biological mother, visiting us mainly on major holidays and during the summer. My son, Tristan lived with us and, having raised him by myself for so many years, we had developed a special mother-son relationship. Jon began to complain that he felt excluded and that I always took my son's side and didn't support him when he felt the need to discipline Tristan.

I realized I just could *not* trust Jon with disciplining Tristan or even being fair with him. Tristan didn't trust Jon either. A vicious circle of disrespect had built up due to the fact that Jon was hardly around to validate and encourage Tristan.

When Jon was around he would always find something to criticize and chastise Tristan about. I soon realized this was just another ploy to justify Jon leaving for the night. He would incite arguments to justify running off to his other lovers.

Deep inside, I believe Jon was looking for the respect from my son that he didn't have for himself or me. I also came to realize that Jon's envy of the bond between Tristan and I stemmed from the lack of relationship between him and his own mother. He couldn't recall his mother's protection, defense or love. Through counseling, I found that my being a nurturing mother was one of the things that attracted Jon to me but that repelled him now. I could not deny that during his growing up years Tristan had become accustomed to getting what he wanted from me. By the time Jon "settled into our lives," the controversy between them often put me right in the middle as I tried to blend our families peacefully.

Loving both my son and my husband, I also wanted to be an example and a Christian witness to them both. When Jon and I were not getting along well, I found myself being irritable with my son. I experienced many lonely, sleepless nights, pondering why my husband didn't want me. After all, I took pride in staying in shape and taking good care of myself physically. As I tossed and turned during my many sleepless nights, waiting for the telephone to ring or for Jon to come up the stairs and embrace me, my thoughts sometimes drifted to the many opportunities I'd had to marry former boyfriends who loved and adored me. Now, the very man I yearned to cherish me was trampling all over me. Something was really wrong with that picture. I just didn't understand it!

I prayed that God would show me signs of Jon's infidelity; but what I wanted more was for Jesus to change my husband's heart and bring about submission and true conversion within him. I also prayed that God would give Jon the strength he needed to overcome evil and lean on the Lord.

Happy Anniversary!

Through many prayers and much submission to God's purpose, I'm grateful to say that my walk with the Lord was amazingly enriched through the challenges of my first year of marriage. There was so much confusion about my life with

Jon that it was hard to find the balance between trust and reality, but I learned to journal my thoughts, feelings, prayers, and hunches, as well as the inconsistencies that sparked my suspicions. Too often, I had no idea what to expect from Jon so I treasured those special times when I could see the caring and sentimental man I had fallen in love with. I was ecstatic when my romantic Jon showed up on our first wedding anniversary by serving me breakfast in bed.

I had learned a lot about Jon during my first year with him. It seemed his life was filled with deep sorrow and regret. He had many sleepless nights, tormented with an inward battle which he was reluctant to share with me. I would sometimes awaken and find him lying on his side, propped up on his elbow, half asleep.

At first, I thought he was praying, but when I asked him he said he was "talking with his father." I was not comfortable with the idea of Jon having regular conversations with his deceased father fearing he was being deceived by Satan so I would silently pray for Jon. Ecclesiastes 9:5, 6, 10 tells us that, "For the living know that they shall die: but the dead know not any thing, there is no work, nor device, nor knowledge, nor wisdom, in the grave, whither thou goest."

Though I yearned to start my own personal training fitness business, I was afraid to step out into it completely so I decided to return to public speaking. Fulfilling another of my lifelong aspirations, I became an independent contractor for a speaker company, Making College Count. I enjoyed the speaking end of it but wasn't completely thrilled about the inconsistency of work. Consequently, I continued to teach aerobic classes at various health clubs in Sacramento, as I traveled by plane and car between five states conducting public speaking engagements at various high schools. Traveling and being away from home often left me feeling a little uneasy about Jon having so much freedom, but it gave me some assurance to know he would be home to care for Tristan in my absence. Traveling was also a nice break from the drama of my marriage.

I was a health enthusiast and continually felt that God was leading me to start my own health and fitness business so I took advantage of every opportunity to share my vision with my husband. Finally, one day he told me to stop talking about it and do it. That's when I decided to take my fitness interests to the next level and I became a personal fitness trainer.

Dad's Final Days

During my speaking engagement travels, the news came that my Dad's progressively failing health had taken him to the hospital. Dad was a fighter and I wanted to convince myself that his illness was just another bout of pneumonia. I wanted to believe that within weeks he would bounce back as he had so many times before and it would be life as usual. After all, I had just seen him at Christmas and he seemed fine. He was only 78 years young and although his old lifestyle had taken its toll on him he seemed to be as strong as could be expected.

In the hospital, we laughed and talked with Dad and took pictures with him as he dozed in and out of sleep. While sharing in the optimism my family held of Dad's condition improving and his release from the hospital, Jon shared as lovingly as he knew how, his feelings of Dad being very ill and probably not having very much longer to live. I was upset by Jon's premonition and refused to accept that my life-long hero was on his death bed. I was truly in denial of the fact that my daddy was dying.

On my return home from another speaking engagement, Jon was waiting patiently at curbside near the Sacramento Airport's baggage claim area. When I hopped into the car, Jon broke the news, "Honey, your dad is very sick! I really don't think he's going to make it this time." Very tired from my trip, I burst into tears telling Jon again that he didn't know what he was talking about and that Dad *was* going to make it.

I could hardly wait to get home to call Dad at the hospital. He made several weak attempts to speak with me, but was very incoherent as he tried to figure out which of his four daughters he was talking to. Somehow, it gave me great comfort just to know he was talking and that's all I needed. A couple of days after speaking with Dad, he was released from the hospital; within a matter of hours he drifted off to sleep, never to open his eyes again.

I was deeply saddened by my father's death and could only hope that he found the Lord Jesus in his life, and received the gift of eternal life here after. My father, being a highly educated college professor, always liked to be spoken to in quiet tones, not shouted at. I remember while growing up that he preferred not to join us in worship services at my maternal grandmother's church because he felt that there was nothing but confusion there. To him it was foolishness, saying the music was too loud, the people spoke in tongues which he could not understand, and it was nothing but a show of emotional gibberish. Dad also believed that most of the people in the church were hypocrites and he wanted no part of that.

It had been my sincere desire to share Christ and my new-found faith with Dad but it was generally taboo to speak about religion with Dad. I prayed as my brother asked the visiting pastor to share the plan of salvation with our father. I knew God gives every man a lifetime of opportunities to know God for ourselves. The Bible tells us in Romans 14:12, "So then each of us shall give account of himself to God."

All of us as beings are blessed of God with reasoning powers, with intellect skills and judgment, but we should also acknowledge our accountability to God. The life He has given us is a sacred responsibility and no moment of it is to be trifled with for we shall have to meet it again in the record of the judgment. In the books of heaven our lives are as accurately traced as in the picture on the plate of the photographer. Not only are we held accountable for what we have done, but also for what we have left undone. We are held to account for our undeveloped character and our unimproved opportunities. (Ellen G. White, "That I May Know Him," 93)

Jon and I made it through two very long years of marriage with our share of drama, arguments and blow ups. My prayer had not changed! I continually reminded the Lord that I did not want to be in a marriage where my husband continued to cheat and lie. I also asked the Lord to quickly reveal to me when I needed to pray for Jon if he was tempted to cheat on me. I truly hoped 2002 would be a fruitful year. Off and on, Victoria would call to tell me that Jon was "at it again." Jon had often said that if a couple could survive the first five years of marriage, it was a good possibility they would last. We had just braved two, and so I held onto my hope.

More Doubt...More Inconsistencies

On one particular occasion, while filming a basket ball game with the Sacramento Kings, Jon called and said he would be leaving from there and heading to NBC Channel 11 in the Bay Area. When I called his cell phone and it was off, my suspicions were aroused. Jon was not in the habit of sharing his work schedule with me in advance; rather, he would just "spring things on me." I decided to insist that Jon give me advance notice of his schedule and keep his cell phone on 24/7. There were still so many issues that challenged my becoming one with Jon. Our marriage was on and off in the sense that Jon "did his own thing," but I faithfully prayed for comfort and a better understanding of the man I married.

Jon avoided me whenever he was angry, sometimes staying away from home for days at a time. I worried a lot and got very little sleep during those times. When he calmed down, he would return as if nothing had happened. Whenever Jon was angry with me and stayed home, he would punish me by sleeping downstairs on the couch or in the back bedroom. Those were indeed my loneliest nights. In my mind there was nothing more miserable than being married and being lonely. Given the choice, I would take singleness over loneliness any time. Believing that sleeping in separate beds gives the devil a foothold to destroy a marriage, it was my desire for us to sleep in the bed together every night, even when we were angry, remembering the exhortation of Ephesians 4:26; "Be angry, and do not sin, do not let the sun go down on your wrath, nor give place to the devil."

My stress and loneliness eventually created a few health challenges as the drama persisted. But I held my ground, stayed put and continued to be the best mother I could be to my son and step-mother to Jon's children in spite of my roller coaster marriage. There were times when I could see Jon putting forth more effort with Tristan and in fact, taking an interest in the things he liked, obviously trying to connect and understand him. It was those times that I received the encouragement I needed to hang in there and I made it a point to commend Jon for doing a tremendous job with my son.

At it Again

Periodically, his on and off girlfriend Victoria would call to remind me that she was having relations with my husband again. Her calls always left me numb and on edge in anticipation for what I might hear next. I continued to pray for patience and I knew for sure that my faith was being tried. Prior to my close encounter with Christ, I would have left the marriage with no questions asked. The truth of the matter was that, deep in my heart, I felt dreadfully sorry for my poor husband.

As handsome as he was and as kind and loving as he could be at times, he was pitifully weak and extremely deceived. He seemed to be totally unaffected by my exhausting efforts to live a Godly life before him.

I had a Savior who was seeing me through and holding me up, but Jon was constantly on the run looking for love and nurture in all the wrong places. Then he would have to deal with guilt and remorse every time he cheated. Jon didn't set out to hurt me, he was sick and needed help. I knew he needed someone who would stick with him through this experience and look beyond his faults and see his need. I was determined to stand by him but I knew God was the only one who would not only stick with him but watch over him and love him through it.

God is the ultimate example of unconditional love. He never complains and He is patient and goes to great lengths to save us from ourselves. It was my love and deep pity for Jon that anchored me to him but even more my love and dependence upon God. I knew God was the only one that could make the vision I had of Jon as a man of God come to reality.

At Wit's End

I found myself in that place again where I truly needed to talk to someone. Finally, I swallowed my pride, called my

Mom and told her just about everything. In her cool and calm manner, Mom comforted and encouraged me as only as a wise loving mother could do, but I knew that my situation disappointed and upset her greatly. She knew that I loved Jon dearly and she didn't want to come between us.

One day, I desperately prayed asking God to stop my pain. Even as I pray now, sometimes I reflect back on that time of pain and trouble that are only a memory. But as I listened to the sermon on television the preacher brought out the three ways God goes about getting our attention. "The first way is pain," he said, "Pain is the megaphone that God uses to get our attention." God had already had my attention but obviously not my full attention since I married Jon in spite of His numerous warnings.

When I heard him say that the second way was sorrow, I could relate because my life was filled with so much deep sorrow. I was truly in love with my husband and wanted my marriage to work but I felt full of regret and guilt for marrying Jon. I sometimes wondered if I was being punished for not listening to God.

"The final way," the Pastor said, "that God gets our attention is with love."

I am so thankful God has shown me love and continues to show me how to love even when I am hard-headed and acting like a strong willed child.

As things between Jon and I grew continually worse, I recommended we go for marriage counseling. Skeptical about counseling, Jon suggested that we talk to his Christian friend and wife. Desperate, I agreed and we began to meet with them. After about the second counseling session, the couple suggested we seek professional help.

They recommended one of their counselor friends because he was a pastor with more counseling experience, and they admired his skills. They shared with us that they had turned to this pastor with their own early-marital problems. The pastor's counseling seemed to be successful in helping them, so I was sold and willing to travel to the Bay Area to get our marriage on track. I had never stopped yearning to know the man I married, and I sincerely believed a good counselor would get through Jon's "tough shell."

In Spite of Counseling

From my perspective, the counseling sessions were supposed to bring order to our home and to somehow get Jon to see that he needed to work on restoring my trust in him. I needed him to see how he had defiled our marriage bed and violated his own very sacred oath. I needed to know that he was committed to the necessary behavioral changes to make all of these things happen.

There were weeks when I lived from counseling session to counseling session. The reality was that each session seemed more futile. We left the same way we came: broken, frustrated and confused, but I didn't want to give up too soon. Believing firmly that nothing is too hard for God to handle, all I could do was hope and pray that if we continued with the sessions we would get a breakthrough. Sometimes both of us would be so angry at the end of our session that there would not be one word spoken between us during our hour-long return trip home. I knew if things did not change, in spite of our love, eventually one or both of us would "throw in the towel." The counselor was a man of God who came highly recommended, so I remained optimistic. There was no doubt, though, that I needed a miracle and I needed it fast!

One thing I learned from our many arguments in counseling was that Jon loathed the fact that I had not changed my last name from Gardner to Johnson. We had discussed it before we got married and he said it didn't matter to him whether I used my maiden or married name. At the time I felt it was for the sake of my son that I had kept my maiden name but because of our rough start, I think I was also insecure in using Jon's last name. I think in the back of my mind I wondered if our marriage would last.

Jon often threw around the big "D" word so I believed it would be just a matter of time before we would be in divorce court and then go our separate ways. But, in an attempt to "make peace," I changed my name hoping Jon might begin to treat me like his wife, instead of a stranger. Looking back I believed my name change at that time was a part of God's will in my life.

The many sleepless nights and deep sorrow brought me to my knees, and prostrate before the Lord, I eventually came to the place where I had to "let go and let God" so I could keep my sanity and keep the peace in my home as God worked in both of us.

The steps of a good man are ordered by the LORD, and he delights in his way.

(Psalms 37:23)

Young men and women will often be brought into positions where they are uncertain what to do. Their inclination leads them in one direction, and the Holy Spirit of God draws them in another direction. Satan presses his temptation upon them and urges them to follow the inclinations of the natural heart. But those who desire to be true to Christ will listen to the voice that says, "This is the way, walk ye in it" (Isaiah 30:21). They will decide to take the course of the righteous, although it is more difficult to pursue and more painful to follow than the way of their own heart.

We need to receive divine wisdom in the daily concerns of life in order that we may display sound judgment and choose the safe path because it is the right one. He who acts upon his own judgment will follow the inclination of the natural heart, but he whose mind is opened to the Word of God will prayerfully consider every way of his will. Remember that "even Christ pleased not himself," and we should consider it a great privilege to follow in His steps. He will take his perplexities to God in prayer and ask the guidance of Him whose property he is. He will realize that he belongs to God, mind, body, soul and strength. (Ellen G. White, "That I May Know Him," p. 251)

Chapter Eight

Changing Hearts

The combined facts that my stepchildren lived three hours away from us and were not at all accustomed to the ways and practices of my Christian lifestyle, seemed to present an insurmountable challenge for us. My values and the way I dressed, ate, parented and socialized made the blending of our two families an interesting dynamic in and of itself. In addition, we were further opposed as a couple when our children felt threatened by our marriage. Although dealing with two boys and one teenage stepdaughter was extremely challenging, I still looked forward to the summer months when my nephew, Daniel, and my step children, Tangela and Tray visited. Jon spent more time at home, I enjoyed our family outings and he slept in our bed and not on the couch.

Tristan and Tray were the same age so they related well to each other and looked forward to their summers together.

They understood their roles as children and were respectful to me. On the other hand, Jon's daughter Tangela was a different story. She was now sixteen and definitely "Daddy's little girl," but now Daddy had a new girl; a wife whom she despised. When Tangela was expected to pitch in and help out around the house, she was extremely disagreeable. As she grew older, she often made arrangements to stay with her girlfriend instead of with us. I loved her the best way I knew how and desired to connect with her on a deeper level, but most of the time she shunned me. We were both strong-willed and I came to the point where I demanded that she treat me as an adult and not disrespectfully as her equal.

In no way was I trying to take the place of Tangela's mother, and made that crystal clear to both of my stepchildren, but I faced resentment and ingratitude on every side. Tangela did not like going to church and she especially didn't like my observance of the 24-hour Sabbath day. It was her father's desire that she attend church, but she resented me for it because she had no say in the matter. Tangela only knew that since her daddy married me he had made some changes that she did not like.

Sadly, Tangela also did not understand that, in marriage, "the two shall become one." Her father was the head of his household and I was second in charge. She believed *she* was second-in-command. She was under the impression that Jon had purchased the house we were living in before our marriage and that it belonged to her dad and I was just a "gold digger." She also hated it when her father supported my decisions over hers.

To his credit, Jon support my disciplining his children and put forth great efforts to fulfill his duties as a father. He was as diligent in his child support payments as he was actively involved in their lives.

He would often make the round-trip drive to their home and then head directly to work in the Bay Area, without any rest. In the process of trying to build family togetherness and offer support to my husband, I found myself picking up the slack by making the trip to pick up my stepchildren so that Jon could rest or work. Of course, it gave me much pleasure to bond with my stepchildren and for my husband to acknowledge my efforts by expressing his appreciation.

Jon had settled down with me because he wanted a Godly wife, someone who could nurture, accept and embrace him and his children. He was seeking something in me he didn't have within himself and couldn't find with others. He loved the fact that I had a close-knit, large and loving family. Jon loved my family and became the grill master at every family gathering.

Bountiful Opportunities

As a talented cameraman, producer and visionary, Jon had many phenomenal opportunities to earn tremendous salaries. One time in particular he was offered a nice contract to work with a professional basketball team on the East Coast. The package came with a hefty six-figure income, relocation bonus, a house, travel and other perks. It sounded very appealing to me, for I had nothing holding me back. At the time, Tristan was 13 and he would have adjusted where ever we were.

The more Jon told me about this once-in-a-lifetime opportunity, the more enticing it became. God knows we could have used the money and the change of scenery; therefore, I desperately wanted Jon to take the position but in the spiritual realm an awareness was taking place. I knew this could be a distraction for both of us to take our eyes off Jesus. The money and the fast life could be a further detriment to our marriage and I didn't want us to get too caught up in material things. I knew that making that kind of move would require Jon to travel and work on the Sabbath. The Lord impressed upon me to advise him not to take the position and to share the reasons why.

I told Jon that I would support his decision but my concerns were his inability to keep the Sabbath and his children's need for him to be close to them. I went on to explain how Tangela needed him the most. She was confused and was entering into a very critical time in her life where she needed her Dad's love, guidance and firm discipline. I also shared with him that Tray, who was timid, shy and very impressionable, was also in need of his father's guidance. I expressed to Jon that he would be making a grave mistake by leaving his children to pursue his dream across the country. He pondered the offer for a while and then rejected it.

I knew that Jon loved his children dearly and would bend over backwards for them. Their happiness meant the world to him; if they were happy, Jon was happy. I saw some illumination from a light at the end of our tunnel that kept me striving as a wife, mother and woman of faith. I believed that Jon and I loved each other and that, despite our wars, we were both determined to make our marriage work and make a good home for our children.

Signs of Change Begins

From the rocky beginnings of our marriage, my mind was made up to fight no matter how devastating and challenging it became. I saw great potential in Jon and in the future of our marriage. I knew if Jon had a close encounter with Christ his soul would be healed from all the hurt and shame of his past and experiences. As for me, I was hungry for restoration and took up private counseling to help me work on forgiveness. I never faltered in my belief that God allowed us to be together for a reason. I fastened my seat belt and held on! The good news is that the more afflictions we went through, the closer I was drawn to Christ and the stronger my faith became. One thing I knew for sure was that God hates divorce. I began to realize that forgiveness was an ongoing thing and made it a process and a part of my marriage to Jon.

As we continued to experience marital ups and downs, I began to confide in my best friend Esmie and her husband Arthur. Jon had had it with counseling so I sought their Godly counsel and wisdom. Esmie and Arthur knew and loved Jon dearly and wanted to see our marriage work. They under-stood Jon and yet treated him with love and respect. Yearning to handle my husband and marriage from a biblical view point they coached and supported me maintaining my Christian values as a wife and mother while not wavering through the trials. In retrospect, it was nice to gain Christian counsel from close friends who loved us both.

Though my mother was always at my disposal and would always listen to my marital problems, I knew it was very hard for her. Hearing about the things that were not going well between Jon and me upset her and I knew being upset wasn't at all healthy for her, especially at her age. Jon was her son-in-law and I wanted her to be able to embrace him warmly, therefore, I limited the things I would tell her.

I was beginning to feel I was getting a handle on the main challenges I faced in becoming the godly wife I knew Jon needed me to be: how the two shall become one, how to trust my husband even after he had cheated on me time and time again, and how to forgive and move forward.

"Happy is the man who finds wisdom, and the man who gains understanding."

(Proverbs 3:13)

The Perfect Career

Working in the television industry for Jon was a life of long hours, deadlines, travel, pagers, cell phones, women, multiple projects, and very little accountability. It seemed to be the perfect career for either a bachelor or the unfaithful. He also volunteered his time working with foster children, when he wasn't working evenings and weekends at Arco Arena. Then there were the last-minute calls from Fox Sports and other freelance projects that kept him constantly on the go.

A day's work of going from story to story and meeting deadlines could sap Jon's energy to the point he needed to unwind in front of the TV for an hour or so before addressing issues with the boys or spending meaningful time with me. By the time he came home at night, it was around ten or eleven o'clock, pretty much past my bedtime. There were many times I waited patiently for time with my husband only to find him fast asleep on the couch. Trying to keep track of him with his many business dealings and making sure he had time with his children was very stressful.

Jon had no browbeating boss and no nine-to-five desk job. He was a free mortal agent unwilling to cooperate and be accountable to me, therefore I had no way of knowing when he was at work or spending time with someone else. I was not privileged to the things most wives knew about their husbands. I had no access to his personal mail, car, post office box, cell phone, call records, income tax information and when he was angry with me definitely not his paycheck. Jon kept his business private, some of it even under lock and key. He had so many deep, dark secrets and showed little interest in teaching me how to assist him with managing his life or help me to trust him.

Many Facets of Jon

There were times when Jon seemed to be an empty shell or in a deep trance with nothing to say. Sometimes I wondered if he was vexed by another spirit. On the flip side though, Jon was out going and a great host, often the life of the party at family gatherings. It was during our fun times with extended family that Jon really came alive. He loved to do impersonations of public figures and his ability to take on the mannerisms of his subjects made our time together as a family very special and fun.

Jon's supportive side gave me the freedom to pursue my life's goals. To my delight, he endorsed my career choices and encouraged me to follow my dream of starting my own consulting health and fitness company. In 2004, I developed "For Him Only Foundation" but later renamed it, "Try 7 Fitness for Heaven" to teach health principles God's way. At its inception, I used television media to develop and teach programs on health/fitness, did healthy cooking demonstrations and gave personal fitness instruction utilizing God's natural laws of health. Today we have expanded to include health consultations, boot camp fitness training, lectures and seminars.

Jon and I began purchasing exercise equipment and turned our three-car garage into a fitness studio while I continued to train at the 24-Hour Fitness Health Club. I also continued to educate myself while producing my own health and fitness exercise TV program. Jon tenderly assisted me with the necessary production tasks by performing on-location shooting and editing. I really enjoyed being able to accomplish my career goals while working alongside my husband.

Early in our relationship, my husband shared his passion and vision for helping "discarded children," and eventually founded his own nonprofit company, "Assist One." It's slogan became, "there are no unwanted children—just unfound families." It's twofold mission was to assist foster children in finding loving, adoptive families and generate an awareness regarding the plight of innocent children being tossed from foster home to foster home. The vehicle to sound this loud cry was Jon's camera lens. He effectively used the media to tell the stories of the many orphans and displaced children in Northern California.

The Struggles Continue

Jon and I had been married four years and although Jon was still away from home and for much of the time without any accountability, we both still had hope for our marriage. Of course, there were days when I just wanted to give up but I never wanted to lose hope. I didn't want to allow failure to become an option. I still felt a lot of fight within me though there were times I would become distracted by the debilitating negativity between us. I was in constant need of confirmation of my calling and ministry.

One day I had an early breakfast appointment with a faithful woman of God. Even though I arrived 15 minutes behind schedule, I enjoyed breakfast with Sheri who was filled with wise Godly counsel. She reminded me to return to my daily journaling and that I could do nothing without faith. God had called me to a ministry of health and I needed to stand firm with my faith in Him to carry it out. From time to time, other fellow believers would feed me spiritually and confirm my understanding of God's calling on my life.

At other times I would pray, "God, you are an awesome God! I thank you from the bottom of my heart. I have always known that I am different. I now know why. When I look back on my life and think of the many times I have been close to death or in grave danger, You saw fit to give me another chance for repentance. I want You to become more necessary to my life than food itself. God, I want my ministry to change lives. Please show me how I can make this a life changing experience. Show me my flaws and help me to work on my character. Help me to be more like You. I pray in Jesus' name."

My commitment to journal was much easier said than done. Sometimes six months passed before I picked up my journal to make an entry. Given the state of my life and my marriage, my emotions were often in a ball of confusion. Sometimes I would be so far down in my spirit that I had absolutely no desire to journal or do much else.

Let's Grow the Boy Up

In spite of Jon's love for children and me wanting to marry a man that would be sensitive to my child's needs, my son had become a very sore subject between us. Jon thought I babied him too much and believed Tristan, who was turning 16, needed to grow up. According to Jon, it was time for Tristan to go away and experience life apart from mom. I was not opposed to Tristan growing and maturing, it was just difficult for me to send him away for an entire summer. But, in another attempt to "make peace" and for the sake of Tristan's development, I surrendered and enrolled him into a literature evangelism program through the church conference. Jon helped me to understand the benefits of releasing my hold on Tristan so he could grow and develop. I finally agreed to Tristan's summer away with one condition: I would accompany him to see firsthand if the program would be held in a safe area.

On June 10, 2005, Tristan and I flew to Baltimore, Maryland, for our first major apron-string-cutting event. What a culture shock for Tristan! He could hardly believe his eyes! I had forgotten my first cultural shock when I went to Washington DC at the age of 15. Now looking at the sights, I remembered my trip as we traveled through Bronx New York with my high school band in 1976. It was very sobering and difficult to think of leaving my baby so far away for the entire summer. I sincerely wanted Tristan to grow spiritually, mentally and emotionally, but still wasn't sure this was the way to do it. So I prayed for his protection, that it would be a positive experience and give him a whole new perspective on life. I sincerely hoped I was doing the right thing and knew this was the precursor to him leaving home for college.

Tristan's summer home was located in a very impoverished part of the city. The drive to his place of residents was a concrete jungle of abandoned cars, vacant houses and the hustle and bustle of city life. It was definitely not what I had in mind for my impressionable son's first time away from home. The house my baby was staying in was hot, musty, old, and dark. It was hard leaving him behind but I kept telling myself it was for his good. I surveyed the area around the house and quickly determined the streets were very harsh and unkind. I interrogated my nephew who was to keep a close watch over Tristan while he was there. My objective for going with my son was to see if it was a safe place to leave him. So far things were not adding up and my spirit was grieved. After getting Tristan settled into his room I left to stay overnight at my nephew's.

I hardly slept a wink that night fearing for my son's health and safety. When I awoke the next morning, I just couldn't get over the horrible feeling I had in the pit of my stomach. When Tristan called he reported the house was extremely hot, dirty, roach infested and full of mildew and he hardly slept because of having asthma attacks. Tristan's literature evangelism program wasn't scheduled to start until Monday, so we went to my nephew's place after church.

It seemed like anything that could go wrong did go wrong from Tristan's hideous place of summer residence, the plumbing backing up at my nephew's house, to my nephew and his wife having a falling out while we were there. I began to wonder, what next?

I had made Sabbath lunch from some old veggie "meat" that I had found in the cabinet. I remember being in the kitchen and thinking aloud, "I can't wait to get back home!"

Tristan heard me and responded, "How do you think *I* feel, Mom?"

Suddenly, how Tristan was feeling hit me like a ton of bricks. He begged me not to make him stay describing it punishment rather than a rewarding Christian summer experience. I knew I would face the wrath of Jon if I gave in, so I made an attempt to call and convey the terrible living conditions and talk to him about the change in plans. Glad I was unable to reach him I called Mom and Pat to get their feedback. Without a moment's hesitation, they each gave me their blessing to abort his trip.

Jon was indeed unhappy with my decision not to leave Tristan in Maryland for the summer, but the decision was mine and we had to live with it. I made arrangements for Tristan to return home one day after me. I knew that Jon would punish me by withdrawing his affection, but that was something to which I had grown accustomed to. It may sound bizarre, but it was true.

Final Events 2005

As the end of summer drew near, Jon had been working on "Daddy Hunger," a documentary project that exposed "dead beat dads" in society and the fatherless children that grew up in a life of brokenness. They would often get involved with drugs, gangs, prostitution and the penal system. Because of Jon's love for children, this project was very near and dear to his heart, and he endeavored to tell the stories of the children, particularly the African American children. I was very supportive of the project because it was a story that needed to be told and was one I was very familiar with, having been a single parent myself because my son's father was one of those dead beat dads.

When I wondered aloud why he had hardly been home, he informed me that he had been working in Los Angeles, Oakland and Fresno with the project and became very angry with me for questioning his whereabouts. He went on to punish me by refusing to go on our big family vacation; a five-day Thanksgiving cruise to the Bahamas. In spite of

Jon's fear of water, I was happy when he had promised to join us, but now angered he reneged. Although Tristan, Mom, my brother Ronnie, sister Pat, cousins, aunt and uncles were all on board, I felt sad and alone without my husband. I had hoped and prayed he would get over it and change his mind but he did not. Once again I found myself lonely even though I was surrounded by a loving family.

'Tis the Season

Christmas was an electrifying time around the Johnson house. Jon usually turned into a big kid himself and because he had such a big heart he loved shopping for the kids and for me. Jon had bragged about how he completed his Christmas shopping early for the whole family and seemed very content knowing he had enough money this year to satisfy us all. Jon was in a very cheerful mood, even helping me in the kitchen as we prepared to host the big family Christmas dinner.

My sister Pat and my step children were already staying with us. Mom, my brother, nieces, nephews and other family members would be joining us a little later. We were off to what seemed to be a wonderful start when Jon announced that we needed more sweet potatoes and headed off to the store to get some. After being gone for several hours, he checked in with the report that he had stopped at many stores but they were all closed. In need of his assistance and worried, I tried unsuccessfully to reach him by phone. When Jon returned home, he was in great spirits; so I didn't want to spoil our holiday. I made the choice to have a good time and went with the flow!

Hopeless New Year!

As the 2006 New Year approached, Jon suddenly needed to fly out to Milwaukee to see a sister whom he said was dying of cancer. His plans were to leave on Friday and return home Sunday evening. Saddened by the prospect of entering the New Year, a new beginning, without Jon I asked him to wait until after the New Year. My spirit not feeling right with his decision I told him it was important to bring in the new year together as a couple. In spite of my opposition he went leaving me behind again.

My Mother invited us over for a spaghetti dinner the day Jon returned home from his trip. However, when he arrived, he rushed in, dropped his bag, barely acknowledged me, brushed his teeth and left again. Later, he called to let me know he would be on his way home after his truck was fixed. When he didn't return in a timely manner, I attempted to reach him by phone but to no avail. When he finally called, he said his truck was still on the rack. It was already past 6:30 in the evening and I was upset about keeping Mom and Cherryl waiting. I knew they had planned to leave after dinner to see my Uncle Terry.

When I mentioned it to Jon, he suggested I go to Mom's house, pick up the food and bring it home so he and I could eat and spend quality time together when he got home. When I returned home with dinner, Jon was in his truck talking on his cell phone. After about half an hour, I went back outside to discover he was *still* on the phone in what appeared to be a heated conversation. By the time he finally came into the house, an hour had passed and I was just too angry to be bothered.

Seeing that he was preparing to leave again, I wanted to explode. I knew this pattern all too well. He was planning his escape so I went into the piano room where he was ironing clothes. He didn't respond to anything I had to say. I went into our bedroom to shower before going to bed.

Lying down next to me in bed, Jon inquired, "You want to talk?"

I was hotter than a firecracker so I started venting. Inflamed by my tone and choice of words, he jumped out of bed, declared he was not going to listen to my harsh tone, packed a bag and took off. My anger gave me the courage to tell Jon that if he left, it would be the last time. I was so tired of holding my tongue, tired of the pent up stress, tired of all the lies, tired of him running at the first sign of confrontation and tired of his refusal to deal with our problems head on.

As he headed to his truck, I yelled, "Don't come back!" I had had enough!!!

Hosea and Gomer

When my anger cooled, I picked up my Bible to do my daily reading and wouldn't you know, I opened up to the story of Hosea and Gomer. In Chapter One, God speaks to the prophet Hosea telling him to go and take a prostitute for his wife. Can you imagine God telling you to marry a man that will cheat on you or a prostitute that will not be loyal to you? But God did just that and Hosea obeyed. Gomer went out and cheated on him over and over again. Sometimes Hosea would go searching for her and he would find her in the town square selling herself and he would buy her back, take her home and clean her up.

She would stay for a while, but then her need to go a whoring would overwhelm her and she would rise up again and find herself on the streets doing what came natural to her. She got pregnant on several occasions and had children from other men. Hosea took those children in and made them his own. God gave him names for each child and told Hosea to care for them as though they were his own flesh and blood.

In fact, Hosea watched over another man's children while his wife was still cheating on him. That's not human, that's divine! Only a heart like God can do that. I realized I needed the heart of God to do what I was called to do as well.

Through all of this, God was testing Hosea's loyalty and his willingness to forgive and press on despite what others may think about him. He was obedient to God even though he didn't quite understand the pulling in his heart toward this wayward, lying, cheating woman. He had no control of the ties that bound him to Gomer, his prostituting wife. I can only imagine how Hosea must have wanted to leave and save the embarrassment of having to go buy back his own wife time and time again. Because Hosea's heart was willing and his will belonged to God, he was able to love the unlovable.

As I read through the rest of Hosea, I saw that God had great love and mercy for his wayward adulterous children. He had forgiveness toward them and a heart filled with pity and sorrow. I wondered how God could love people who hurt others and commit adultery like Jon was doing to me. Then I realized that the Book of Hosea was not just talking about an unfaithful spouse like Jon and the suffering spouse like me. It's a story about all of us. We have all gone astray and have searched after our own idols and gods. We have committed spiritual adultery; we have gone out and cheated on God. But just as He instructed Hosea to do with Gomer, He keeps buying us back and begging us to be faithful to Him. With open arms and forgiveness He receives us back each time. What a great God!

The Lord knows it's not easy to be forgiving when someone you love hurts you, but I have found in my own personal experiences that God won't give us more than we can handle. I have experienced God's graciousness and tender mercy towards me time after time as I stood my ground against Satan and his ploy to snatch and destroy my husband. All God wanted in me was to be surrendered to Him and be a vessel through which He could work to call Jon to repentance and to experience His love. I realized then that Jon and I may never be the ideal couple, but I was not willing for any other woman to have him and destroy his soul. Through the story of Hosea and Gomer I realized my fight for Jon was no longer about me or even our marriage, it was for his soul. Just like Hosea became a vessel to save his wife, I was called to be a selfless worker for Him so that Jon could taste and see that God was truly good.

As I set out to fulfill this call, God heard my desperate cry and Jon began to show signs that change was occurring. Our dear friend, Pastor Branner, started to call Jon on a regular basis, just to talk and build a deeper friendship. He felt Jon needed an outlet and another man to talk to who could be honest with him and love him as well as inspire him without condemnation. Arthur felt there were some serious truths about Jon that needed to be unveiled and laid on the table for discussion and for Jon to face up to them.

At first Jon ran and wouldn't return the calls from Arthur, but Arthur continued praying for Jon's heart to be softened and receptive. After some months of consistent calls, and patient responses from Arthur, Jon began to open up slowly but surely. He could see that Arthur was not about to condemn him or lay guilt on him. Arthur showed Jon genuine love. It came to the point that when Jon didn't hear from Arthur he started chasing Arthur down and leaving messages for him to call him so they could get together.

As Arthur began to see that Jon was sincere and truly desiring to change, they decided to read and study the Bible together. Arthur promised confidentiality and encouraged Jon to share what was in his heart. Arthur wouldn't tell me what they were discussing, but the change in Jon's spirit was evident. Jon was becoming more tender and loving. He expressed a desire to attend Church together as a couple again. I was beginning to feel respected and cherished. I remained prayerful and hopeful that it would be real and ulti-mately complete.

Taking Business to the Next Level

On Friday, March 10, 2006, I decided to become a business partner with an associate I had met through networking named Roberta. She had been mentored by a very successful businessman whom I had turned down repeatedly because of the clashes it would cause with my spiritual walk. He hired Roberta instead and she had become very successful in her field. Roberta was impressed by my passion for health and by my natural ability at public speaking. She desired to work with me to promote health and envisioned us becoming financially successful together. She had the facility, the network of people and the marketing dollars to make it happen.

I really wanted to make it happen but I needed to let her know that I would not be available to work on Sabbath from Friday at sundown to Saturday sundown. Although Roberta expressed her thoughts that Sabbath would be primetime to yield a huge return on our investment, she agreed to the terms and we struck a compromise. She would promote my end of the business on Saturdays even though I would not be there. This didn't sit right with me because I felt I would still be breaking the fourth commandment[10] but I rationalized the compromise and agreed to the partnership. I still didn't feel like this was in line with God's will but I was tired of struggling

---

[10] Exodus 20:8

and decided to help God along by taking matters into my own hands.

I shared the particulars with Jon. He knew of Roberta's success and agreed that she and I would make a great team. Feeling that was the validation I needed, I continued to move full steam ahead while she continued to make plans to expand our market to the Bay Area. Though things were moving according to plan, I was doubtful. Roberta and I continued to talk in preparation of our upcoming meeting in the Bay Area. We were to meet with some of her business contacts the evening of March 25th before our first launch in Sacramento. As the day drew near, my spirit became more unsettled with the business venture but instead of being straight forward, I began to look for excuses not to meet with Roberta.

The Perfect Alibi

Jon had been away for four days and I yearned for his attention and affection. He told me he would not be home on that Friday evening, but would come on Saturday morning and we could go to church together. I decided not to tell him about my appointment with Roberta for that Saturday evening knowing he would tell me to fulfill my obligation. I allowed my husband to be my perfect alibi and made plans to go on our date night that Saturday evening with Jon instead of meeting with Roberta.

It was wonderful to experience the subtle changes in Jon that I had waited so long for and having a date night was one of our new experiences. My husband was becoming more spiritual and more loving. I knew it wasn't complete, but I did know he was making the effort to be more in touch with God and with me. For the first time in our marriage I was beginning to sense the light at the end of our long dark tunnel.

Chapter Nine

March Night

As I anticipated our date night, thoughts of peace ran through my mind. Jon and I were finally beginning to walk together in unison. I was thanking God for bringing me through thus far and for helping me to hold on so I could witness this marvelous change in my husband. Today was a new beginning for us, it was a day filled with loving thoughts, tenderness, and time to spend with each other. Jon was so contemplative and in a different realm than I had ever seen him before. Earlier Jon had called all the people he loved and family members that he cared deeply for. It was just so incredible to see.

Jon was finally ready to start something new, something pure, something everlasting. His honesty and integrity that day was truly a divine experience. Sincerity had taken hold of Jon. Christ had won the battle and Jon had surrendered his weapons. It would be a daily struggle, but with both our hearts committed to God we would make it. That's all I had ever wanted, to see him make a commitment to God once and for all.

With the promise of more date nights, quality family time and time spent together with God, we took off on our night of love, fun and laughter. We arrived at our destination which was only ten minutes from home to grab a bite to eat before setting off to visit some friends and then stop by to wish my mother a happy birthday to cap off our evening together. Everything that day had slowed down into poignant increments of time filled with meaning and purpose, while at the same time I could sense a divine presence of approval from heaven above.

When Time and Chance Ignite

On the other side of town the opposite was taking place. Lives that had been struggling for peace and happiness were now hopeless, distraught, and ready to erupt. Pain, resentment, hatred and death had filled the thoughts of a man named Aaron Dunn. Slowly but surely the thoughtful plans he had imagined over and over again would soon become a reality. As Aaron packed his car that night to go out on his mission, all the pain of a broken relationship with his wife had become his motivation. The lost job and all the other failures he had experienced while attempting to make life worth living stood up and taunted him right in his face.

With the help of the large amount of methamphetamines, Aaron felt equipped and ready to release his anger and frustration in one final battle. Filled with an evil spirit of destruction, Aaron was prepared to maim, kill and destroy anyone who might cross his path. He took off armed with a twelve-gauge shotgun, an arsenal of bullets, and a Satanic Bible. Aaron left his hometown and headed for another man's with music full of satanic advice blaring on his radio. He felt a false sense of security as he thought he was finally taking charge of his life.

On his body was a tattoo that sealed his mission; the Grim Reaper, the Angel of Death. He had given himself over to another power that had turned him into a living monster. There was no stopping such an evil creature. His actions from here on were no longer his as the satanic power he had given control over his life set out to accomplish what in his frail human self he had been too afraid to do.

Choices

The Bible warns us that we become like the one we chose to lead us and allow to control our lives. God has given us the power of choice so no one we can say the devil made me do it. God reaches down daily, moment by moment, calling us to walk with Him.

Isaiah 65:1-2 says, "I am sought of *them that* asked not *for me*; I am found of *them that* sought me not: I said, Behold me, behold me, unto a nation *that* was not called by my name. I have spread out my hands all the day unto a rebellious people, which walketh in a way *that was* not good, after their own thoughts."

No one has an excuse when we have a heavenly Father who sent His son to die on the cross for us so that we can choose and make right decisions. No matter what life brings, God is still greater and able to heal all of the abuses, attacks, hatred and emotional pain. The supply of grace and power is always so much more than the supply for defeat and failure. We can live victorious lives if we so choose. Many who have come from dysfunctional homes have risen to the top, because they chose to follow the right path. Romans 5:20 says, "Moreover the law entered, that the offence might abound. But where sin abounded, grace did much more abound."

The Restaurant

We had eaten enough and it was time we left the restaurant, but Jon just sat there staring off into nothing as if in a strange kind of trance. I thought it was odd as he seemed in no hurry even though we were running late for our visit to Dwayne's. I felt a chilling presence but knew not to disturb him while he was in this deep far away place. He eventually surfaced and rose to his feet, immediately pulling out his cell phone to tell his friend Dwayne we were on our way. I began to walk more hastily toward the door, inadvertently trying to hurry Jon along. It was about 8:00 p.m. by the time we left the restaurant and the parking lot was quiet and still, almost eerie. Unbeknownst to us, a night of terror had already begun to unfold just a few short blocks away.

What had begun as an evening celebration for the 84th birthday of their dear elderly mother had turned to grief when one solid gunshot to the face had taken the life of a beloved father, husband, son, uncle and brother. As Jon and I walked across that parking lot, we had no idea that a crazed killer was on the loose as he searched for his estranged wife and her lover to annihilate them.

We didn't hear the gunshots fired or witness the car accident that had just taken place a few yards from the restaurant where we had eaten. We had no idea that a man had just shot and tried to kill two police women when he blasted out the rear side window of their car. No one told us that a young couple had been shot at by someone they claimed looked like "a Terminator" dressed in a dark hoody and carrying a long black shot gun. We had no indication that such chaos was happening all around us when we left the restaurant and stepped into that dark March night.

I was instantly chilled by the cold night air so I ran swiftly toward our car, getting way ahead of Jon. I unlocked it, hopped inside and immediately started the engine. I turned up the heat and rubbed my hands together trying to get warm. While waiting for my honey, I marveled at the fact that I was on a date with my love. I smiled as I reflected on God's goodness. After all that we had been through we had finally made it to this point and were enjoying our night together. Still on his cell phone but apparently having trouble connecting with his friend, my husband approached the passenger side of the car.

Finally, I heard him say, "Spoon," his friend, Dwayne Witherspoon's nickname.

I remember Jon's voice, so cheerful and full of life. I patiently waited for him to finish his call but wished he'd hurry up and get inside the car so we could be on our way. At that very point in time, the terrible chain of events that had begun earlier that evening 45 miles away, was hurled into motion. The demon possessed perpetrator, who had plotted all day how to make his big impact, had reached his final destination. Keyed-up on drugs and enraged by all of life's injustices, he was prepared to make somebody pay in a BIG way! The grim reaper, the angel of death had arrived.

I heard Jon say in a calm but determined tone of voice, "Man, get that out of my face."

POW!!

I heard a loud sound like a car had back fired. Then there was silence. I patiently waited for my husband knowing in a few short seconds he would be off his cell phone and grace me with his presence once again. A still small voice seemed to be telling me to "be still" so I remained in the car, thinking maybe my husband had gone back to the restaurant to talk privately with Dwayne. After a few more seconds of silence, I turned and looked toward the passenger side of the car but Jon was not there. Still unaware of what was happening around me, I resumed my forward position and as if prompted by the Holy Spirit, continued to sit still and wait.

I sat motionless for a few more seconds, then, as if instructed "now's the time," I turned and looked over my left shoulder in the opposite direction. Shocked and terrified by what I saw, I gasped for air and trembled in fear while clutching my chest in disbelief.

Trying to keep my wits about me I knew my next move was critical. In a fixed crouched down position, I saw a Caucasian man wearing a hooded brown sweat jacket with a shotgun raised above his head as though claiming victory. As

I watched, he placed it on his shoulder as if ready to shoot at anything that moved.

Without my permission my mind quickly started to place things into perspective and put two and two together. My heart sank as I played back in my mind the sound I had heard just seconds earlier. I suddenly came to the startling conclusion that the "POW" I had heard was a gunshot that had been fired at my husband. The calm tone of his voice I had heard just before the shot was his attempt to prove his bravery and not startle the deranged gunman. Jon had successfully walked away from many near death experiences both as a television photo journalist and growing up in the rugged parts of East Oakland, CA. This time Jon was not to escape the wrath of another.

Realizing I needed to take action, my instinct kicked into high gear to run to my husband's rescue. Not thinking about my own safety I quickly opened the car door and immediately knew I had made a grave mistake. Hearing my car door open, the shooter robotically turned around and looked in my direction. I just knew he was going to come back and finish the job. It appeared as if he was looking right through me even though he was only a few yards away. I quickly ducked but kept the door slightly cracked not wanting to make a sound so I could keep an eye on him. From my vantage point, I watched him pan the parking lot, looking for his next victim.

I was trembling uncontrollably, my heart was racing and I remember saying to myself, "he's going to kill me, he's going to come back and kill me because I can identify him."

In my mind I was crying out to God, do you see me God? Are you there? God heard my plea and shielded me, while the deranged gunman looked right at me. "I was covered" by God's safety and protection. Unable to see me, the demon possessed man did an about face and walked away from the scene of the crime.

And it shall come to pass, that before they call, I will answer; and while they are yet speaking, I will hear. (Isaiah 65: 24)

I anxiously waited in terror for the right moment to safely exit the car without the gunman seeing me. After one final scan of the parking lot, the shooter headed toward the street on foot shooting round after round into the cold night sky. It was then the Holy Spirit impressed upon me to make my exit quickly. I flung open the door and bolted around the car to the passenger side.

I gasped as I saw my strong, handsome 6'2" husband sprawled out on his back, motionless on the cold damp pavement. Jon's face was unrecognizable, his chin and jaw were gone and there was a pool of blood around his head. I wanted so badly for him to moan or move so I could see some signs of life.

Numb and in shock, my adrenalin kicked in and I frantically ran back to the restaurant shouting at the top of my lungs, "My husband's been shot, my husband's been shot!"

But the music was blaring, the huge wall mounted big screen televisions were on at full blast, people were laughing and talking while sipping their alcohol and no one heard me!

Desperate for help, I belted out a second time, "My husband's been shot!"

Again there was no response to my desperate cry. In a state of confusion, wondering why they weren't getting it, I changed my plea and with all the energy I could muster up I belted out, "Somebody call 911, my husband's been shot!"

Gasping for air from the adrenalin rush, finally two guys asked me to repeat myself. Shaking and crying with tears of relief I said, "My husband's been shot, please call 911."

They bolted out the door running to the scene of the crime, as I pointed to where my husband lay between our white Mercedes and a Silver Honda. Once outside, they saw the gunman off in the distance still shooting in the air as if it were the fourth of July. My adrenalin pumping, I told the men I was going back to be by my husband's side.

One of the good Samaritans said, "No, you can't go back. It's too dangerous, Mam."

Shaking uncontrollably, with tears streaming down my face, I pleaded with them to let me go back. I couldn't leave him out there by himself. As the gunman continued shooting round after round, it hit me like a ton of bricks. The image of my husband's disfigured face, his juggler vain pumping blood out his body, and the right side of his lower jaw mush like hamburger meat on the pavement. I realized I couldn't bear to see him again in that lifeless state. Confused and afraid, I wanted to hold his hand and comfort him until help arrived, but I suddenly felt weak and sick to my stomach from the sight of my husband's blood. After they convinced me it wasn't safe and assured me they would stay by his side, I gave in and went back inside the noisy restaurant, anxiously waiting for help to arrive.

Anxious and afraid, I tried to calm down. I could hardly breathe. Crying and trembling, I kept asking those who stayed with me why it was taking so long for the ambulance to arrive. Still not convinced I should be inside while my husband laid outside in the dark on the cold pavement fighting for his life, I kept telling the people around me Jon needed me.

They kept assuring me that I did the right thing by taking shelter from the gunman and tried to calm me down. I had never felt so desperate, helpless and alone in my life.

I started going through a roller coaster of emotions and irrational thinking. Guilt and condemnation began plaguing me telling me I should not have gone to that particular restaurant bar and grill. My husband and I were Christians, we didn't drink, do drugs or party. We just went out for an innocent evening of dinning, but the fact of the matter was, we probably shouldn't have been in a place like that. If I would have followed the prompting of the Holy Spirit telling me to leave that place when we first set foot in that establishment, Jon would not be lying on the cold wet pavement with half his face blown away. I beat myself up even more as I remembered how I had run to the car ahead of Jon for shelter and safety. I even wondered why Jon was the one hurt and not me.

As guilt and pain started to overwhelm me, one of the most amazing acts of love and kindness I have ever experienced in a public setting began to unfold. As I sat there feeling like no one understood what I had just witnessed outside, Christ began to move in the hearts of all the believers in that restaurant. They started rallying around me, laying hands on me and earnestly praying and interceding for us out loud. I was seeing the forces of good come against evil in a mighty way. God was moving in that place and calmed the storm in me. My mind flashed back to a passage of scripture I've heard and read many times. Our God is a present help in time of trouble and will not leave us comfortless; He will come to us.[11] God came to me in that restaurant that night.

---

[11] See Psalm 46:1

The Battle Between Good and Evil

The eyes of the LORD are on the righteous, and His ears are open to their cry. The face of the LORD is against those who do evil. To cut off the remembrance of them from the earth. The righteous cry out, and the LORD hears, and delivers them out of all their troubles. The LORD is near to those who have a broken heart. And saves such as have a contrite spirit. Many are the afflictions of the righteous, but the LORD delivers him out of them all. (Psalms 34:15-19)

What blew me away more than anything was the battle between good and evil that was unfolding right before my very eyes. A demon-possessed man was outside shooting at the police and innocent by-standers, while inside believers put away whatever they were doing and shifted their energies to the spiritual realm calling on God as they prayed for my husband and me.

Feeling as if I was playing a role in a movie, I was keenly aware there were two distinct camps in the restaurant that night, those who feared God and were spiritually aware of the intense battle raging around them and those who had no clue at all what was going on. I realized how dark and destructive the world could be outside of God and never wanted to be part of that world ever again. As a Christian I knew God had called me to live in this world but not be a part of it. Christ, Himself, was hated by the people of the world.

"I have given them Your word; and the world has hated them because they are not of the world, just as I am not of the world," Jesus told His disciples. Then He prayed for His followers and all of us that would come after. "I do not pray that You should take them out of the world, but that You should keep them from the evil one. They are not of the world, just as I am not of the world."

(John 17:14-17)

As I sat there in the restaurant, surrounded by praying believers, I could hear the piercing voice of the intoxicated woman who had been sitting next to us as we tried to enjoy ourselves amidst the loud noisy crowded restaurant. I remembered how her disregard for other patrons had annoyed Jon as he tried to watch the game. He glared at her, but said nothing. Though it had annoyed me, too, I chose to focus my energies on my husband and savor each minute with him. Little did I know those would be our final few minutes together on this earth. With all the commotion going on around me the good Samaritans, the drunks, and the Christians, my mind suddenly flashed to a quote from a Christian book titled, "The Great Controversy."

Before the Flood, after Noah entered the ark, God shut him in and shut the ungodly out; but for seven days the people, knowing not that their doom was fixed, continued their careless, pleasure-loving life and mocked the warnings of impending judgment. "So," says the Savior, "shall also the coming of the Son of man be" (Matthew 24:39). Silently, unnoticed as the midnight thief, will come the decisive hour which marks the fixing of every man's destiny, the final withdrawal of mercy's offer to guilty men. "Watch ye therefore: lest coming suddenly He find you sleeping" (Mark 13:35, 36). Perilous is the condition of those who, growing weary of their watch, turn to the attractions of the world. While the man of business is absorbed in the pursuit of gain, while the pleasure lover is seeking indulgence, while the daughter of fashion is arranging her adornments – it may be in that hour the Judge of all the earth will pronounce the sentence: "Thou are weighed in the balances, and art found wanting" (Daniel 5:27). Conformity to worldly customs converts the church to the world; it never converts the world to Christ. Familiarity with sin will inevitably cause it to appear less repulsive. He who chooses to associate with the servants of Satan will soon cease to fear their master. When in the way of duty we are brought into trial, as was Daniel in the king's court, we may be sure that God will protect us; but if we place ourselves under temptation we shall fall sooner or later. (Ellen G. White, "The Great Controversy, The Global War on Freedom,"188)

As I panned the restaurant, I was ashamed to be in such a place and wondered what my Pastor and church family would think when they saw the reports from all the news media and newspapers. My earth shattering experience showed me how easily I had gotten caught up in the cares of this world. On the other hand, I was grateful God had placed other Christians there that night to pray for and comfort me until my family and friends arrived. "The Lord is nigh unto them that are of a broken heart; and saveth such as be of a contrite spirit" (Psalm 34:18).

As my fellow brethren gathered around me, I remember one lady in particular. As I sat there crying after they had prayed for me, she knelt down to my eye level and asked me if I had any nearby friends or family members that she could call to come and be with me. I could not seem to pull myself together enough to come up with anyone. As she persisted, I thought of my best friend Esmie. When she came back and said she had not been able to reach Esmie, she asked if there was family nearby she could call. Not wanting to break the news to my elderly mother, I bypassed her and asked that she try my other girlfriend, Felicia. Successfully reaching Felicia, she came back and asked me again if she could call my mother. I told her my Mom had been sick and I was afraid she might have a heart attack upon hearing the news.

With profound wisdom she said, "That's what mothers are for, give me her phone number."

Instantly, the light bulb went off and I gave her my mother's telephone number knowing I did indeed need her with me.

As she handed me her cell phone, I could hear Mom answer but all I could say between sobs was, "Mom?"

"What Karen, what?"

"Jon's been shot!"

Mom immediately sprang into action and asked me where were we. I tried to give her directions but my brain was so foggy I couldn't think straight. Seeing my confusion and frustration, the dear lady took the phone from me and calmly gave my mother directions to the restaurant.

Chapter Ten

No Time To Say Good-bye!

The restaurant suddenly went quiet. The police had arrived and quickly brought order instructing the restaurant personnel to turn off all TV's and music saying no one was to leave. When I asked them how they got there so quickly they said they were next door at the Chevron gas station. Realizing the ambulance still hadn't arrived, I told the police that if help didn't arrive soon Jon would die, but all the police would say was the ambulance is on their way.

Another woman approached me saying she was a nurse and said she had offered to give Jon CPR but the police wouldn't let her. Sadly shaking her head, as she looked me in the eyes, I realized either Jon was dead or she didn't expect him to make it. Her words confirmed what I had been thinking, as the picture of Jon's face flashed again across my brain.

Shortly after our exchange the ambulance arrived on the scene. I wanted to run outside and be with my husband in the ambulance but the police said I would not be going with him. When I asked why, "because your husbands too sick," a lady replied. The gruesomeness of Jon's disfigured face again began to haunt me, so I dared not press the issue.

After the ambulance left, patrons remained in the restaurant while police questioned witnesses. I was anxiously waiting to be united with the familiar faces of my mother, son and friends but no one was allowed to enter the restaurant. As the police finally allowed the others to leave, I was detained. They said my car was part of the crime scene and I was going to be escorted by a detective to the police station. Exhausted I just wanted to go home and act like it never happened. The two dear ladies stood by my side until I was escorted away. They each gave me their telephone numbers and told me to feel free to call them any time. Unfortunately, in the commotion of the next few days, I lost their telephone numbers and never saw or spoke to those two dear women again. I am forever grateful to those two dear ladies and the two men who helped me that night. I regret that I never got to thank them personally for their heroic act of love and support in my time of despair.

He shall cover thee with His feathers, and under His wings shalt thou trust; His truth shall be thy shield and buckler.

(Psalm 91:4)

As the patrons slowly filed out, the Chaplain and a police officer stayed with me in the restaurant. I remember telling the officer I was afraid to go outside but he assured me the gunman was subdued and they would be escorting me out to safety. When the detective arrived to escort me, I timidly walked out of the restaurant and down the sidewalk across from the crime scene.

I turned in the direction of the car looking for Jon's body but the detective quickly ushered me away. I couldn't help but notice the multiple news teams with their satellite dishes all lined up along the street.

As the detective put me in the car, I wanted to scream out to the reporters, "It's Jon, the man you're reporting about, it's our beloved Jon."

Instead, I told the detective, "They don't know the person they are reporting on is one of their colleagues."

Silence filled the air as I was escorted to the police station. When I got out of the car I was united with my mother, my nephew Carl, my son and Tristan's friend D'Artangan. Other friends and family were waiting for me inside as I was ushered into a conference room. As family members called other family members, my son called his stepbrother and sister to tell them their father had been shot. I stood by in a trance still not believing what was happening. While I waited to hear from the hospital regarding the status of Jon, more and more people began to file in to the conference room. Jon's Chaplain friend from the Sacramento Kings, our doctor friend Brett and my girlfriend Felicia arrived shortly after I arrived at the police station.

As people were being notified of what happened, calls came pouring in. My pastors and their wives had just left town but I did get to speak to them by phone and Pastor Williams prayed with me. Still unaware of the extent of Jon's condition, we were all on pins and needles, hoping for the best but braced for the worse. When another Chaplain arrived to talk to me, I knew that Jon was not going to make it.

Though the nurse at the restaurant alluded to it, this Chaplain sealed it by telling me shortly after his arrival at the police station, Jon had expired. I had "no time to say good-bye." I just couldn't wrap my mind around what happened. One minute we were together and he was full of life making future plans, then the next minute he was dead. His beautiful face disfigured and his lifeless body on some hospital slab.

At the time it felt like such a waste but now I understand that Jon's death was not in vain. As I tell my story and give God the glory for covering and keeping me through the whole ordeal, I now see how God used it to bear much fruit in His kingdom. I clearly see how He took a mess and turned it into a message. "Unless a grain of wheat falls to the ground and dies.....it cannot bear much fruit..." (John 12:24).

Sadly, I had to break the news to Jon's daughter, Tangela over the phone. She was living in Colorado at the time. As I shared what had happened, we just cried and cried together. After I got off the telephone the Chaplains offered me food but I had no appetite.

Exhausted, I just wanted to go home, process through all that had happened and go to bed. But I was told I had to stay until the detective arrived to take my statement.

Please Hear Me

While friends and family members waited for me in the conference room, I was escorted to a tiny room to wait for the detective. I don't remember his name or how he looked. All I can remember was his gentleness while he questioned me over and over again about what happened and what we did leading up to the shooting. He asked me if Jon had an exchange of words with anyone, and I told him no. He asked me if Jon got into a fight with anyone. Again I told him no. He asked me how I knew that and I told him because we never left each other's side once we entered the restaurant; not even to go to the restroom.

I told him Jon was a nice man. He asked me if Jon had anything to drink. I told him neither of us drank liquor. He asked me to describe the man I saw in the parking lot which I did to the best of my ability. It seemed he kept asking me the same questions but each time a little differently. I was tired and getting frustrated with his line of questioning. I was already extremely upset that they denied me the right to be by my dying husband's side. All I knew was my beloved Jon was dead and I just wanted to go home, sleep this whole experience off and forget everything that happened. I begged him to let me go home. He said he would as soon as I answered his questions. Then he asked me the same questions again.

He finally escorted me back into the conference room where I was reunited with my loved ones. My mother drove me home, passing the restaurant where the shooting took place. By now, it was late and the strip mall was dark and deserted. There were no more police, news trucks, cameras or reporters. It was as if the final scene of the production had finally been played out and the cast and crew had gone home. The star of the movie was dead and I was on the outside looking in.

Home Alas

I was relieved to be heading home to get much needed rest. As we turned the corner and drove toward the house the first thing my eyes beheld was Jon's silver Ford Expedition sitting in the driveway were we'd left it just a few hours earlier. It was then the startling reality that Jon was dead and would never drive his truck nor set foot in our home ever again hit me full force. This painful reality brought on fear, loneliness and a sudden sense of deep sadness in my heart. I had hoped by going home I would be comforted and somehow negate the tragic events of March 25, 2006. Instead, I was faced with the grim reality that Jon's life had been senselessly snuffed out. Jon had been suddenly snatched away and in the twinkling of an eye I went from wife to widow.

In silence, I slowly retraced our steps through the garage where just a few hours earlier my husband had so lovingly asked me to drive my car as we embarked on what we thought was going to be an intimate date night. Too exhausted and scattered to try and figure things out, I walked into the house. Finally at home I didn't know what to do. I guess in some strange way I thought that being home would make it all go away, but instead it magnified my sense of loss. I had hoped to come home and go right to sleep but I trembled in fear even though the police assured me the murderer had been caught.

I was so afraid I asked my mother to stay the night and sleep in the bed with me. That night and for many nights to follow my mother, niece and sisters had sleep duty with me as my fear of the dark and being left alone was too much to bear.

I Couldn't Stop It

Exhausted and home in my bed I tried to sleep but when I shut my eyes I was gripped with fear. The gut wrenching images of Jon's disfigured face kept flashing across my brain every time I closed my eyes. Lying in the darkness with my mother sound asleep beside me, tears streamed down my face as my whole body shook with fear. Confused by what the Lord had allowed me to see and experience, I desperately tried to erase the last image I had of Jon. I kept having flash backs. One minute I was walking beside my healthy husband, happy and in harmony with one another. The next instant Jon was lying motionless, flat on his back in a cold dark parking lot, with shotgun pellets sprayed in his face. The mush, blood and gore kept flashing in my brain and I couldn't stop it though I desperately wanted to erase it.

I had hoped to quickly fall asleep in a place of quiet and solitude but when I closed my eyes, there was no peace, only horror. Unable to sleep but not wanting to wake mom or Tristan, I jumped out of bed and paced the floor until daybreak. I kept the lights on in the hall way and downstairs, still battling the fear of all I had experienced that long night. With dawn approaching and sleep impossible, I decided to call my friend Vicky to tell her about Jon.

Not realizing in was only 5:00 a.m. but needing someone to talk to, I continued to pace until Vicky picked up the phone and whispered a groggy, "Hello?"

Sad and confused I said, "Vicky, Jon's dead. He was murdered last night and we won't be meeting today."

Shocked by what she heard, Vicky said "shut up" and asked me to repeat myself. This time I told her Jon had been shot and killed last night while we were out on a date. Still sounding groggy, she asked me what night I was talking about. As I tried again to explain what happened, she suddenly processed what I was saying and asked if there was anything she could do. Crying, I told her no I was waiting for my sisters to arrive and that some of my family was here with me, then I hung up.

Very weary now, I walked into Tristan's room. Tristan's television was on so I quietly laid on his bed as the morning news came on. I wondered if any of the reporters knew it was Jon they were talking about. As I suspected, the police had not released his name. I wanted to call the station and tell them it was one of their own that had died but I was so confused and weak, I just got up and walked out of Tristan's room back to the family room. Then the phone calls began to come in from people sharing their condolences and wanting to help but I didn't even know where to begin to sort out what I needed. I just thanked them and continued walking around in a daze.

I wanted to get my car back and my girlfriend Felicia volunteered to pick it up and bring it home once the police released it. I waited in the garage after she called to say she was on her way. Just as I opened the garage door, an SUV pulled up. It was Vicky, her husband and their kids. They were on their way to church and though I had told Vicky I didn't need any help, she decided to stop by to see how I was doing. Seeing my mental and emotional state, Vicky decided not to go to church and took control of everything that needed to be done. On my behalf, she contacted the news media, the funeral home, the coroner's office at UC Davis Medical Center, and Arco Arena telling them what had transpired and making arrangements for what needed to be done.

Understanding there were pressing things that needed to be done but not having the energy or the mental capacity to handle them, I welcomed her help. The Citizens of Elk Grove had begun a memorial outside the restaurant where Jon's body once laid and the news media wanted a story. When the news media arrived at my home, Vicky knew I was in no condition to face the cameras and took over naming herself the Johnson Family Spokesperson. Vicky handled so many important things that I was unable to do; I knew she had been sent by God in my time of need.

Traumatized but still unable to eat or sleep, my mother asked our friend Brett who Jon referred to as "Doc" to write me a prescription for sleep medication. Though I tried to sleep, lovingly my church family and friends kept coming up to my bed room to visit until my mom had my aunt tell everyone to leave so I could get the rest I needed for all that was still ahead.

Monday and Tuesday

For the next two days the majority of the media came by to cover the story and I was glad my mother was with me to oversee all that was taking place around me. Mom sat at the downstairs kitchen table where she could watch all the various activities going on, making sure things were being done decently and in order. Slow in physical mobility but sharp as a whip, Mom watched the news reporters enter my home and listened as they interviewed Vicky on my behalf. Then she came upstairs, told me to get myself together and talk to the reporters. She said Jon was my husband and I was there that night and no one could tell the story better than me. By the grace of God I pulled myself out of bed, showered and dressed then went downstairs to receive guests and interview with reporters.

The days leading up to the funeral were filled with interviews with newspaper and television reporters, talking with police, detectives and pastors, besides making arrangements with the funeral home.

After Jon's family and children arrived, we had our time of weeping and reflecting on the life of Jon. We were all hurting over the sudden death of Jon and as much as I wanted to disappear, I knew I had to get a hold of myself and make decisions that only a wife can make. I wanted to keep him in Sacramento but I set out to honor his wishes that he be buried in Arkansas next to his daddy's grave.

I had been trying to reach my girlfriend Esmie to tell her what had happened but she was away in the mountains on a weekend retreat. When she finally got a signal and heard my solemn voice on her voicemail, she and her husband Arthur rushed back as quickly as they could. I needed their wise counsel and knew I could trust them to keep my private matters confidential.

Even though I was extremely busy during the day, I still couldn't sleep at night even with the help of sleeping medication. I had no appetite and by the time of the funeral I had lost 16 lbs going from a size 8 to a size 2, from 131 pounds to 116 pounds. Between the lack of sleep and the lost weight,

I looked like a walking zombie. The pain of my loss coupled with the fear of my near death experience made every breath I took an effort.

During this dark time, I experienced a range of emotions which included being afraid of the dark and loud noises. For the first two weeks after the loss of my husband, my mother, niece and sister slept with me. After they left I slept with my lights on for more than a year. I was afraid of parking lots and men with features similar to Aaron Dunn. Loud noises like gunshots, fireworks and sirens set me on edge. Movies and television depressed me, especially the news because of the negativity and violence. To keep my sanity, I basically avoided anything connected with death and loss.

Although I knew I was a child of the most High God, I walked around in a state of constant fear and experienced Post Traumatic Stress. Death was constantly on my mind as I kept anticipating something happening to more of my loved ones or me. When I tried to express my fears to those around me it felt as if no one really understood what I was going through. Although I was constantly surrounded with people, I felt so alone. It was as if someone took me and threw me into a deep dark abyss that I had to find my way out. I achieved moments of peace during my times of Bible reading and listening to Christian music but for the most part my days were filled with chaos and pain.

Once Upon a Time

As I walked through the darkest time of my entire Christian journey, I remember thinking back to a time when my mother and I had fellowshipped together. Sunday after Sunday this one particular lady testified about all the turmoil she experienced in her life before she came to Christ. If Sister Riley was in the church that day, you could count on hearing her shout about God's goodness. I remember turning to my mom on several occasions saying I had no sad stories to tell. Mom agreed with me and said she didn't have any either. Now as I reflected on my husband's murder, my entire perspective changed. Although I had experienced the loss of my father and brother, I never totally related to that level of grief or God's sustaining love until I had my own tragic experience.

This earth shattering experience hung over my head like a dark cloud day and night for many months. Death permeated my thoughts as I battled post-traumatic stress and personal guilt for choosing the restaurant and leaving my husband's side after he was shot. I visited Jon's grave almost daily as I found great comfort and an unexplainable peace there as I prayed and talked to God. As I focused my thoughts on Him, I saw Isaiah 26:3 become a reality in my troubled life. "You will keep him in perfect peace, whose mind is stayed on You, because he trusts in You."

I'm so glad I was grounded and rooted in the word of God. At first, I didn't think I could make it but even as the clouds got darker and darker, God knew my weakness. He dispatched His holy angels and surrounded me with prayer warriors to intercede on my behalf day and night to give me strength and calm my spirit. He provided what I needed to endure the crisis that was raging all around me. The Bible says we can each walk through whatever life throws at us by, "casting all your cares upon Him, for He cares for you" (1Peter 5:7).

I will lift up my eyes to the hills - from whence comes my help? My help comes from the LORD, who makes heaven and earth. He will not allow your foot to be moved; He who keeps you will not slumber. Behold, He who keeps Israel shall neither slumber nor sleep. The LORD is your keeper; The LORD is your shade at your right hand. The sun shall not strike you by day, or the moon by night. The LORD shall preserve you from all evil; He shall preserve your soul. The LORD shall preserve your going out and your coming in from this time forth, and even forevermore.

(Psalms 121:1-8)

I can tell you I experienced this promise first hand following the days after my husband's death.

Just a few days after the tragedy a grim reality set in, I worked with my step children, Tangela and Tray, to sort through our differences and grief so we could deal with all the business matters that now needed handling. Hubby and Daddy were gone. Oh, how I yearned for his guidance as we strove to bring order to our shattered lives.

In the mean time I sent my brother to scout out a funeral home. After giving me his report I decided to go with Thompson's funeral home. My stepchildren and I met with two ladies from the funeral home and shared Jon's wishes to be buried in Arkansas next to his father. Though his grave would be too far for frequent visits, we wanted to honor his wish.

We picked out Jon's suit and the coffin together and even decided to go with Jon's favorite colors, blue and orange. He was an avid Denver Bronco's fan and loved those colors. After our meeting, the two ladies assured me they would attempt to carry out Jon's request and have him buried in Arkansas next to his father's grave. They left my house eager to go to work. However, the search for Jon's father's grave in Arkansas was not successful.

Still trying to wrap my mind around all that had happened, I knew I had to somehow pull myself together and take care of settling our affairs. There were times I thought I was going to go insane but even as I walked through this fiery trial, I clung to God's everlasting promise.

No temptation has overtaken you except such as is common to man; but God is faithful, who will not allow you to be tempted beyond what you are able, but with the temptation will also make the way of escape, that you may be able to bear it. (1 Corinthians 10:13)

As the family gathered together to cry and reminisced about Jon, our circle of intimacy began to crumble because the murder was such a high profile case. It happened in the small bedroom community of Elk Grove where the man that shot Jon had also killed Michael Daly, a man who was out celebrating his mother's 84th birthday with his family at a nearby restaurant. There were other victims shot but not killed that night. A gruesome shootout between police and Aaron Dunn ensued on Laguna Blvd right after he shot Jon in the parking lot of a strip mall, which is why Jon did not receive the immediate medical attention necessary to preserve his life. To top it off, we received a lot of media attention since many reporters knew and loved Jon. A talented and highly successful photojournalist with over 24 year's experience in the television industry, Jon's sudden death left many friends and colleagues shocked and needing to know what happened. It got to the point all this attention began to invade our families' privacy.

Jon's Deepest Darkest Secret

Things got even worse when one of Jon's skeletons dropped out of the closet just four days after his death. As Pandora's Box was opened, Satan had a field day playing on the hearts and minds of my bonus children, certain members of Jon's family and the community. It seemed like things were happening in rapid succession as people tried to get a hold of me because of the breaking news coverage. I'll never forget the day Esmie, Mom, and I sat upstairs in my bedroom while Vicky talked on the phone with the coroner's office making arrangements for Jon's body to be taken to the funeral home. Vicky loved to call me her twin even though I was ten years her senior. Our birthdays and even our wedding anniversaries were on the same day. We grew up in San Jose just blocks away from one another and attended the same elementary school.

As she started to tell me when the funeral home would be picking up the body, she received a call back from the coroner's office asking her to fax them my marriage license. Thinking it was proper protocol to get the body released, I went to my files to retrieve it and we faxed it over. A few hours later the coroner's office called again asking Vicky more questions about my marriage. In a calm professional manner she spoke with the coroner relaying information back and forth to me. With so much to do and very little time to do it, I began to get agitated with the Corner. I could not understand why the holdup and after having been on the phone for quite some time, I asked Vicky what was going on.

With tears in her eyes, Vicky sadly said, "Twin, they won't release Jon's body to you because he has another wife."

Taken aback, I couldn't believe what I was hearing but calmly asked, "Who are they saying is his wife?"

Vicky said nothing; she just looked at me with deep sadness in her eyes.

Anxious for a response I asked, "Diana?"

Looking somewhat relieved, Vicky sadly shook her head yes.

My husband of five and a half years was indeed a Polygamist and his other wife Diana was at the hospital refusing to release his body to me. Both of us insisted we were the current legal wife. I had broken up with Jon nine years earlier, after finding out he was married to Diana. He had convinced me he was in an arranged marriage for the sake of her kids. When I discovered her and the children living in his condo, he had assured me he was not living there nor was he in love with Diana. He just didn't want her to lose her kids. After our blow up and months apart, we came back together, were baptized and recommitted our lives to each other because he assured me he had filed for divorce. Now, nine years later it had come back to haunt me. I didn't understand how we were able to get our marriage certificate while Jon was still married to another woman. Wouldn't that have shown up on his records?

But no matter how ugly and bad things got, Isaiah 54:17 reminded me, "'No weapon formed against you shall prosper, and every tongue which rises against you in judgment You shall condemn. This is the heritage of the servants of the LORD, and their righteousness is from Me,' says the LORD.'"

The devastating news that Jon Johnson was still married to Diana and was leading a double life really rocked my world. It added doubt of his love for me to the multiple layers of grief I was already experiencing.

Anger and despair threatened to take over yet I drew even closer to God as He reminded me of His promise to be my refuge and strength and a very present help in times of trouble.[12] I knew the answers to my questions could only come from God and that God would give me the peace I needed to survive this. So while I had to endure the embarrassment and added stress caused by this latest information, God took me on yet another journey into the heart of His love.

When you pass through the waters, I will be with you;
And through the rivers, they shall not overflow you.

---

[12] See Psalms 46:2

When you walk through the fire, you shall not be burned,
Nor shall the flame scorch you. (Isaiah 43:2)

The Battle Rages On

In the days to come, a battle raged within my mind. I was a devoted Christian woman, why did God allow this to happen? I now know that it was God's permissive will that allowed Jon's life to be taken at that moment in time. God gave me confirmation through Pastor Banner as he shared with me the types of conversations he had with Jon leading up to his tragic death. He shared how Jon had started to unveil himself and wanted to be more accountable. I thank God that He allowed me to see that Jon wanted a closer walk with Him. Even when I got into my husband's truck days after his death to sort through and clean things out, to my surprise he had the radio dial set on a Christian radio station.

In spite of all that happened in the days following Jon's death, it was these things that gave me great comfort and hope that I would see my husband again. God is merciful and let me see that Jon had turned to Him prior to his death. God also revealed to me that it was my guardian angel that protected and shielded me from the deranged man who shot the fiery blast from his shotgun from the passenger side of my car. I likened myself to being tucked away safely in the cleft of the rock so the gunman didn't see me to destroy me, too. God knew that the road would be long and the battle for my soul wasn't over, yet He had not left me to do battle by myself.

Finally, my brethren, be strong in the Lord and in the power of His might. Put on the whole armor of God, that you may be able to stand against the wiles of the devil. For we do not wrestle against flesh and blood, but against principalities, against powers, against the rulers of the darkness of this age, against spiritual hosts of wickedness in the heavenly places. Therefore take up the whole armor of God, that you may be able to withstand in the evil day, and having done all, to stand. Stand therefore, having girded your waist with truth, having put on the breast plate of righteousness, and having shod your feet with the preparation of the gospel of peace; above all, taking the shield of faith with which you will be able to quench all the fiery darts of the wicked one. And take the helmet of salvation, and the sword of the Spirit, which is the word of God.

(Ephesians 6:10-17)

Angels are sent on missions of mercy to the children of God. To Abraham, with promises of blessing; to the gates of Sodom, to rescue righteous Lot from its fiery doom; to Elijah, as he was about to perish from weariness and hunger in the desert; to Elisha, with chariots and horses of fire surrounding the little town where he was shut in by his foes; to Daniel, while seeking divine wisdom in the court of a heathen king and in the lions' den; to Peter, doomed to death in Herod's dungeon; to the prisoners at Philippi; to Paul and his companions during the tempest on the sea; to open the mind of Cornelius to receive the gospel; to dispatch Peter with the message of salvation to the gentile stranger – holy angels have ministered to God's people throughout the ages.

A guardian angel is appointed to every follower of Christ. These heavenly watchers shield the righteous from the power of the wicked one. In Job 1:9-10 we see that even Satan recognized this when he said, "Doth Job fear God for nought? Hast not Thou made an hedge about him, and about his house, and about all that he hath on every side?" The agency by which God protects His people is presented in the words of the psalmist in Psalm 34:7, "The angel of the Lord encampeth round about them that fear Him, and delivereth them." The Saviour Himself said in Matthew 18:10, "Take heed that ye despise not one of these little ones; for I say unto you, that in heaven their angels do always behold the face of My Father." The angels appointed to minister to the children of God have at all times access to His presence. (Ellen G. White, "The Great Controversy," 198).

God's people are assured of the unceasing guardianship of heavenly angels and God's promise that what Satan means for bad, God means for good. Knowing this and that there was a battle going on for my soul between good and evil, I begged God to help me stay strong in Him. I felt guilty and the need to know why my life had been spared and Jon's was taken caused me to draw even closer to God. I knew this was a spiritual battle that I was in and God alone would deliver me from my enemy.

Chapter Eleven

Shifting Love

As the devastating news of my husband's polygamy came
to light amongst the family and a few close friends, the
tragedy of his death took on a whole new twist. I was angry at
the system for not catching the fact that Jon was still married
when we applied for our marriage license and I was infuriated
with Jon for leaving me hanging with this legacy. I desperately
wished I could close my eyes, click my heels three times and
miraculously wake up from this terrible nightmare and be back
in the safety of our home with Jon. I not only had no time to
say good-bye, now I had no way to know what was truly in my
husband's heart at the time of his death.

I knew Jon had filed for a divorce from Diana but what I
didn't know was that it was never finalized. My anger at myself
for believing Jon in this matter went to a whole new level and
once again I felt duped. I felt like everything I had experienced

in my five-and-a-half-year marriage to Jon was a LIE. The gaping hole in my heart now included an incredible amount of doubt that he had ever really loved me. I was left alone to try to put the missing pieces together and fight this new battle as his last few words to me kept playing over and over in my head like a broken record.

"Honey," he had said to me, "this is going to be a great year."

My emotions were shot as I remembered all the red flags there had been throughout my relationship with Jon. I felt like I had gone against my Heavenly Father's wishes for my life and was being punished for those decisions. I desperately tried to understand as I cried myself to sleep in the nights that followed. My Mother shared a steady stream of comfort but I knew I needed God's assurance that I was not alone in this storm. I desperately struggled to be positive amidst the depression and remember God's loving kindness and precious promises of hope. Although my spirit knew God was still on the throne and in control, my flesh was weakened by the apparent chaos all around me and my intense battle with guilt.

With each passing day, my physical body grew weaker and I began to experience constant excruciating pain in my left side. I knew I had no time to wallow in self-pity. I needed an attorney to help me prove I had a legal right to claim my husband's body since my marriage license apparently wasn't sufficient. I desperately needed to know if I had a say in the funeral arrangements including having his face reconstructed before too much decay had set in. It seemed like everything was out of my hands so I cried out to the Lord to take control.

He reminded me of the words of Jeremiah 29:11-13 which assured me He knew exactly what I was going through.

For I know the thoughts that I think toward you, says the LORD, thoughts of peace and not of evil, to give you a future and a hope. Then you will call upon Me and go and pray to Me, and I will listen to you. And, you will seek Me and find Me, when you search for Me with all your heart.

I also knew I needed to break the news about Jon's "other wife" to his family. They knew of his children's mother, Janice but only Tangela and Tray had met or even heard Jon speak about Diana. Shocked and furious, Jon's family promised their allegiance to me. They were not happy with the precarious situation we all found ourselves in at such a grievous time and expressed to Tangela and Tray their disapproval of Jon's double life.

As the breaking news hit the television, Diana found out Jon was married to me and tried to persuade others to side with her as the more prominent wife. I put forth every effort to maintain the integrity of the marriage Jon had with me and poured all my energies into making sure he was laid to rest decently and in order. Despite the fact that my brain was still scrambled and my senses were off kilter, I hung on as God carried me through yet another tempest blast.

In the Mean Time

Unable to give friends and family the funeral date and location because of my conflict with Diana, the Holy Spirit impressed me to ask Tangela to meet with Diana and ask her to release Jon's body to the Thompson Funeral Home. Tangela welcomed the opportunity to meet with Diana so Mom, Vicky and I coached her on how to handle the meeting. I felt that if anyone could get through to Diana, Tangela could. After all, she was still daddy's little girl and technically, Diana was her stepmother, too.

When Tangela arrived back from her mission, she was filled with excitement in her eyes and a smile on her face. I wanted to leap for joy when she reported that Diana had indeed signed Jon's body over to the Thompson Funeral Home. But the whole atmosphere changed as she also reported that Diana gave her full authority over *all* the proceedings for Jon's funeral and burial. My mind raced trying to ascertain the magnitude of such nonsense. Just the day before, she and I had been making plans to together to bury Jon in Arkansas, choosing his suit and coffin together. I was stunned at how quickly Tangela had shifted her allegiance from me to Diana.

Though Tangela and I had experienced our differences in the past, I was surprised and angered as she showed more love and support to a woman she barely knew than to me, so she could have her way and take control. As I witnessed Tangela's enthusiasm, my anger toward Jon was rekindled for the ugly mess he had left behind. "How dare he leave me in this predicament?" I thought. Tangela was Jon's daughter, but she did not have the authority that I had as his wife. I knew I had rights and I would not stand by and allow my stepdaughter to take over all of the arrangements for my husband's funeral.

It was at this point, my girlfriend Esmie and her husband Arthur decided to step in and mediate this whole situation. They spoke with Tangela with gentleness knowing that her behavior came from a place of shock and deep hurt. She was missing her father. They carefully helped her see the dynamics of relationships and the various roles each of us play. They showed her the difference in Jon's relationship as a father, husband and step-parent. They created a scenario for her to help her really get the picture. They made her switch shoes and asked her how she would feel if she married a man who brought children into the marriage and the daughter of her husband took over the funeral arrangements, ignoring the relationship that she had as his wife.

It was then that the blinders were removed and she broke down sobbing profusely. At the same time my strong will emerged, I put my foot down and let Tangela know that she would not be "calling the shots" and Jon would be buried where I thought best for him as his wife! Jon's sisters wanted to have Jon buried in Richmond, California, about 65 miles southwest of Sacramento.

However, I knew that Jon hated Richmond and I couldn't stand the thought of him being put so far away. Once Arkansas was out of the picture, I overruled that decision and moved forward with arrangements to keep Jon in Elk Grove.

How Could She?

Once I found an attorney to inform me of my legal rights, I became so embroiled in business matters that I could hardly respond to my personal phone calls. Away from home much of the time, handling other pressing matters, I was far too busy to continue with interviews from the press or even receive guests whose visits to pay their respects would have been welcomed. One particular afternoon when I was out taking care of my business matters, Tangela took it upon herself to bring Diana, Jon's other wife to my home. My family members knew I would be displeased with Diana's violation of my privacy, so my aunts urged her to leave before my return. I was incensed by her arrogance and insensitivity in doing such a thing.

In the meantime, Vicky, who had been *so* helpful since the Sunday morning after Jon's death, began to overstep her bounds in her role of assisting me. Not only naming herself as the Johnson Family Spokesperson, she began to put inappropriate demands on representatives from the Maloof organization and reportedly made attempts to manipulate their kindness to me and my family. Aware of what was happening to me and recognizing that Vicky's behavior did not appropriately represent me, my childhood friends began to more actively oversee details between the Maloof organization and me. When Vicky tried to get her name on the bank account when the Johnson Family Trust was being established, I began to see she was doing too much. She eventually so dishonored the confidence between us that our friendship was destroyed. You really know who your friends are in times of tragedy and loss.

Jon's true "friends" turned out to be Jon's work family and at of Maloof Sports and Entertainment. Jon had been a dedicated team employee there for more than 16 years. I had seen for myself how important this job was to Jon. There were many occasions when Jon was ill or seemed too tired to report to work at the Arco Arena and I would encourage him to stay home. Not wanting to disappoint his employer, he'd usually mustered the energy to meet his obligations. He had often spoken of his admiration and respect for his employer's kindness and how privileged he was to work for such a fine organization.

Upon learning of the tragedy, the Maloof's Organization took on the entire fiscal responsibility for Jon's funeral arrangements. They made sure his final journey on this Earth was first-class. From the reconstruction of Jon's face to his final resting place, the Maloofs paid for *everything*! In addition, they kindly organized two fundraisers to allow the community to share with my family in our time of grief. It became crystal clear to me why Jon was so devoted to his employer and I will be forever grateful to the Maloofs for their compassion and generosity during our time of need.

I watched as God continued to send those to me that would walk with me through these trials and even provide the financial assistance I needed. God promises to help those who are committed to Him as they go through life's challenges.

The more I turned toward God, the more He took charge of the mess that Jon created, even when things appeared to be spiraling out of control.

Oh taste and see that the Lord is good; blessed is the man that trusteth in Him.

(Psalm 34:8)

Praise Be to God!!!

When the issue was being disputed over who the legal wife of Jon Johnson was, I began to reflect on the numerous times Jon expressed his desire for me to change my last name during our marriage counseling sessions. As my mind raced back to the many arguments Jon and I had over my last name, God showed me even in that His will was being done. Looking back I'm glad I gave in and changed my name even though at the time I didn't want to for fear I would have to change it back if we divorced. At the time, I did not understand the significance of changing my last name to Johnson but how glad I am I did. I am enamored at how God so lovingly orders our steps and then He shows us what He was doing and why. As you read more of my story you will understand this concept even more clearly.

A representative from the Thompson Funeral Home notified me when they finally received Jon's body. I was assured they would honor my wishes and my wishes only and they didn't give it a second thought as to who the "real" Mrs. Johnson was. With that settled, the mortuary was in position to ward off *anyone,* from Tangela and her mother Janice, to Jon's siblings and Diana. They immediately proceeded with plans to lay my husband to rest taking guidance from me and me alone.

O God, You are my God; Early will I seek You. My soul thirsts for You, My flesh longs for You in a dry and thirsty land where there is no water. So I have looked for You in the sanctuary. To see Your power and Your glory. Because Your loving kindness is better than life. My lips shall praise You. Thus I will bless You while I live; I will lift up my hands in Your name. My soul shall be satisfied as with marrow and fatness, and my mouth shall praise You with joyful lips.

(Psalms 63:1-5)

Jon's Remains

Now that we were finally moving forward with the funeral arrangements, I remembered how gruesome Jon's face looked after he was shot that awful night. I was apprehensive about what Thompson's would be able to do to make him presentable for viewing. Even though they had one of the best forensic artists traveling in to do the job, Thompson's professionals were not sure they would be able to reconstruct Jon's face because of the damage to his lower right jaw. I was on pins and needles waiting to hear whether it could be done or not due to the decay from the long delay.

After a few days and a few delays, Thompson's called to announce that Jon's body was ready for viewing. They felt certain that I would be extremely pleased with their work.

Eager to view Jon's remains, we called Jon's children to notify them that their father's body was ready for viewing. Other family members were also notified so they could drive in from Oakland and meet us at Thompson's.

The Viewing

I'd always had an aversion to funeral homes and was very apprehensive about Jon's appearance; I was grateful for a full set of family members "in my corner." After entering the viewing room where Jon laid, I walked timidly over to the casket to behold my beloved Jon. After my first initial wave of grief, I carefully examined his face. Due to the trauma and severity of the injury, he didn't quite look like himself from the nose down but I felt the professionals had done a beautiful job in their reconstruction work. Mom, Tristan, my brother, sisters, aunts, uncles and nephews stood around me as we viewed Jon's body together. Members of the funeral home staff were very helpful and efficient as they attended to our needs.

Not wanting to linger long at my husband's casket, I gave my stamp of approval, said my good-bye to Jon and then waited in another room for the rest of my family members.

When Tangela arrived I could clearly see she was still fed up with me for not allowing her to make certain decisions about Jon's estate; like who would get his truck and how his money would be dispersed. As she worked herself up into frenzy, I stood my ground and tried to keep a clear head and be fair about what decisions she could be part of. Quite frankly, I was disgusted with her thoughtless actions and continuous demands before we had even buried her father.

At that point, my top priorities were to make it through the funeral and have Jon buried. Once the funeral was behind us, it was my plan to get Jon's financial obligations squared away and then we could deal with the other matters. Though I tried to explain myself, Tangela nitpicked every little thing, especially if it appeared to give me more recognition than her. She even took issue with the blurb on the obituary that highlighted my life with my husband. It seemed her grief again escalated as she viewed her father's body and needed to blame someone for the loss, confusion and pain her dad had left behind. Consequently, she chose to take out her resentment on me.

Of course, Diana was also entitled to view Jon's remains. I wanted to avoid crossing paths with her so I requested that the funeral home personnel inform me when she arrived. They were careful to guard my privacy. From what my family members reported, it was good I had made arrangements not to be in the viewing room when Diana arrived. My relatives were shocked by her public performance. I'm sure I would have been extremely uncomfortable witnessing her uncontrollable bawling, kissing on Jon and carrying on like she was going to climb into his casket. My aunties wanted her removed but she and I were both given the same polite consideration by the funeral home staff.

Funeral Day

Although I dreaded it, the day had finally arrived when we would lay my beloved husband to rest. Much like the night Jon was shot, the day of his funeral dawned cold, wet and dreary. Still groggy from the sleep-aid medication, I desperately struggled to get my bearings and get myself dressed. Feeling overwhelmed and afraid, I told my two sisters I didn't want to go to Jon's funeral. As family arrived downstairs, my sister Pat stayed with me and helped me prepare myself for the day ahead. When my Size 6 skirt suit swallowed me, Pat scurried around looking for safety pins to alter my skirt closer to a Size 2. Once dressed, I slowly walked downstairs to join my family for a word of prayer. I had no doubt this would be the saddest day of my life.

Jon never professed to have many close friends, but in his line of work many people knew and respected him. He was very active in the community with his softball league, video projects and the Assist One Foundation.

I was actively involved with my networking group, my church, running my health ministry and with our boys' schools. The number of people coming to pay their last respects numbered more than 1,000 mourners. There was standing room only in the large Sacramento Central Seventh-Day Adventist Church. The television media was also there to report the services and pay tribute to their colleague, Jon R. Johnson.

With the inclement weather and traffic backed up on Highway 99, we were delayed at least an hour getting to the church. At long last, we arrived and were ushered to the small chapel to wait until it was time for the family processional. On our way in, I caught Pastor Doug Bachelor off guard and requested he offer expressions during the service.

The sanctuary seemed to be completely transformed. On the huge video screens, there Jon stood, much larger than life. A gigantic poster at center stage portrayed the image of my handsome husband flashing his signature smile. As I fixed my eyes on the screens, I couldn't believe this was really happening. Then my eyes were drawn to the shinny, blue casket that contained my beloved Jon's remains and sadness gripped my heart. I was awestruck by the beauty of the floral arrangements that flanked Jon's casket. It was all so surreal; Jon was a celebrity in his field of work. According to reports from family members and others, his ex-wife Janice and Jon's daughter, Tangela and son Tray, were there as well as his other wife,

Diana, and his alleged girlfriend(s), and "other" children. I had no idea what was going on "behind the scenes."

During the lengthy funeral services, I was sorely distraught and cried woefully. Though Mom diligently tried to calm me, she understood that it was a very sad day for me. At times, my mind wandered to the plans I had of retiring, traveling the world and growing old with Jon. As my thoughts were reeled in by the fact that Jon had been gunned down in the very prime of his life by a senseless act of violence, I could not contain my grief. I began to experience pain so severe in my side that I had difficulty breathing and requested crackers and water in hopes of calming my nerves and easing my physical pain. I was just not prepared to face the finality of this day.

Many pastors attended the funeral and several shared parting words that brought great comfort to my family and me. But the main officiating minister was our own dear Pastor Arthur Branner who had performed our wedding ceremony just five and one-half years earlier. Now he returned home from Iraq to officiate at Jon's funeral. Pastor Branner knew that more than anything, I wanted some good to come out of our tragedy and souls to be won to Christ. I had asked him to present the call to Discipleship, inviting Jon's grieving family members, friends and colleagues to surrender their lives to Christ. But with all the delays, there just wasn't enough time for the invitation. The mortuary had called several times informing us to hurry because they would be closing.

As I sat there, listening to family members speak about Jon, I began to pull myself together. I don't know what it was that made me feel so compelled to share my own final moments with Jon, but I wanted everyone to know that, in spite of our struggles, I truly loved Jon and I knew that he sincerely loved me. I wanted everyone to know I was not angry with God, that I was thankful I had been spared. I wanted everyone there to somehow see the Christ in me.

As the massive crowd left the sanctuary at the end of the services, the casket was opened for one final viewing by the family, but particularly for Jon's mother. My sister Cherryl had directed the funeral ceremony and now watched as family members had their final viewings. Each of Jon's siblings solemnly approached the casket and sadly said their good-byes. When the time came for Jon's mother to view his remains, she was pushed to the casket in her wheel chair.

My sister said that with a total lack of emotion, she took one quick glimpse and said, "Okay," before asking to be rolled away.

The estrangement between Jon and the woman who birthed him into this world had always been a mystery to me. Now, on the day of his funeral his mother could not muster even one ounce of emotion as she said good-bye to her dead son. She displayed the same rock-hard shell Jon had so often described. I am, however, thankful that no matter how much we sin or how grotesque our crime, God is a loving and forgiving Father. It is true He hates the sin but He loves the sinner.

Final Salute

The family walked closely behind the team of pallbearers as they carried the dark blue casket down the path toward the hearse. I felt the streaming tears return as I walked slowly with my head bowed, wanting to avoid having my doleful face captured by the TV cameras. However, those surrounding me repeatedly urged me to lift up my head. Curious about the urgency in their voices, I complied. Amazed, I saw the honor and respect the TV industry was showing Jon; an industry Jon loved and worked in to make a difference in this wicked, twisted world. I was swept away by the love and respect that Jon's colleagues showed for him by their acts of love toward my family and me.

Struggling with the reality of our loss, the funeral procession slowly followed Jon's casket as cameramen from all over Northern California lined the long path from the church, through the courtyard to the waiting hearse and limousines. Jon's colleagues saluted his loved ones with cameras pointed down at the ground. I was so touched by their display of honor, affection and respect that I could not hold back the tears. I was grateful that Jon had been so highly respected in his work and saw how his tragic death so deeply touched the hearts of those who knew him.

As I rode in the limousine from the funeral ceremony to the cemetery, my mind flashed back to scenes of my life with Jon. As I relived the horrible night of Jon's murder, I wondered if I would be strong enough to endure seeing his casket lowered into the ground.

I rode in reflective silence from the church in Sacramento to the cemetery in Elk Grove. The weather was cold, the ground was wet and so were the chairs. A small intimate group of family and close friends witnessed as Jon was put to rest. I watched the lowering of his casket into the ground; then threw my flowers on his casket and silently said good-bye. In a way though, I looked forward to the finality that Jon's April 6th funeral day would bring as Tristan and I struggled to move forward with a life without him.

Deathly Fears

I believe some people know when their time is coming to an end and sometimes God even sends warnings. I believe Jon had many warnings from God about his wayward lifestyle. In retrospect, I sincerely believe my beloved Jon knew his life was winding down as just a few weeks before his death he came to me like a humbled little child, afraid that something bad was going to happen to him. I remember I was fumbling around in my closet trying to find something to wear when Jon entered our bedroom, walked past me and over to his face bowl.

"Honey," he said, "I think I'm going to die!"

Startled by such a strong statement, I stopped what I was doing, walked over to him and asked why he would make such a strong statement.

In a calm tone, he responded, "Because I'm getting everything I'm praying for and I'm scared."

With a sigh of relief, I realized he wasn't involved in any life threatening illegal activity so I assured him that didn't mean he was going to die; he was just being blessed by God. He paused, thought about it, shrugged his shoulders and changed the subject. At the time, I didn't give it any real serious thought, but after his death, the conversation Jon and I had replayed over and over in my mind.

As far as I knew, Jon had no illness or concrete evidence that his life was coming to an end. From time to time, he and I engaged in general conversations about death and dying. There were times Jon insisted he would not live to see a ripe old age, though I envisioned us raising our kids and enjoying a long life together. I had learned about his apprehension about deep bodies of water during a vacation we took early in our relationship. We had stayed near the water in Jamaica and that is where I discovered Jon couldn't swim. Jon had promised our boys he would take them fishing, but it never happened because he was afraid of drowning.

Jon also told me that a psychic had advised him that something bad would happen to him if he rode on a motorcycle. He took that warning seriously and stayed away from motorcycles. Then there was the fact that his father died from cancer when Jon was but a youth, so Jon lived with the fear of contracting an incurable disease and took yearly check-ups very seriously. Although Jon felt he would die in his mid 50's, he had just turned 46 when we spoke again about death; just a few weeks before the night of his murder.

When I think back, I wish I had prayed with my husband instead of changing the subject. I often asked Jon to pray with me but he always said he had his own prayer life and he didn't feel comfortable praying with me in our bedroom. The only time we prayed together was as a family after Sabbath, and often times I would be the one to lead in prayer. I would get very frustrated with him feeling he wasn't living up to his commitment to be the priest of our home and lead our family in Bible studies and family worship.

I realize that because Jon and I didn't share a prayer life together, I rarely knew the exact challenges my husband struggled with or his secret sins and his temptations. I saw only the side of Jon he wanted me to see. Perhaps it was the side he thought I could love and accept. My advice to Christian couples is they should always pray together because it will bring them closer to God and to each other. Praying together allows Christ into the relationship and helps develop transparency and trust in a relationship.

You will keep him in perfect peace, whose mind is stayed on You. Because he trusts in You. (Isaiah 26:3)

Chapter 12

The After Math

Before settling on East Lawn, I visited one other cemetery in Citrus Heights but immediately knew it was not the place to lay my beloved Jon's remains. With no time to spare Esmie and I dashed to East Lawn Cemetery in Elk Grove hoping it would be the appropriate burial home. As we drove through the huge metal gates my eyes were captivated by the beautiful cascading waterfall, in an instant a peace emanated from me and I knew it was the answer to prayer.

It wasn't until a few weeks after the funeral that I realized God had led me there. Since we lived in Elk Grove, I had passed that cemetery many times. My husband had even told me rumors about black people being lynched on that same property before the cemetery was built which is why at first it wasn't even an option. I am so glad the Holy Spirit impressed upon me to bury Jon there because every time I visited Jon's grave my afflicted mind experienced peace and comfort.

God's Ministering Angels

One of the other blessings of East Lawn was the cemetery director, John. Seeming to understand the hurt and pain I was suffering due to the nature of Jon's death, he took a sincere interest in me and listened patiently as I tried to process through all that was happening in my life. At first, I was embarrassed to be sharing all my personal problems with this perfect stranger but he truly went above and beyond the call of duty as he allowed me to cry my way through, not judging my husband or me. He had a very sympathetic ear and listened to me talk about my bonus children, my husband's infidelity, my fears, financial affairs and, what seemed at the time, my insurmountable problems.

What a godsend he was as he sympathetically explained the cycles of grief and helped me understand what I was feeling through each stage of it. God even used him to help me face my fears of death taking me on a tour of the different rooms at the cemetery and looking at the various coffins. As I did, I reflected on my own mortality and praised God for covering and protecting me that horrible night. Had He not I might very well have been laying there beside my husband. I am forever grateful that John allowed God to use him during my time of grief. He was like an angel sent from above sitting with me for numerous hours during the days and months after the funeral while I processed the enormity of everything caused by Jon's tragic death. His words were seasoned with wisdom as he gently counseled me through the stages of grief in my new life journey.

Another gift from God was my Christian therapist, Delores who helped me compartmentalize all that was happening to me as a result of Jon's tragic death. Not only did she deal with the issue of step-parenting, but also reminded me who I am in Christ and who I was as Jon's wife. She also helped me to see that although Jon had left this world never to return, he was still a very real part of my life.

At first, I didn't understand what she was talking about thinking she was referring to some reincarnation new age thing. But her gentle coaching helped me to understand that though Jon was gone physically, he would always live on in my memory. That realization brought me great comfort and I began to feel the darkness gradually replaced by an ever so small glimmer of hope.

Revelation

Between my therapy sessions and trying to move forward in the grieving process, I was often drawn to Jon's grave site. I didn't understand the pull and even though sometimes it felt like I was losing my mind, I remained in tune with my spirit and went whenever I was being pulled. One day, after meeting with my therapist I decided to stop by the gravesite. As I drove through the gates and passed the cascading water fall, I played the instrumental version of Via Della Rosa. The beauty of the music brought tears and images of Christ hanging on Calvary's cross and I began to ponder the life of Jesus and how terrible sin is. I ached as it became very evident that my sins put Christ on the cross. In a very vivid way through Jon's death, He showed me my sinful self and why He had to die. I realized the very ground beneath my feet reeked of death and sin. It was this revelation that helped me understand the importance of salvation and a savior. It was a sobering glimpse of this *great controversy* we are all a part of. As I listened to the song and viewed the multiple tomb stones my mind flashed back to the pain Jesus' earthly Mother must have felt as she watched the closing scenes of His life. What intense anguish and sadness His heavenly Father must have experienced as He willingly gave His life for the salvation of all mankind. This made such an impact on my spirit that from then on, every time I went to the grave site I played Via Della Rosa as a reminder of the sacrifice Jesus made.

On one hand I grieved over my personal loss, but at the same time I felt the impact of Calvary. As I sought to understand why my husband was snatched away so suddenly, God helped me to see the cross of Calvary and the tremendous price Jesus paid to redeem us from the clutches of sin and evil. As God ministered to my heart, I began to reach out to other grieving souls in the cemetery and share the blessed hope of Christ and His imminent return.

Each visit to Jon's grave brought further revelation from God as He lovingly answered my "why" questions. As I pondered the events of our life together, it became crystal clear why God allowed this terrible tragedy to happen to Jon and why I was spared. God helped me to see Jon's double life but also the repentance he was experiencing at the time of his death. God knew Jon's heart and responded to Jon's prayers at the very moment he secured an eternal future. A peace I could not really describe began to overtake my mind and gave me an assurance of where Jon Johnson was. All of his lying and manipulating had come full circle. Never again would I need to second-guess his whereabouts or feel wrong for questioning his activities. As more and more of Jon's life were revealed to me, it made sense. And as morbid as it may sound, I even felt vindicated.

Weeping may endure for a night, but joy comes in the morning. (Psalm 30:5)

Finally, the five-and-a-half years of yearning for Jon's love and the endless nights of waiting for him to come home to me had ended. Though I continued to mourn Jon's tragic death, my heart was finally coming to a place of peace and rest. I knew it was all in God's permissive will and my years of prayers questioning his whereabouts had been answered.

Satan Launches Yet Another Attack

Even as I came to a place of acceptance of the brutal attack that had taken Jon's life, I suddenly had to face an attack of a different kind as the integrity of my marriage was again being questioned. A cruel internet character assassination against me was being led by my step-daughter, Tangela. As I read the ruthless, unfounded attacks being launched against me, I liken my situation to the story of Job. I was confused and tormented for months as I wrestled against this new wave of guilt sparked by Tangela's accusations. There were many times over the next several months that I felt like I was being punished for stepping outside of God's will and choosing who I thought was best for me. God had repeatedly reminded me not to be unequally yoked and to wait on Him for His choice of my life's mate.

For the LORD God is a sun and shield, The LORD will give grace and glory; No good thing will He withhold from those who walk uprightly. (Psalm 84:11)

As I read again the Book of Job, I began to experience a break through. The spirit of the Lord showed me that even when we fall short and follow our own dictates God does not place guilt and condemnation on us but instead rescues us from the torment of the devil. God patiently showed me that even though Jon was not His desired will for me, that as Jon and I began to turn our lives around, God could use it for good.

Genesis 50:20 says, "But as for you, you meant evil against Me; But God meant it for good, in order to bring it about as it is this day, to save many people alive."

The Holman Concise Bible dictionary says, "The book of Job wrestles with issues all people eventually face, and the two important issues are the cause and effect of suffering and the justice and care of God. Job begins by accepting suffering as part of human life to be endured through trust in God in good and bad times. He moves to human frustration with problems for which we cannot find answers. Yet, he refuses to accept his wife's perspective of giving up on God and life.

Rather, he constantly confronts God with cries for help and for answers. He shows faith can be struggling in the dark for answers struggling with God, not with other people. His friends note that suffering will not last forever; punishment is not as bad as it could have been, sin is forgivable, suffering can be endured, and God's word should be heeded. Job's complaint is that he cannot find God to present his case to Him, get his name cleared and his body healed. God's speaking to job shows that God cares and that He still controls the world even a world with unexplainable suffering. His creative acts and the mysterious creatures He has created only prove that humans must live under God's control.

People must be content with a God who speaks to them. They cannot demand that God give all the answers we might want. God can be trusted in the worst of circumstances as well as in the best."

Job 5:6-8 states, "for affliction does not come from the dust, nor does trouble spring from the ground; yet man is born to trouble, as the sparks fly upward. But as for me, I would seek God, and to God I would commit my cause."

Dealing with Death

Death was no stranger to my family and me. Coming from a very large family, we had experienced a few losses along the way and so at a young age I was introduced to the concept of death as two of my favorite uncle's battled cancer. When I was 18, I experienced the sudden death of my maternal grandmother who died of a heart attack at the age 78. She was a godly woman and the matriarch of the family. I was deeply saddened and felt the void of her absence. At the age of 26, death came even closer as my brother Donnie died unexpectedly after an epileptic seizure. Fifteen years later and six months after my marriage to Jon, I was heartbroken at my father's death after a prolonged illness.

The loss of a father and a brother is different from the loss of your spouse. So much more is shared in a relationship between a husband and wife than even between a parent and a child or a sibling to a sibling. God designed men and women so that the emotional, spiritual, and physical intimacy they would experience as husband and wife would make the two become one.[13] Therefore, when you lose a spouse, the effect of that loss is greater than that of any other family member. The grief is deeper as though a part of your own flesh dies because as Genesis 2:23 says, "This is now bone of my bones and flesh of my flesh; She shall be called Woman, Because she was taken out of Man."

We never know when sudden death might come our way. This experience made me realize how important it is to have

---

[13] See Genesis 2:23-24

a relationship with Jesus and walk in obedience to the Lord's commands. If sudden death should come to any of us, we must know we are ready. 1 John 5:10-13 tells us how we can have that assurance.

He that believeth on the Son of God hath the witness in himself: he that believeth not God hath made him a liar; because he believeth not the record that God gave of his Son. And this is the record that God hath given to us eternal life, and this life is in his Son. He that hath the Son hath life; and he that hath not the Son of God hath not life. These things have I written unto you that believe on the name of the Son of God; that ye may know that ye have eternal life, and that ye may believe on the name of the Son of God. (KJV)

Jesus is coming friends and we must be ready. We are called to enter into His sufferings and bear our crosses as He did. In this world, we will have tribulation but remember Christ has overcome this world.[14] Therefore but for the glory that was laid up in heaven, Jesus bore the cross of Calvary. We too must keep this heavenly vision in front of us so that we, too, can bear our burdens along life's journey. Take your eyes off

---

[14] See John 16:33

the temporal things and look to those things that are unseen and claim the great promises of God.[15]

I called to the LORD, and he answered me. I called for help and you listened to my cry.

(Jonah 2:2)

Time to Face my Fears

After Jon's death, though counselors, family, and friends assured me Jon loved me, I could not wrap my finite mind around that fact, especially after discovering all his hidden secrets. As the weeks went by, the desire to know if my husband truly loved me grew stronger and stronger until one day I decided to call Jon's close friend, Dwayne. I suddenly realized that the man Jon had asked me to get along with just hours before his death might hold the key to answering the question as to whether Jon really loved me. Though my husband had said he loved me in cards and words, his actions went completely against our marriage covenant. I needed to know his proclamation of love for me was real.

I knew the time had come to face my fears and deal with the reality of my relationship with Jon and his love for me. I needed to talk to the man I had jealously despised because

---

[15] See Colossians 3:1-17

of my own insecurities and the special bond they had. When I called Dwayne, he didn't seem at all surprised to hear from me. In fact, it was as if he had been expecting my call, though he didn't actually say so. Sensitive to my desire to meet with him, he honored my request.

The Moment of Truth

As I stepped inside Dwayne's house, I thought of how Jon and I had left the restaurant with intentions of stopping by for a festive social gathering just before Jon's life was ended. Afflicted by the many thoughts that ran through my mind I settled myself on his comfortable couch, not sure how to begin. I knew Dwayne was hurting and could see that he was struggling to hold back the tears over the loss of a friend that held a special place in his heart.

After a few minutes of small talk, I came right out and asked Dwayne, "Did my husband love me?"

Dwayne paused for a moment and then said, "Yes."

Not fully convinced, I asked, "How do you know?"

As I pressed for more details, Dwayne finally shared with me that a few weeks before the murder; Jon had asked if he thought we should get a divorce. Jon had told Dwayne we were separated and even introduced his new girlfriend to him. When I found out Dwayne knew about another woman in

Jon's life, I let him know how disappointing it was to learn he did not stress Christian counseling. The fact that Jon told him we were separated came as a big surprise to me because I had never agreed to a separation. I knew if I did it would have only been a license for Jon to cheat and our marriage would have been over. Dwayne told me he always counseled Jon to do the right thing and work on his marriage to me which confirmed what Jon told me just hours before his death.

Dwayne then told me the last time he saw Jon, he answered Jon's question with a question, "Do you love Karen?"

Dwayne went on to share with me that Jon paused, thought about it, and then he told him yes, he loved me. Once Jon clarified that, Dwayne said he advised him to end the affair and make things right with me. Jon assured Dwayne he would which brought a great amount of relief to me. I was able to accept this as truth as it explained why Jon had been so receptive to my request for him to spend more time at home and to begin our date nights again. Jon had been doing what he had promised Dwayne he would do and was trying to make things right with me. However, as we talked further I discovered Dwayne didn't know about Diana. He said Jon had never talked to him about her and he was just as shocked as the rest of us about Jon's marriage to her.

We went on to talk about the night of Jon's death. Dwayne recounted, Jon had just made the phone connection. Dwayne said he heard Jon call his name, when suddenly there was an abrupt disconnection. One moment he was talking with Jon, and then there was nothing but silence. He went on to say he had actually been in the vicinity where the incident happened. He heard the sirens and saw the rush of police cars, ambulance, fire trucks and television news vans. He said he called Jon back to tell him to be careful because something bad had happened and wanted to make sure he was safe.

When he couldn't reach Jon by phone and we never arrived at his house, he drove over to our house to see if Jon was all right. He said he was relieved when he saw Jon's truck in the drive way but went into shock when I told him Jon had been shot. We talked in my upstairs office where just hours earlier Jon asked me to make amends with Dwayne.

As I remembered that conversation with Jon, I apologized for the ill feelings I had harbored toward him and asked Dwayne for his forgiveness to fulfill the vow I made to my husband before his death. I no longer blamed Dwayne for any of our marital issues.

As I sat there in Dwayne's living room I was so thankful he had agreed to meet with me. He played a very significant role in helping me to place the pieces of the puzzle together and put my heart at rest regarding my husband's love for me. We also learned we shared the same concern about Jon's infidelity and his double life. We were able to validate our respective places in Jon's life and offer each other assurance about our relationship with a man that wore many different faces.

More Secrets in the Truck

The day after the murder my brother came to my aid and pulled everything out of Jon's truck so I could go through it. I knew eventually I would need to get a handle on his current jobs, business deals, outstanding invoices, outstanding debt, future projects and the dollar value of all his video equipment. Jon's entire life was in the oversized duffle bags he kept under lock and key in his truck.

I asked my brother to put everything in my closet and put new door knobs with locks on my bedroom doors because people kept barging into my bedroom when I was trying to rest and when I wasn't home. I especially wanted Tangela to stay out of my bedroom since I had already caught her trying to steal one of the bags with Jon's possessions.

Now, as I sat in my closest going through the endless mound of papers, cards, invoices and documents, I hoped to begin to piece together all the parts of Jon's life and determine how to make this new life without him work. However, I found I was facing more of Jon's deep dark secrets as I searched among his personal possessions. Not only did I have to come to grips with and accept the fact that Jon had another wife, but he also had a girlfriend in the Bay area that was very much in love with him according to Dwayne. She had apparently been hopeful he would marry her until finding out about his death and his marriage to me from the television reporting the tragedy.

While sitting in my closet going through his red bag, I came across a document that stated Jon was 98.8% positive he was the biological father of another young woman whose mother had previous relations with him. Surprised at this new revelation and confused why he had repeatedly denied he was her father, this well-mannered young woman had been seeking the truth since she found out that the man that raised her was not her biological father. Furthermore, I found out she was not the only estranged child in his life; Jon had fathered a total of seven children from five different mothers and two of them were living in Sacramento. Traumatized, I added all of this new information to the steadily growing pile of confusion concerning this man I had loved and was married to.

Still the Chosen

As time went by, I realized that God loved Jon more than I did and that everything leading up to that night was divinely ordered. God's word teaches us that nothing in this life happens without God allowing it to happen. I truly believe God used me to lead my husband to Christ and through it all; I grew stronger and deeper in my relationship with the Lord as well.

I truly believe that on Jon's last day on this earth, something spiritual took place in my husband's heart. I have a peace in my own heart that Jon made a sincere decision to walk right with the Lord and put away all his lying and cheating. As I look back, I remember several times that day when Jon seemed deep in thought. For the first time in our five and a half years of marriage, I felt we were on one accord. There was a distinct harmony between Jon and Tristan as well as a major change in his attitude toward our relationship. Jon didn't put up a fight or complain as we talked about some important decisions just before we left for the restaurant that night.

I do not know what happened in the four days Jon was away from me, but I believe he repented from all his sins and surrendered himself to Jesus. During the week prior to his death, he decided to attend Bible studies again with Pastor Branner. We believe Jon turned the corner and did all he could to stand blameless before the Father when his time was up. I know God allowed our lives to be intertwined to help bring about his deliverance and I am truly honored that God chose me.

As I continued to process all God was revealing to me, I was reminded of the story of Moses and how his generation was not permitted to enter into the promise land due to dis-obedience. God permitted Moses to view the Promise Land atop a mountain just before he died. As I have reflected on that story, I remembered the statement Jon made as we drove through Elk Grove looking for a restaurant just a few hours before he was killed.

He said, "Honey, this is going to be a great year."

In spite of his plans, God had other plans for Jon. Jon saw a glimpse of the future, but God's plan did not include him par-taking in anything else in this life. As I accepted that God had spared my life for a purpose, I vowed not to let go of God's hand and determined to stay nestled in His bosom. I clung to Him and His promise that He would never leave me nor forsake me.[16] It was this specific promise that gave me hope and helped me live from day-to-day. At first it felt like I was learning to walk with and take God at His word all over again. I had faced challenges in the past trusting Jon and God with all that Jon was doing. Now God was teaching me to trust Him completely as He walked me through this tragedy.

My mind, body and spirit were stirred by the struggle going on all around me. While I sensed the battle between Satan and the sovereign God, I would close my eyes and visual-ized Jesus carrying my frail tattered body. I felt my Lord and Savior standing in the gap for me and assuring me that many

---

[16] Hebrews 13:5

people were praying for me. It was as if each day was a test of my loyalty as God taught me how to walk in faith. God was strengthening and refining me every step of the way.

Beloved, do not think it strange concerning the fiery trial, which is to try you, as though some strange thing happened to you; but rejoice to the extent that you partake of Christ's sufferings, that when His glory is revealed, you may also be glad with exceeding joy.

(1 Peter 4:12-14)

I was experiencing a closeness with Christ that I had never experienced before. I no longer looked at life the same way or related to people in the same manner. Life was short and very precious. I was on a new journey to find out the deeper meaning and purpose for my life. I was hyper-sensitive to everything and paid close attention to the little things of life. I was determined to savor every moment I had, cherishing my family and loved ones even more. I wanted to walk in the presence of God twenty four seven, but more than anything I had to figure out how to restore my faith in man. I asked God for discernment and relied heavily on the Holy Spirit to lead me as I walked through each new day.

Ups and Downs

John, the worker at the cemetery, told me of the roller coaster ride I would be on, especially in the next three to six months. There would be intense anguish, he told me, of such magnitude that I would feel I couldn't live through the pain. It was extremely difficult to wrap my mind around what John was trying to tell me. I knew I did not want to die but at the same time I could not see how my life would look from here on. John said my life would begin to move calmly along like the beginning climb of a Ferris wheel. As I climbed up, he told me I would feel good, like I was making progress and was out of the woods. All of a sudden, he warned me, it would seem like the bottom was dropping out and my life would become tumultuous again. But just before I hit the bottom, things would become bearable and calm again. I didn't really understand it at the time but knowing what to expect and what stage I was in brought me great relief especially as I passed each milestone. As I walked through the grief cycles, realizing what was coming brought me some comfort plus God continued to assure me I was not alone. God was by my side riding each tidal wave with me.

It had been three months from Jon's passing and I was feeling quite strong and felt the worse part was over. Then in June of 2006 I had to go to court, and there he was, Aaron

Dunn, the murderer. I was so angry that I wanted his hands cut off so he could never pull another trigger. I wanted him to experience what it felt like to suffer. What Aaron Dunn did was a heinous crime against two innocent victims; Jon R. Johnson and Michael Daly. I wanted him to get the death penalty for the two lives he took. Then I remembered what God said about revenge "Vengeance is mine sayeth the LORD" (Deuteronomy 32:35). Though my mind knew that, I was filled with rage every time I thought about it; I wanted him to suffer like I was suffering. Every time I saw Aaron in court, I was disgusted by his lack of remorse.

I knew as a Christian I had to turn it all over to Jesus and often during my devotions I cried out, "Lord, teach me how to forgive this man. I know I have to but I don't know how and I don't want to."

Another Cross Road

Emotionally, I was unable to work for an entire year. I am thankful that God made a way financially so I could be still and seek His comforting face, doing what would eventually bring about total emotional and physical restoration and healing. I found great comfort in attending Bible studies, listening to Christian music, praying and exercising. I knew the key to my restoration was abiding in Him and after about six months, I weaned myself off the sleep medication though I continued to sleep with the light on.

As I began to feel stronger, I decided to direct my attention toward keeping Jon's dream alive and resurrect his non-profit organization. "Assist One" brings awareness about the plight of children caught up in the foster care system in California through extensive media campaigns. Our mission is to bring about awareness and facilitate positive connections for children through adoption. This project brought me great satisfaction and comfort because I was doing something that was so near and dear to Jon's heart.[17]

More Trials

My biggest fear in losing my husband was how I was going to keep my home and provide for Tristan and myself. Somehow we had to live on my small savings, money donated through the family trust and my meager income. My husband had made good money but he had also left me with a lot of debt and there was no Life Insurance policy.

Two days after Jon died; Vicky took me down to the Victims Crime Division office where I filed for spousal support and other benefits but with all that was going on, I completely forgot

---

[17] See further information about the "Assist One" foundation at the end of this book.

about it. I had no idea what I was entitled to until Ahmanal my advocate called asking if I had started receiving my support money. When I told her I had not, she encouraged me to find out why. When I looked into it I found out Jon's other wife had filed for support as well so now they didn't know who to give the money to. When I asked how much money I would be entitled to, the lady told me up to $70,000 max depending on his salary. I knew I would get the max because Jon's salary was well over that if I could convince the lady I was Jon's true wife. Again I was finding Jon's polygamist lifestyle left me with a mess to clean up. Diana was also claiming she was entitled to the support money.

Diana wouldn't let up so once again I had to plead my case and prove I was entitled to Jon's benefits. The Victim's Crime Board wanted me to prove that Jon resided with me by sending them all the bills that had his name on them.

Fortunately, Jon had insisted I changed my last name to Johnson and that his name be on all the bills after we got married therefore that wasn't hard to do. I had numerous current bills, his check stubs, and 1099 stubs which I quickly submitted them.

During this trying time, I fell in love with this particular Psalm 91:1-16:

He who dwells in the secret place of the Most High shall abide under the shadow of the Almighty. I will say of the LORD, "He is my refuge and my fortress. My God in Him I will trust." Surely He shall deliver you from the snare of the fowler and from the perilous pestilence He shall cover you with His feathers and under His wings you shall take refuge; His truth shall be your shield and buckler. You shall not be afraid of the terror by night, nor of the arrow that flies by day, nor of the pestilence that walks in darkness, nor of the destruction that lays waste at noonday. A thousand may fall at your side and ten thousand at your right hand. But it shall not come near you. Only with your eyes shall you look, and see the reward of \the wicked because you have made the LORD who is my refuge, even the Most High, your dwelling place. No evil shall befall you nor shall any plague come near your dwelling; for He shall give His angels charge over you to keep you in all your ways. In their hands they shall bear you up lest you dash your foot against a stone. You shall tread upon the lion and the cobra. The young lion and the serpent you shall trample under foot. Because he has set his love upon Me therefore I will deliver him; I will set him on high, because he has known My name He shall call upon Me and I will answer him. I will be with him in trouble; I will deliver him and honor him with long life I will satisfy him My salvation.

Approximately two weeks later the decision ruled in my favor and Diana received nothing. God had fought and won another battle for me.

God now had my undivided attention. I was seeking His plan for my life and needed to know if I was on the right path with my health ministry and whether it would sustain me financially. I was at a crossroads and needed to choose wisely. My ministry of health and fitness meant the world to me and I wanted it to reflect the health God wants us to have. I prayed and asked God for a ministry that would change lives and give Him the glory.

The number seven symbolizes wholeness, completeness and perfection as God completed the work of creation and rested on the seventh day. Seven is also important as it pertains to the Sabbath being the LORD'S true day of worship as described in Deuteronomy 5:12-15. As I prayed and God verified my decision to continue in pursuing the health and fitness ministry I had started, but I renamed it, "Try 7 Fitness for Heaven."

Prayer

When a loved one like a spouse, parent or child is snatched out of your life suddenly, where there is no closure, and when there is a lot of unfinished business, and unanswered questions, it adds up to the enormity of the grief one is experiencing. This dynamic can create a tremendous amount of anxiety that leaves a trail of devastation, brokenness and emptiness for loved ones to process through. It is when you are at your lowest Satan seeks to destroy you through suicide, drugs, alcohol; by any means necessary.

However, if anchored in Christ while in that dark valley, it will strengthen your faith. The Bible says, "Daniel went to his house and made the decision known to Hananiah, Mishael, and Azariah, his companions that they might seek mercies from the God of heaven concerning this secret, so that Daniel and his companions might not perish with the rest of the wise men of Babylon. Then the secret was revealed to Daniel in a night vision. So Daniel blessed the God of heaven."[18]

As God revealed more and more of the pieces of Jon's double life to me, I was thankful that He not only heard my prayers but the prayers of the saints who were interceding on my behalf. When the confusion, distrust and dishonesty of my marriage threatened to overwhelm me, I knew as I prayed to my heavenly Father He would give me the strength and wisdom I needed to move through each and every day.

Prayer is a powerful dialogue between God and His covenant partners. I learned first hand that prayer enables us to receive from Him. Prayer is not to bring God down to us, but

---

[18] Daniel 2:17-19

brings us up to Him. When I was bombarded on all sides, too weak to fight my own battles, I would go into my closet, lie prostrate on the floor, and cry out to the Lord for deliverance. As I turned the situation over to God, a great sense of peace would come over me. I can definitely say that my prayer life sustained me through the difficulties, gave me hope and kept me holding on when it seemed there was no way out. It was in that same closet I felt safe and sought God's guidance for the many important decisions I had to make but knew would be met with opposition.

Chapter 13

When Tragedy Clouds the Mind

Approximately six months after Jon was murdered, a dear friend told me about a woman who experienced a similar tragedy, losing her fiancé in a senseless act of violence in a town about 45 miles away. Her fiancé and a few of his friends were on a road trip shortly before they were to be married. They had stopped at a gas station to fill up and buy a few snacks. The driver and everyone but her fiancé went into the convenient store deciding not to disturb their friend's sleep. Out of nowhere a man came up to the car and shot the young woman's fiancé in the head killing him instantly while his friends were in the store. The young woman had become so distraught and angry that she blamed God for her misfortune.

When I heard the story, my heart ached for her and I yearned to meet with her to bring her encouragement, comfort and hope by sharing how God had helped me walk through my personal tragedy. She knew I was a woman of God, but she was so bound by pain and anger that she could not stand to hear my story. I realized right then and there that had it not been for the grace of God I would have been the same way. It made me realize how important it is to identify who the enemy really is and not blame God. I've also come to realize that true healing and restoration is a choice and that it comes only from God and being in right relationship with Him.

For our light affliction, which is but for a moment, worketh for us a far more exceeding and eternal weight of glory; while we look not at the things which are seen, but at the things which are not seen for the things which are seen are temporal: but the things which are not seen are eternal. (2 Corinthians 4:17-18)

As I walked through the next few months, I was comforted by the following quote from one of my favorite writers.

If our minds are fixed upon the things that are eternal, and not on the things of earth, we shall grasp the hand of infinite power, and what can make us sad? We need not be left a prey to Satan's power. . . . The children of God should not permit Satan to place himself between them and their God. If you permit him to do this, he will tell you that your troubles are the most grievous, the sorest troubles that any mortal ever bore. He will place his magnifying glasses before your eyes, and present everything to you in an exaggerated form to overwhelm you with discouragement. . . . Take the Word of God as the man of your counsel, and humble your doubting soul before God, and with contrition of heart say, "Here I lay my burden down. I cannot bear it. It is too heavy for me. I lay it down at the feet of my compassionate Redeemer." When Satan tempts you, breathe not a word of doubt or darkness. You may have your choice as to who shall rule your heart and control your mind. If you choose to open the door to the suggestion of the evil one, your mind will be filled with distrust and rebellious questioning. (Ellen G. White, "Our High Calling")

My husband's death was so shocking that the effects were never far from the surface. At times I found myself questioning God, not so much out of anger but more out of my confusion. In fact I wrote in my journal, "God, please give me some answers. Why Jon?" Then my thoughts turned from "why" to guilt. My heart ached as I wrote, "I blame myself because I picked the restaurant and I insisted on going. What's with that LORD? I feel like I led him right into harm's way." As I fluctuated back and forth between wanting to know why and blaming myself during the grieving process, I wondered how our dinner date had turned into such a horrible tragedy.

Suddenly God showed me the selfishness of my questioning. In shame I realized what I was really saying was, "Why did it have to be Jon, why couldn't it have been someone else's husband?"

As God reminded me of the pain He suffered being separated from His son as Jesus died a violent death on the cross as a ransom for my sins, it helped me to understand the love He had for me.

For God so loved the world, that he gave his only begotten Son, that whosoever believeth in him should not perish, but have everlasting life. For God sent not his Son into the world to condemn the world; but that the world through him might be saved.

(John 3:16-17)

Hold On To God

In the wake of all my discoveries, I thought my nightmare would never end. As Jon's secret life continued to be unveiled, I felt like Job and feared I would lose one of my greatest possessions, my physical health. As I studied the life of Job, I discovered the secret of his great patience; he never let go of God's hand. When I read about the many attacks on Job's life, it gave me strength and hope as the battle raged on in my life. Like Job, I held on tight to my faith, not once turning my back on God knowing that would be utter foolishness. I knew my only recourse was to turn toward God, press into His bosom for His divine guidance, rely on His enduring strength and seek understanding of His purpose. I knew God was sustaining me and that if I persevered, He would carry me through and reveal His perfect will for my life. I prayed and searched the scriptures and God revealed what I needed to know right when I needed it. He did it for me, and He will do it for you.

God's Natural Laws of Health

The Creator of the ends of the earth neither faints nor is weary. His understanding is unsearchable. He gives power to the weak. And to those who have no might He increases strength. Even the youths shall faint and be weary. And the young men shall utterly fall. But those who wait on the LORD shall renew their strength; they shall mount up with wings like eagles, they shall run and not be weary, they shall walk and not faint.

(Isaiah 40:28-31)

You might be wondering what health has to do with my personal tragedy. My background is in physical fitness. I am a Personal Fitness Trainer, health reformer and a Literature Evangelist. Prior to this life altering experience, I had made many changes in my life by embracing God's Eight Natural Laws of Health and, I believe beyond a shadow of a doubt, it was because of my health practices that I was strong enough to endure the attack against my physical body; my life. Please take note and give careful consideration to this part of my testimony.

My son, give attention to my words; incline your ear to my sayings. Do not let them depart from your eyes; keep them in the midst of your heart; for they are life to those who find them, and health to all their flesh. (Proverbs 4:20-22)

The best way I can explain these principles can be found in a book called, "The Ministry of Healing."

PURE AIR, SUNLIGHT, abstemiousness, rest, exercise, proper diet, the use of water, trust in divine power – these are the true remedies. Every person should have a knowledge of nature's remedial agencies and how to apply them. It is essential both to understand the principles involved in the treatment of the sick and to have a practical training that will enable one rightly to use this knowledge.

The use of natural remedies requires an amount of care and effort that many are not willing to give. Nature's process of healing and up building is gradual, and to the impatient it seems slow. The surrender of hurtful indulgences requires sacrifice. But in the end it will be found that nature, untrammeled, does it work wisely and well. Those who persevere in obedience to its laws will reap the reward in health of body and health of mind.

Too little attention is generally given to the preservation of health. It is far better to prevent disease than to know how to treat it when contracted. It is the duty of every person, for one's own sake, and for the sake of humanity, to inform himself or herself in regard to the laws of life and conscientiously to obey them. All need to become acquainted with that most wonderful of all organisms, the human body. They should understand the functions of the various organs and the dependence of one upon another for the healthy action of all. They should study the influence of the mind upon the body and of the body upon the mind, and the laws by which they are governed.

We cannot be too often reminded that health does not depend on chance. It is a result of obedience to law. This is recognized by the contestants in athletic games and trials of strength. These men and women make the most careful preparation. They submit to thorough training and strict discipline. Every physical habit is carefully regulated. They know that neglect, excess, or carelessness, which weakens or cripples any organ or function of the body, would ensure defeat. . . .

In view of the issues at stake, nothing with which we have to do is small. Every act casts its weight onto the scale that determines life's victory or defeat. The scriptures bid us, "So run, that ye may obtain." (Ellen G. White, "The Ministry of Healing,"127-129)

If one were to ask me how I was able to come through this ordeal, I would tell them I had embraced these principles as a part of my lifestyle prior to the tragedy. Even though I experienced deep depression and post traumatic stress right after the tragedy, I knew the way back would come from the training I had already built my life upon. To this day, I adhere to them and counsel all my clients to follow these principles in regaining health in mind, body and spirit.

Each area of our lives requires us to make deposits of success. Tiny withdrawals with no deposits will lead to physical, spiritual and emotional bankruptcy in relationships, jobs, and finances. In times of crisis, the area of most pain gets most of our attention, but by making extra deposits in other areas, we can bounce back to success in our depleted accounts. (Dan Miller, "To the Work You Love," page 13)

As I began to battle my way back from depression and post traumatic stress disorder, I took some simple steps to change my environment from negative to positive influences. I cut off all negative energy like television news, depressing telephone calls, and avoided toxic relationships with friends and even certain family members. I also found I needed to find positive, peaceful places to spend my time. In the beginning, my home and the city of Elk Grove were sources of stress rather than peace. I desperately needed to find a place where I felt safe, where no one knew me or what had happened to me, though I really didn't want to venture too far from home.

A long time friend knew I needed to get away and lovingly made all the arrangements for a trip to Palm Springs for a week of rest, pampering and new scenery. As soon as I arrived at the hotel in Palm Springs, I saw couples and families vacationing together and remembered our last family vacation together. Seeking real comfort and a quite spirit, I decided my healing needed to go to the next level so some weeks later I took a trip to Weimar and visited the lifestyle center just outside Sacramento where I could embrace and apply God's natural remedies of health and restoration. As I checked in I will never forget what the kind gentleman told me when I shared with him why I came to Weimar. His Godly response was that if I came for healing, I came to the right place because many people find healing at Weimar.

However, shortly after I laid my weary body down to receive a good night's rest, I was startled by a presence I felt in my room. At first, I thought I was dreaming but it was as if something was holding me down. As I struggled to wake myself, I prayed asking God's help and the presence left. Once I was fully awake, I jumped up and called Esmie and shared my experience with her. She and her husband told me I was under demonic attack so they prayed with me until my spirit felt settled and the presence left. I was able to get a good night's rest.

Weeping may endure for a night but joy comes in the morning. (Psalm 30:5)

After that first encounter and the intercessory prayer from my two dear friends, Satan had to flee. My stay from then on was very therapeutic bringing the healing and restoration I so desperately needed. While there, I ate a total vegan diet, got lots of fresh air and sunshine, massages and hydrotherapy treatments to bring my body back into balance. I attended health lectures, rested, and wrote in my journal. This was a new season of my life and I allowed the Holy Spirit to guide and lead me as I walked by faith learning to be temperate through this trying time.

I had to get away from my house, my problems, the drama and all the things and places that reminded me of Jon. Though I was steeped in fear and plagued by conflicting feelings as my spiritual battle seemed never ending, the battle was eventually won.

The Grieving process

The word of God says I can do all things through Christ who strengthens me.[19] That includes going through the grieving process to get to my ultimate healing and recovery. It's not an easy road, but as the song says, the Savior is with me and grieves with me, gently caring for me every step of the way. It's easy to blame God for the good, the bad, and the ugly while forgetting there's a devil out there who loves it when we get angry and blame God for the pain and affliction

---

[19] See Philippians 4:13

that come into our lives. God weeps with us at the loss of our loved ones then He gets blamed for it as well. I can truly say that I made it through my grief by concentrating on the everlasting love of God and meditating on His faithfulness on a daily basis because the true battle is not an outward one but inwardly fought.

The Battle Ground

It took me a while but I discovered that the hardest part of dealing with my grief and moving on to total healing was battling my own morbid thoughts and irrational thinking. The guilt that I had to deal with was unbearable; I had to take that to the Cross. In His great love, God showed me I had to picture myself taking the heavy burden of guilt I was carrying and giving it to Christ. As I did this I saw Him take it from me and put it on His shoulders. He showed me how Jesus took everything to Calvary and replayed it for me over and over and over again until I got it. Jesus said, "Come unto me all ye that labor and are heavy laden and I will give you rest."[20] Not only did Jesus take the guilt that had haunted me throughout my marriage but He swallowed it up in His death.

What He did for me He will do for you. The great revelation I received during this time of prayer and focus on God is

---

[20] See Matthew 11:28

that as we linger at the Cross and look at the face of Jesus He looks back at us with tender pity. He asks us to give Him all our pain telling us it was for this purpose that He came to this world. God poured out His healing ointment and "He covered me and kept me." He washed my tears away and gave me hope and peace. The truth is grief can either drive you away from God or closer to Him. If you are grieving, let God embrace and comfort you as He did for me. Trust Him to administer all the right medicine to you. God is willing and able to surround you with His angels who will tend to your every need.

One of the worst times for me was at night when I would lay down and try to rest. As my heart ached and I felt like I couldn't make it through another long, dreary, lonely night, I would drop to my knees and pray. As I cried and spoke of all my painful thoughts and memories, God sent His ministering angels to remind me that my Savior was near and all I had to do was turn my eyes toward heaven and receive the peace and comfort that only Christ can give. As I obeyed, the atmosphere changed in my room and I sensed His presence. His peace filled my heart as Christ lulled me back to sleep. I began to trust in God's loving concern and protection over me.

I need to assure you that it is alright to grieve, cry and weep. It's a part of the healing process and don't let anyone hurry you along. Take the time you need as long as Christ is in it with you. You will still miss your loved one but your grief should not last forever. In order for you to be whole and complete and able to carry on with life you must work through the grieving process.

I knew I had made it through when I began to want to reach out and help others. I realized I could use all that I had learned through the grieving process to lead others to the fountain of healing. I knew I was not to remain in despair forever as one who has no hope. God wanted me healed so I could be His witness and show others His grace is sufficient to heal and restore. I won't tell you it was easy but don't be afraid of setbacks. Some days I felt like I was back to square one, but He would remind me I was making great progress in spite of how I was feeling. Never let your feelings govern you or make you believe a lie, instead believe that you are being healed, long for it and you will have it.

Prayer is truly the key, for in prayer you are literally practicing the presence of God. Tell God how you feel and talk with Him concerning the challenges you are facing. Always remember He knows all things and waits for you to open up a conversation with Him. He waits patiently for you to come to Him. He never gets tired of talking with us and never hangs up on us. You can openly talk about your feelings. He is the best therapist any human being could ever have, plus He is always available day or night. He's never too busy and He's free.

Four Years Later

I know I could never have made it through the next four years had it not been for God and the healing and restoration that had taken place daily since Jon's death. Things seemed to have quieted down and life was back to as normal as possible after such a tragedy.

I was still dealing with some of the issues and the financial struggles left behind after Jon's death but God had been there every step of the way, supplying all our needs and teaching me to trust Him when I didn't see how I could make ends meet. God always came through and our needs were met.

It was the end of the work week nearly four years after Jon's death and I was eagerly looking forward to some much needed rest and some uninterrupted time with the Lord. As I scurried around putting things together for my Sabbath date with the Lord, I decided to go through my e-mails from the day before shutting my computer down for the night. I opened one up from Scott Triplet, the Deputy District Attorney in the Aaron Dunn murder case. It stated that the jury selection should begin February 1st, and the trial was scheduled to begin in March of 2010. I was also informed for the umpteenth time that subpoena's should be going out any day now. I suddenly realized that if things went as planned, we would be in the midst of the trial exactly four years from the day of the shootings. I was relieved to know that after waiting four years justice would finally be served in the death of my husband.

Though we had received similar notices in the past, somehow I knew this time it was really going to happen. Finally the two grieving families, the Daly's and the Johnsons, would have their day in court and bring final closure to the death of our precious loved ones. I hoped all the unanswered questions surrounding the motive and the missing pieces leading up to the events that rocked my world and changed my life, would now be revealed. I had waited a long time to see the perpetrator prosecuted to the fullest extent of the law, but I could see that the long delays had better prepared me for what would come next. In fact, I was assured God had prepared me for such a time as this and that I was indeed ready for complete closure from the horror of March 25th, 2006.

As I met with the prosecuting attorney and went over my statement, photos, sensitive issues about Diana and what to expect in the days to come, I knew this new phase of my life would require a special grace and tolerance that only God could give. I was assigned a wonderful court advocate named Ahmanal Dorsey, who stayed by my side from the start of this nightmare, lovingly coaching me through it to the very end. I was advised by Ahmanal to seek counseling from my mental health therapist to properly prepare me for the trial. After we met, I felt better prepared to move into the final phase of healing and closure.

Everything was now in place and the date was set for the trial to begin. However, I still had concerns as to how things would be handled with both Diana and me at the trial. Would the press interview her and what would she say if she was asked about her affiliation with Jon? Would she be attending every day or would she just be there for the first day of the trial? Embarrassed by the situation but needing to have these questions addressed, I asked Scott and Ahmanal how things were going to play out during the trial.

They told me they had been in contact with Diana and she would be attending the trial but I, Karen Johnson, would be declared as Jon Johnson's legal wife. Diana would have no opportunity to get on the witness stand and talk about her personal relationship with Jon since it had no relevance to the case. As far as they were concerned, I was there that night and I was Jon's wife. She had also been informed, they assured me, that it was Aaron Dunn that was on trial and not Jon Johnson.

Chapter 14

Come To Order

As we arrived at the court house, it was evident the news media was out in full force. As I entered the courthouse and made my way through the metal detectors, my nerves almost got the best of me. My head throbbing from lack of sleep, my family and close friends ushered me through the throngs of reporters to Department 20. I was comforted as even more friends greeted us when we stepped off the third floor elevator.

Though even more television, radio and newspaper reporters lined the hallway to the courtroom, Scott and Ahmanal admonished me not to give any interviews until after I testified. Anxious to get a story, members of the press continually approached us wanting an interview to uncover how we felt about the death penalty. Keeping a low profile, I respectfully turned them down promising an interview once I testified.

We had agreed, however, that my dear friends Esmie and Arthur would grant them an interview.

I was not bothered by all the commotion as it brought back fond memories of my husband covering different events and news worthy stories. Many of Jon's colleagues attended his funeral and respectfully saluted the family as we filed out of the church on our way to the grave site. I had nothing but love and respect for them as I reflected back on that day. This was the type of work my husband loved and I knew many of Jon's colleagues looked forward to the day justice would be served as much as I did. I was amazed by how many family, friends, pastors and church members had turned out in support of our two families as we prepared for the trial to begin.

Michael Daly's widow came all the way from Italy and was also surrounded by family and friends as we greeted each other and prepared to await our entrance into the courtroom. After testifying, she headed back home to be reunited with her mother, small children and the new life she had created since her husband's untimely death. Like me, she and her young children had witnessed their loved one shot point blank in the face. As we embraced, we shared the pain a wife feels at the loss of a husband and quietly talked before a hush slowly descended on the hallway.

The twelve jurors and four alternates walked single-file down the hall way toward the courtroom. There was no eye contact with any of us as they silently filed passed us but their solemn faces assured all of us they were ready to do some serious business. Then the families were asked to enter and quickly filled the quiet courtroom. As I sat quietly awaiting the start of the proceedings, I studied the faces of the jurors.

They were everyday people who took time away from their busy lives to hear this case and make a life or death decision for someone they'd never seen before. As I looked at all those who had come to support me, I wondered how long the trial would go on and who would be in it with me for the long haul.

We were asked to turn off all cell phones and then given instructions by the court clerk on what was permitted in the court room. Total silence permeated the air as we anxiously awaited the start of what would prove to be a very emotion-filled experience for each and every one of us.

Then a voice rang out, "All Rise!"

The Judge that would hear this case and make the final determination was a middle-aged man. He walked in briskly and took his seat. It was still too early to tell what kind of a man this judge was as he took his place behind the bench. Then the bailiff brought the court to order, officially signaling the start of this trial.

Scott Triplett, the prosecutor stood at the podium facing the jurors and gave his opening argument. He addressed the jurors directly giving them a summation of what to expect over the next few weeks from the prosecution, the defense attorneys, and the witnesses and then explained their duty as jurors. I can remember sitting there in awe at how Scott so eloquently told the jurors how he was going to prove the defendant's guilt and how important each fact was in the decision making process. I was impressed by his confidence, poise, and professionalism.

Scott Triplett was young, shrewd and determined to let the jury know that Aaron Dunn was not at all innocent and should pay for the carnage he caused that dreadful night. He explained that drugs were a factor but neither drugs nor insanity were to blame. Aaron Dunn, he told them, was in his right mind as he drove 45 miles down the highway with a purpose and mission in mind. He had a well thought out murderous crime planned and even called family members before he left telling them to watch the news later and they would see something they would never forget.

The defense attorneys then made their case known. It seemed to go on forever as they pleaded for Aaron Dunn's life declaring he was insane at the time of the murders. They claimed he was not in control of himself after losing everything through a series of unfortunate events until he couldn't take it anymore. They claimed his acts were all drug induced and that he was heavily under the influence that night and did not know what he was doing.

Then the first witness was called to the stand. Roberta Daly, wife of Michael Daly rose timidly from her seat and walked up to the witness bench. After swearing in, she nervously took her seat in the witness box. My heart went out to her and I breathed a silent prayer for her as I was quietly ushered out of the courtroom until it was time for me to testify. I was not allowed to hear Roberta's testimony so Esmie stayed in the courtroom and took notes of all that was being said so that I would not miss one thing.

Roberta quietly shared how the night had begun as a family gathering to celebrate her husband's 84-year-old mother's birthday. They had just left the restaurant and bid family members farewell. Michael and Roberta's two young children, six-year-old William and three-year-old Julia, were seat-belted in the backseat. As they drove out of the parking lot of the restaurant, they stopped to yield to oncoming traffic. Suddenly, Roberta said she heard a loud noise and was splattered with glass and blood. As she looked to her left, she saw her husband slumped over the steering wheel, blood everywhere. She said she saw no one as she got out of the car screaming for help. Roberta turned to run for help and bumped into her sister-in-law who did all she could to resuscitate her brother though he had a large hole in his cheek. Roberta broke down as she remembered the awful scene and how her little children had witnessed the horrible event.

All through Roberta's account Aaron Dunn showed no remorse. He just sat in his chair looking as though he didn't know what she was talking about. From time to time he would whisper something in the ear of his attorneys, almost as though he was refuting what was being said. When Roberta concluded her testimony, her family whisked her away before the news reporters could get a statement from her. She had a plane to catch and her children awaited her in the new life she had begun far away from the painful memories of four years ago. It was painful for her to relive and she had no reason to hang around once she had shared her testimony.

The next person called to the witness stand was the young driver of the truck that was rear ended by Dunn that night. The young soldier who took the stand was only 16 at the time but he remembered being shaken up by the sudden hit to the back of his blue truck. He told the jury that when he walked around to the back of his truck, there was a white vehicle rammed up underneath his blue truck. He looked around for the injured driver of the other vehicle thinking surely somebody had been hurt by the force of the impact. However, he could find no driver. Thinking the driver had taken off on foot, he was preparing to report the accident when he heard a loud bang in the near distance. He said it sounded like a car back firing.

Next on the stand was Detective Ryan Johnson who was called to the Michael Daly crime scene that night. When the detective described what he saw, Michael Daly's brother and other family members were visible shaken and quietly sobbed as they relived again that horrible night.

A young lady named Stephanie was then called to the witness stand. She and her boyfriend Adam were out that night heading east bound down Laguna Blvd. when she saw a man leaning half of his body out of his car window, both hands clutching a shot gun. He was driving crazy and fast. When he came up on a police car, he fired a shot hitting and shattering the back side window. Then Stephanie described how the driver crashed the car into a blue truck and how the gun fell from his hand landing about five feet from where the car stopped. The driver staggered out of the car, picked up the gun and proceeded to reload it. She and her boyfriend were in total shock, frozen to the spot until the gunman began to walk toward them like the terminator.

She stated he was dressed in a dark hoody and walked with determination as though on a mission. Next thing she knew he fired at their car hitting the front window and shattering the glass. They stepped on the gas, weaving through the congested traffic until they were able to get across some lanes and out of range of the gunman. She concluded by saying her boyfriend Adam was slightly injured by the shattered glass.

As I sat waiting outside the court room, I noticed an attractive young woman sitting across from me who looked very familiar. I became curious to know who she was. She smiled sympathetically at me but I could not place how I know her. As I sat talking with friends and family, I couldn't get her out of my mind. As we waited to be called in, she approached me and introduced herself as Amber Bennett. Suddenly, I remembered who she was and leaped up to embrace her as tears rolled from my eyes. She was the Good Samaritan who prayed with me and comforted me in the restaurant right after Jon was shot. I had hoped and prayed that one day our paths would cross again but as the years rolled by I thought I would never have an opportunity to thank her for her kind attentive support that dreadful night.

While on the witness stand, Amber stated she had seen Jon and I walk into the restaurant and remembered thinking what a nice looking couple we were. She later saw us get up to leave.

"Shortly after they left," Amber said, "Karen came dashing back in hysterically calling for help, and repeatedly shouting that her husband had been shot!"

Amber remembers trying to calm me down and mentioned leaving me for a minute to check to see what was going on outside. She said she saw a man standing over Jon as though he was guarding him. Amber said he wouldn't let anybody near the fallen man, even though she offered to give him CPR. The man would not move telling Amber she could not help him.

Witness Christina Nichols was on her way to dinner at a local Pizzeria when she passed Chili's and saw the commotion of ambulances, fire trucks and police cars. As she drove eastbound on Laguna Blvd, a white car passed her as it moved erratically on the road. She quickly slowed down to avoid being hit by this crazy driver.

"He was all over the place," she told the jury.

Stopping her car, she watched the white car speed ahead of her and crash into the back of a blue truck. The driver immediately got out of the car, dazed but apparently unhurt as he reached for his fallen shot gun. He picked up the gun, cocked it and fired it at the white car, blowing out the front windshield. Then he again cocked the gun again and started to walk toward her car.

"Our eyes connected," she said. "There was death in his eyes as he raised the gun up and pointed it toward me. My instincts kicked in, I stepped on the gas and ran a red light in order to get out of there fast. Shaken but unhurt, I headed for the restaurant to meet up with my friends."

Scott had the witnesses lined up in chronological order as he reconstructed the chain of events of that night for the jury. That is why he began with Roberta's testimony and other eye witnesses regarding the first murder at Chili's restaurant.

I was expected to give my testimony the following day however it was delayed until the following week due to the lengthy questioning from defense attorney's and the many witnesses lined up to give their testimonies before me.

My Testimony

On the day of my court appearance, I sat outside anxiously waiting to be called. I was prayed up knowing it was not my strength but His that would have to carry me through this painful day. It was day four of the trial and the media coverage had died down/ The number of supporters had dwindled considerably though my mother, twin sister Kathie, close girlfriends Esmie and Felicia, my niece Ameerah, nephew Carl and a few other precious friends were still there to give me moral support.

When the bailiff came out to get me, I took a deep breath as I stood to finally have my day in court. I looked around as I walked slowly into the courtroom. The judge smiled and greeted me as I made my way to the front where I was sworn in and asked to take my seat on the witness stand. As I waited for Scott to begin his line of questions, I remember looking at Aaron Dunn and thinking, "You may have taken my power away from me the night you killed my husband, but you're not going to today."

Although I was an emotional wreck from the long wait to share my testimony, I felt a calmness come over me that kept me composed and in control. As I recounted the events of that fateful night, I looked Aaron Dunn straight in the eyes and felt a sense of strength and power come over me. I could see my sister and girlfriend Felicia looking right at me as I testified. I was asked questions concerning what I saw that night, what the perpetrator was wearing and if I could identify the defendant.

After I described what I had witnessed, Scott asked me if the person I had seen that night was in the court room. I shook my head yes and pointed to the defendant. When I described what the man had been wearing, Scott showed me a picture of what Aaron had on that night and it matched my description. I was amazed I still remembered it so clearly. I took a moment while I testified to look at the faces of each juror. Some looked unmoved by my account while others appeared to be trying to hold back the tears and others I just couldn't read at all.

Scott had prepared me for what he was going to do next. He told me the murder had been captured by a surveillance camera just outside the restaurant but didn't want me to see it until I was on the witness stand. He wanted my reaction to impact the jurors. As Scott played back the security tape footage, I saw Aaron run up to Jon, blast him then run away in a victory dance. Then it showed me running from the car and into the restaurant.

When I saw it, I was shaken but again God had prepared me for this long awaited day and gave me strength even for this vivid replay of Jon's senseless murder.

After my testimony I heard comments like, "You're a soldier, you did good, and you're so strong." In fact, right after we were dismissed I granted an interview to a reporter from Channel 13. He told me he'd heard a few comments concerning my testimony such as, "she looks composed, in fact too composed." I'm not sure what they expected to see but after four years of working through the fear and tears along with countless grief counseling sessions and hours of prayer and studying the word of God, I was at peace. My prayer was, "Lord, not my will but Your will be done." Don't get me wrong, the new revelations were chilling. It hurt to watch the gruesome details of Jon's death but God gave me the strength to endure and I kept my mind fixed and focused on Him. I felt as though He was standing right beside me and supported me through the whole ordeal.

Dr. Weisner, the trauma doctor on duty that night, testified concerning Jon's condition when he arrived at the Emergency Room. He described how he tried to get a breathing tube into the lung, but found the injuries were too extensive. Then they tried an oxygen needle in the neck, but nothing was working.

Finally, they were able to put a tube directly into the wind pipe, but to no avail. Jon succumbed to his massive injuries not long after he arrived at the ER.

Aaron Dunn's Wife

On March 22nd, 2010, Aaron Dunn's wife, Sarah Pack walked into the court room and took the oath swearing to be truthful. She was a short, stocky woman with long brown hair and a pleasant face. Dunn looked at her with no apparent facial expression and Sarah barely looked at him. It was obvious no love was lost between them. She stated she had met Dunn in December of 1998 when they were both using Meth. At first they would get high together but Sarah told us she straighten her life out and stopped using when she became pregnant with their one and only daughter, Kaitlin. She encouraged Dunn to also stop which he did, but she said she knew Aaron continued to struggle with the addiction. They were married in 2003 and separated in 2005.

Sarah was the daughter of a 27-year police veteran who did not approve of Sarah's relationship with Aaron and discouraged it as much as he could. Sarah explained that Aaron had a criminal record and had spent four years in the California youth authorities program causing him to develop a bitter hatred for Cops or "Pig's" as he referred to them. Even after they married, her policeman father would not allow Dunn to come to the house for Christmas and other holiday gatherings which just added more fuel to the already burning rage within her young husband.

Sarah stated that their rocky on and off relationship included both of them being unfaithful to their marriage vows. While still married to Dunn, Sarah started chatting on line with single men telling them she was separated from her husband. Quite a few took an interest in her and she began dating these men.

In the summer of 2005, Sarah met and began dating Brian Clauson telling him she was separated from her husband. Dunn, who was always suspicious of Sarah, would tap into her chat room conversations and found out about Clauson. Clauson later testified that one day he thought he was conversing with Sarah when the person he had connected to wrote, "You better kiss your babies goodbye." Clauson, who lived in Elk Grove, told Sarah they needed to cool off because her old man was threatening to hurt his kids.

That same summer things came to a head with Aaron and Sarah. She was tired of Dunn's drug and alcohol binges and told him she was leaving him for good. She continued her relationship with Clauson and added another lover who was a Stockton Police officer, also from the Elk Grove area. Sarah stated how she messed with Aaron's head by keeping his daughter from him all the while taunting him by staying with her lovers in Elk Grove.

On March 25th, 2006, Aaron called her saying he wanted to see her and Kaitlin but Sarah refused not wanting to put her daughter through the emotional pain of such a visit. She said Dunn sounded angry, started crying and yelling at her. Later that evening, Sarah was with one of her lovers watching movies when she got a call from Aaron's sister telling her to turn on the news. When she did, she saw Aaron's car and remembered his earlier call. She flagged down a police car and told him everything she knew of the events of that day.

She later discovered a voice mail Aaron had left on her phone which Scott instructed the jury to listen carefully to. The court room sat in utter silence as we all listened in. First, all we heard was wild screaming music playing but then we heard Dunn in the back ground shouting out, "Whoo Hooo!!" We heard the car crash and a few moments later we heard gunshots, one of which killed my husband, Jon. Thankfully the judge called a recess and we quietly filed out of the court room to get a breath of fresh air.

When the court room was called back to order, Scott began his questioning by asking Sarah how she felt about all that had happened. She stated she felt responsible to some degree since she knew Dunn was angry with her and the men she was seeing. When Scott asked her if Aaron had a history of mental illness, she said no. Then he asked her if he was insane when he killed two innocent men that night. Again she said no, but added she was sure he was high on drugs. Scott then questioned her about her visit to Dunn in jail. Then he played a recording of that visit which left no doubt in anyone's mind how they planned to use the fact that Aaron was high on drugs as a ploy to help him avoid the death penalty. The courtroom was horrified when Dunn's recorded voice declared how he wished her lovers would come to the jail so he could do them in.

"I might have been over the edge that night," he declared, "but not totally. I could have gotten two more but they were women."

The court room sat in stunned silence though Dunn never even flinched.

The rest of the time she refused to say anything but, "I don't recall."

By the time Sarah Pack was finished, everyone had had enough of her. As I listened to her testify, all I could think of was how this one married woman engaging in her extramarital affairs had caused so much death and destruction. I was frustrated and angry with her "I don't care attitude." I realized how cold and callous a heart can be as she displayed no real sorrow for the families of Aaron Dunn's victims that were sitting in the court room that day.

Next we met officer Keith Berry, Sarah's other boyfriend. He stated they dated for about three months on and off. He seemed ashamed of his involvement with her saying he never knew she was a married woman.

Brad Jeffery Allen, Aaron's long time best friend, stepped up to the witness stand.

He said he had seen Aaron the day before the shootings.

"He seemed normal to me even though he was high on meth," Allen said.

"On the day of the shootings," Allen continued, "Aaron called me to let me know that I had been a good friend but he could no longer be around here, meaning his environment and the situation with his wife. Then he told me to say goodbye to my children and his cousins for him."

Before he hung up, Aaron told Brad to watch the news later that night. Brad said he sounded fine. He was coherent and wasn't slurring his words. Brad felt Aaron knew what he was doing.

Blame it on the Meth

The trial took on a whole different bent as the defense attorneys desperately tried to blame the killings on Dunn's state of mind under the influence of meth. Dunn's friends and family came to the witness stand. His brother Patrick, also a drug user, said that Aaron had relapsed just six months prior to that night and was again using daily. One week before the killings Patrick stated he noticed Aaron beginning to get paranoid using 3 ½ grams every day.

Then an established expert in substance abuse and addictions took the stand. Dr. Douglas Tucker, a Psychiatrist who had testified over 200 times in court, explained the effects of Meth. The doctor said he spent a total of 12 hours interviewing Dunn who claimed to have been under attack by Police officers that night. He said that though Dunn's blood had been flushed out twice during his hospital stay, there was such a high concentration of the drug in his system that they still found traces of Meth in his blood stream.

For two days the defense and the prosecuting attorneys went back and forth trying to prove whether the killings were premeditated or the direct result of a mental health disease enhanced by continued meth usage. Scott did a tremendous job proving that Aaron Dunn had used meth for many years and had never killed anyone. He also established the amount Dunn used that night was what he was accustomed to using and not an unusually high dose for him. As I watched the jury processing what Scott was presenting, I felt they agreed the Meth Aaron Dunn took that night was a vehicle that drove him to do what he had already planned in his heart and mind to do.

The choice to kill had been made; the Meth just gave him the boost he needed to follow through with it.

Dunn's phone was also turned in as evidence. The front screen of his phone seemed to reflect Dunn's feelings that all police officers should die: G FDDALLPIGSDIE. Another message left on his sister's phone was also played in court.

"Hey, Sarah, it's Aaron, I love all the kids, tell Pat and everyone I love them, I've been hurt by all the lies from everyone, I've always loved everybody to the end. Bye."

Witness after Witness

My daily schedule now revolved around court. As days rolled into weeks, my support group dwindled down to just Esmie. Each day we would drive together to the court house unless I had to teach a class. If I had to leave Esmie would stay and take notes for me then as soon as class was over I'd race back to the court house. Most days at the courthouse would normally be finished by 4 or 4:30. I looked forward to my evening fitness classes where I could work out and get my dopamine levels up. I don't know how I would have made it through without those times of release.

The line of witnesses continued as everyone shared what they heard and saw and knew. Jen Layton was inside a store nearby when she heard gun shots and then saw a gunman walking across the parking lot shooting his gun into the air. Lisa Kent was rear-ended by the blue truck after Dunn ran into it with his white car. Both described the scene as horrifying! It was all I could do to remain sane as I heard account after account after account. So much was beginning to make sense to me as pieces of the puzzle slowly came together.

I saw people take the stand that I vaguely remembered helping me that night. It was so good to be able to finally let them know how thankful and grateful I was for what each one had done for me. Jim Williams was one of them. He began by saying that he had taken his wife, daughter, mother-in-law and his wife's cousin to Mandangos for a family night out. Jim and his wife's cousin were on their way outside to smoke a cigarette when he saw Jon and me walking toward the door. He waited and held the door open for us to go out into the parking lot ahead of them. He remembered we said thank you and began to weep as he described what happened after that.

"As the couple walked to their car," Jim told the jury, "I also saw a man with a shot gun moving quickly across the parking lot."

Jim remembers asking his cousin if there was a gun shop anywhere nearby. Then as he watched in stunned silence, the gun man went behind a parked van obscuring him from Jim's vision.

Suddenly, he heard a shot ring out, then a brief moment of silence before a woman came running back toward the restaurant frantically screaming, "He shot my husband!"

Jim broke down and cried as did many of us in the court room. Scott gave him a moment to compose himself then asked him what happened next.

Jim said he turned to his cousin and shouted, "Call 911!"

At that point, Jim's testimony stopped as they played a recording of that 911 call for the jury. When Jim was asked to continue, he said he looked back over the parking lot and saw a dark figure walking away and raising his arms high in the air as though he'd just won a victory. Feeling the gunman was leaving the area, Jim took courage and walked over to where Jon was lying. As Jim described what he saw, he couldn't contain himself and broke down again.

Jim struggled to once again compose himself and then said, "I've never seen anything like that in my life."

Thankfully the judge called a recess after Jim's testimony. I found him in the hallway and we hugged and cried together.

After a short walk outside to get some fresh air and sunshine, I prepared myself for the next witness. Vincent Marconi was on a blind date that night at another local restaurant. As he left the restaurant and headed eastbound, he noticed a car as it sped by him. Mr. Marconi then came up on the accident and got out of his car to go check on the driver. A police woman had already responded to the accident and as he approached her, they heard a loud boom. When it happened a second time, the officer pulled her gun and ran behind her car followed closely by Mr. Marconi.

Marconi said the officer shouted to the gun man to put down his weapon but to his horror, the gunman just kept coming at them. The gunman chased them around and around the car firing and ducking. Marconi's testimony took on a more intense tone as he explained how the gunman suddenly did an about face. When the gunman caught up to them, he fired point blank hitting Vincent Marconi in the back with 14 steel pellets. Marconi survived the attack and the pellets were successfully removed in surgery.

The cross examination by the defense attorneys of each of these witnesses was long, tedious and frustrating as they struggled to prove the attack was not premeditated. Over the days and weeks that followed, the trial got more and more intense.

Michael Roper and his little daughter were at a nearby McDonalds. They had just gotten back in their car after eating when they heard a loud bang. When Roper checked his rear view mirror, he saw the silhouette of a man running toward them with a shot gun in his hand. He quickly told his daughter to get down. Then he spotted a female officer not far away and pulled his daughter out of the car and ran to report what he saw. Before he could finish telling the officer what he saw, more shots ring out nearby. The officer pulled out her weapon and an exchanged fire with the gunman. Roper and his daughter sought refuge behind a huge sign, where he said he fell to the ground covering his daughter's body with his own. I was shocked to find out another child had witnessed the horror of that night. I looked at the man who had traumatized so many people as he sat there showing no emotion whatsoever. I wondered if this monster even had a heart.

Donte Higgins was on his way to a birthday party with his wife, brother and friends when they stopped for gas. As they pulled into a Chevron gas station, he noticed several police cars going west on Laguna. Then they saw Stephanie and Adam standing next to a car with a shattered window. They were shaken and told Donte and his group that there was a shooter on the loose.

"Everyone scattered," Donte continued, "when we heard an officer say twice, 'Halt, drop your weapon.' When we turned toward the voices, I saw the man refusing to drop his weapon, and the officer firing three shots in his upper torso."

Jannson DeMoss was at Mandango's with friends that night and had just stepped outside to have a cigarette when he heard what sounded like a car back fire. When it happened two more times, he was convinced it was gun shots and quickly went back inside the restaurant. As he headed back to his friends at the pool table, he said he saw a figure pass by the window, a sudden flash of light and someone crumbling to the ground. Then the figure raised its hands to the sky holding a gun as though he had just won a battle. Next thing he knew a woman came running in the restaurant screaming for help.

Mickey McQuire was also in Mandango's that evening watching the Kings game. He testified that he saw a woman run into the restaurant screaming that her husband had been shot. He got up and went outside and saw a man lying on the ground in the parking lot. He heard gunshots and looked toward the main road where he saw a live gun fight going on between police and the gun man. He witnessed the gun man take upper body shots and fall to the ground as the police fell on top of him. He looked again across the parking lot at Jon lying in a pool of blood.

As the trial continued day after day and week after week, I felt as though I was in a movie theater watching as all the horrifying details revealed as witness after witness testified about that night. I relived the fear and trauma caused by Aaron Dunn as each testimony added to what I already knew, yet the pieces were finally coming together. Scott was always right on target as he questioned the witnesses while the cross examinations done by the defense attorneys were long and seemingly pointless as the same questions were asked over and over again.

One Monday morning we heard that Aaron Dunn had written a letter to a family member saying he wished the judge had drowned while on vacation. The family immediately turned the letter over to the authorities. The Judge was obviously not pleased with this information but he kept his poise and ordered the trial to be continued.

Another law enforcement officer took the stand saying he had heard over his radio that a fellow officer was involved in a shooting and immediately rushed to the scene. Thomas Gland, who had been with the sheriff's department for nine years, said when he arrived at the scene he saw a patrol car and a man lying on the ground not far from it, moaning and groaning. Aaron Dunn had been shot five times and had collapsed on top of his shot gun. Officer Gland approached Dunn, removed the shot gun from underneath him, attended to his wounds and stayed with him until the medic arrived.

Officer Tisha Smith, a ten-year police veteran, said she and her partner Officer Bestpitch were heading for dinner break when they heard the call from a fearful community service officer. As they headed toward the scene, there was a loud sound like someone had thrown a huge rock into the window of their car. She looked around and saw the rear side window of the patrol car was gone and her partner was holding the back of her head with both hands. A piece of the shattered glass had hit and stunned her partner. Then they heard a report on the radio that a person had been shot in the head at the Chili's Restaurant. They did a u-turn and headed toward Chili's but were sent back toward McDonalds where by now Jon had been shot.

Officer Bestpitch took the stand and picked up where her partner had left off. She said that upon their arrival at the scene, they cautiously exited their vehicle. Officer Bestpitch began interviewing a civilian witness, Vincent Marconi.

Then she heard someone say, "He's got a shotgun."

As she turned toward the voice, she clearly saw a man with a shot gun aimed at her so she drew her weapon and commanded him to drop his weapon. When he refused and kept coming at her, she shot at him. Undaunted by her shot, the gunman continued coming toward her and Vincent Marconi. Aaron Dunn came right up to the patrol car and chased both the officer and the civilian around the car several times before doubling back and shooting Marconi in the back.

Hearing the shot behind her, Bestpitch turned and fired four rounds at the suspect while using her vehicle as a shield. Fearful the suspect was once again sneaking up behind her; she cautiously looked through the car window. Hearing no more shots and seeing no movement of any kind, she moved slowly around the front of the patrol car to the passenger's side. At this point she could see Dunn lying face down between the car and the side of the road.

She heard her partner yell, "Move, you're in my line of fire."

Quickly taking cover behind the MacDonald's sign, she said she was relieved to hear backup had arrived on the scene. Scott allowed her to finish then asked her if she had been afraid. As she shook her head yes, tears rolled down her cheeks. Scott reported Officer Bestpitch had fired five rounds, all of them hitting Dunn in the upper torso.

As the testimonies from that night continued, I realized how many people had been affected by Aaron Dunn's acts of violence. After the gripping testimonies, I was sure I was not the only one who was having sleepless nights and nightmares. I was relieved when the Judge called for a recess so Esmie and I could go outside for some fresh air.

Major Victory

As we neared the end of the trial, I longed for this ordeal to be over though I knew it was important that every witness share their story and testimony. It was difficult to process how the law works because though we all knew Aaron Dunn had killed Michael Daly, no one actually saw him do it. Up to this point, it was just speculation. A bullet went through the car window and killed Michael Daly but no one knew where the bullet came from.

Then Patricia Vaca, a crime scene investigator, took the stand. As part of the forensic team that checked out the car that Dunn was driving, she told the jury what she found. There were four shot gun shells, a cell phone and a cassette tape entitled "Whiskey, Rock and Roller" by Simple Man found inside the car Dunn drove that night. In the trunk they found a Satanic bible by Anton Levy and a green duffle bag.

As she examined the car inch by inch, Patricia Vaca said she noticed a very small speck of an unknown substance on the side view mirror. She carefully removed it, jarred it and immediately sent it to the pathology lab for testing. It came back as a blood sample with a positive DNA match to that of Michael Daly. Aaron Dunn had fired at such close range into the face of Michael Daly that the victim's blood had splashed on Dunn's car. This was the evidence that was needed to blow the defense attorneys out of the water. The proof was there; Dunn had killed Michael Daly. This was a major victory for the prosecution!

More detectives took the stand giving short testimonies concerning the other evidence found at the Mandango's crime scene. They found a total of seven shot gun shells at the scene. The officers who questioned the people at the crime scene also came and gave short testimonies. One detective in charge of controlling the crime scene stated Jon was unrecognizable with most of his face blown off. He said he found

Jon's chin and pieces of his jaw with his facial beard attached a few feet away from where Jon was lying.

I gasped as I remembered asking Jon to grow a go-tee several years ago telling him it made him look even more handsome. Picturing again my husband's face ripped apart by shot gun pellets was more than I could bear. The detective went on to say Jon's phone was on the ground next to him and a single live bullet was found underneath my car. That was the bullet meant for me and a reminder that on that night I was truly covered and kept by God! I also learned that the defendant's vision was extremely bad and just before the second shooting, he crashed into the rear end of another vehicle causing his glasses to fly off his face. Thank God, I was hidden in the cleft of the rock.

Then Elizabeth Alvarez, the forensic doctor that did the autopsy on both Jon and Michael gave the official cause of death for both men. Then she went on to describe the extent of their injuries in full explicit detail. She stated that Michael Daly's face was shattered from left to right and that the bullet entered his upper left cheek. My heart sank as I heard the gasps and sniffles from the Daly family sitting behind me. The details were too much for any of us to bear yet we all sat glued to our seats, unable to leave, somehow needing to hear every word. Then she went on to describe Jon's injuries. He received a shot gun wound to the right jaw area, she said, where the pellets exploded and sprayed off into Jon's head and neck.

Next Brian Schell, the fire fighter paramedic who attended to Aaron Dunn that night, took the stand. He stated that Dunn had shots to his upper body, left chest area and under his armpit. He had lost a lot of blood and should have died that night like he wanted to. How ironic that with two single shots two men who had reasons to live died, while this man who had no respect for life took five shots around the heart area and was still alive.

Bruce Moran was an expert in fire arms and described in great detail the Winchester model 1300, 12- gauge-pump-action shot gun used in the killing of both Daly and Jon. He told us this particular gun needed eight pounds of pressure to fire the trigger and described the bullets, shells and pellets used in this type of shot gun. He determined that the damaged police car was not hit by a rock as the police women had originally thought but by a gun of this caliber. He went on to determine the type of gun used for every shot fired that night.

Then, to my horror, they brought the very gun that had killed Michael and Jon into the court room for this expert to examine. I shuddered as I viewed the huge black weapon used against Jon for the very first time. As I stared at it in horror, I realized my husband had stood no chance against that gun at point blank range. Shocked by the sight of it, Esmie and I looked at each other as our eyes again filled with tears.

On March 25th, 2010, exactly four years to the day, Elk Grove Police Officer Jeff McHenry, shared his statement. Officer McHenry had been stationed at the hospital to guard the defendant. He was sitting to the right of Aaron Dunn's bed watching a training movie on his lap top, when a nurse approached Dunn on his left. The officer said he asked the nurse if the defendant was under the influence.

To his surprise, Aaron interrupted and said, "I was on methamphetamine. I knew what I was doing that night; I just don't want to live."

Confirmation of his intent was given by the defendant himself. I wrote in my journal that today's discoveries were very grueling and chilling. The thing that was the most disturbing, I wrote, was the fact that the defendant had a satanic bible and his unemotional response to the vivid portrayals of the death and destruction he caused on that night four years ago.

Chapter 15

Forgiveness is a Process

P rior to dismissing the jurors to deliberate and determine the defendant's guilt or innocence, Scott was able to present victim impact evidence. That means he could call witnesses to the stand to describe how they had been affected by the loss of Mike and Jon. We were told we could discuss the impact of their deaths on our lives by presenting personal characteristics and using specific examples. Scott explained to me the importance of this part of the trial especially because it was a capital punishment murder case.

There are actually two phases of this kind of trial. First, the jury must decide whether the prosecution has proved beyond a reasonable doubt that the defendant is guilty of first degree murder with at least one special circumstance. If the jury finds the defendant guilty, the trial proceeds to the penalty phase of the trial, where the jury reviews aggravating and mitigating evidence to return a verdict of either death or life in prison without the possibility of parole. It appeared pretty obvious to me, my friends and family members that Aaron Dunn was guilty of first degree murder and deserved the death penalty but the law required the jury's decision to be unanimous.[21]

Ahmanal had been assisting me by trying to reach my in-laws and step-children to participate in this important part of the trial. I really wanted them to express their sentiments and love for Jon. But as the weeks rolled by and the time for victim impact evidence approached, she had not been able to reach them. Oh, how I wanted them to take this opportunity to express to the judge and jurors the tremendous impact Jon's death had on their lives. I felt it was crucial for the jurors to see other family members testify concerning how losing Jon had affected their lives. I prayed right up until the day of the victim impact evidence part of the trial began that they would be present and choose to participate.

I was sitting next to my mother directly across from the department 20 court room when Ahmanal called and said my step-children had safely arrived and my in-laws were on their way as well. When my step-children stepped off the elevator and turned the corner, my heart jumped for joy. Tray, now 21, was very tall, mature looking and wearing a go-tee like his father. He looked like a younger lighter version of Jon.

---

[21] Also see *A victim's Guide to the Capital Case Process*, page 1

Tangela, now 26 looked good though she had filled out since I had last seen her at their father's funeral.

Tray made his way through the crowd to embrace first me and then my mother. We talked, happy to see each other again. On the other hand, even though it had been four years Tangela was obviously still harboring ill feelings toward me and made it very clear to Ahmanal she didn't want to sit next to me in the court room. I honored her wishes, gave her space and said nothing to her.

Victim Impact Evidence

The impact statements from the victims' families were emotional, sad and compelling. Each of us told the jury about the pain and emptiness inflicted on our lives by Aaron Norman Dunn the night he went on a shooting rampage in Elk Grove killing our loved ones. We all cried as we listened to each other express the impact of our loss.

Roberta Daly came back and expressed how her husband's death had especially impacted their small children. She said whenever she takes the children to the park her son William sits alone on the slide while other kids play with their fathers. She said that's the worst part because her kid's dad never comes. Tangela broke down and cried as she shared special moments she'd had with her dad and what a daddy's girl she was. Jon's sister described her brother Jon as the rock of their family and how much of a void there was in their lives with him gone.

I told the court about the plans Jon and I had been making to buy a new home. I described Jon's plan to travel to New Orleans to cover the hurricane Katrina devastations and then go on to Africa to produce a documentary about the orphans of the aids epidemic there. I became emotional as I told them how a day that started out with euphoric expectations turned into one of abject grief, excruciating pain, and fear as my husband was shot to death right outside the passenger side of my car. Life seemed so perfect until a mad man named Aaron Dunn barged into our world and changed the course of our lives forever.

I closed my testimony by telling the court how earlier that evening Jon had turned to me and said, "Honey, this is going to be a great year."

As the jury listened to the victim impact evidence, many of them were obviously fighting back tears and others were crying. Now that all of the evidence had been presented, it was time for them to decide Aaron Dunn's fate. After a couple of days of deliberation the jury came back with a unanimous guilty verdict.

Phase Two

We now moved into the next phase of the trial to determine Aaron Dunn's sentence. Would it be life in prison or death by lethal injection? I was still very torn concerning the issue of the death penalty. Though I saw no display of remorse on the part of Aaron Dunn during the court proceedings, he was still a human being. As the facts of his misguided life were revealed during the trial, I found myself actually feeling sorry for him. Don't get me wrong, I wanted Aaron Dunn to pay for the crimes he'd committed but at the same time. I thought about how God had used former murderers like Moses, King David and Paul to do great things for the Kingdom of God once they were converted.

Jury Weighs Killer's fate

Deputy District Attorney Scott Triplett argued that the circumstances of Dunn's March 25th, 2006, attack should tip the scales toward a death sentence. "The shootings," Triplett said, "annihilated the men's lives right in front of their wives, and, in Daly's case, his two young children. The random shootings that night could of taken out anybody you know."

Then the defense pleaded their case acknowledging the horrific nature of the crimes but they reminded the jury that

Dunn's life had been shattered by the loss of his wife and his job. They pointed to his sick life's path that began with a father who shot up heroin in front of him and a mother who emotionally abandoned him. They pointed out that the methamphetamine he had ingested ruined his capacity to reflect on what he was doing that night.

"Ladies and gentlemen, I'm asking you to be compassionate, strong and noble," Defense Attorney Rogers said, "Reject death; come back with a verdict of life without parole."

Judge Michael W. Sweet gave the jury a list of 12 aggravating and mitigating factors to consider in deciding whether to impose the death penalty on Dunn or to send him to prison for the rest of his life.[22]

After the six men and six women who made up the jury heard both sides and received their list of instructions, they exited the courtroom with grim looks on their faces and the weight of a man's life on their shoulders. What appeared to the family and friends of the victims to be an open and shut case turned into a lengthy process that took nine days. As family and friends of the victims waited with great anticipation we talked among ourselves in the cafeteria and in the hall way. From time to time the jurors walked past us with blank expressions, but one day my eyes locked with one of the jurors. As he pass by me he winked and kept walking.

[22] Taken from a report by Andy Furillo Sacramento Bee

From his exchange I immediately knew he was in favor of death by lethal injection and was fighting for our cause. As the days drew on, I knew Aaron had received due process of the law and that the jurors did not take their civic duty lightly. With each passing day, my prayer was "Lord not my will but your will be done."

After the first two days of waiting outside the courtroom, I decided to resume my normal life. I put everyone on notice that I could get the call at any time telling me the jurors had reached a verdict. On day nine, I was indeed at work when I received the call. I told my client I had to go, quickly changed into a suit and hurried to the Superior Courtroom. The judge, defendant, attorney's, media, the Daly family, jury, victim advocates were already there but Ahmanal assured me they would wait until I arrived before reading the final verdict.

Final Verdict – May 12, 2010

Aaron Norman Dunn's random shotgun killings of two good men and the night of danger he presented to an entire region convinced a Sacramento jury that the meth-fueled murderer must answer with his life. The blood drained from Dunn's face as he heard the six-man, six-woman panel declare, "the penalty shall be death" to the courtroom's capacity crowd. It was Sacramento County's first death-penalty verdict in a little more than three years.

In weighing death vs. life for Dunn, jurors said the horrific post-mortem photos of murder victims Jon Johnson 46, and Michael Daly 45, brought over the last panel member who had held out for a life sentence with no parole term. They said they were deeply moved by the testimonies of the victims' families and not convinced by the "meth psychosis" theory put forth by Dunn's defense team.

Mostly, though, they said they were overwhelmed by the brutality of Dunn's March 25, 2006, attack that imperiled a community, stretching from his residence in Olivehurst to the family restaurants along Laguna Blvd. and blasted homicide from the barrel of a shotgun.[23]

"Surely for your lifeblood I will demand a reckoning; from the hand of every beast I will require it, and from the hand of man. From the hand of every man's brother I will require the life of man. Whoever sheds man's blood, by man his blood shall be shed; for in the image of God He made man" (Genesis 9:5-6).

---

[23] Taken from a report by Andy Furillo, Sacramento Bee

My prayer for Aaron Dunn was that before his death, whenever that was to be, he would be given an opportunity to know Christ. Nothing happens in this world by accident so it was my hope that Aaron's heart would soften and he would repent for his sins against his victims, their families and God. I had come to accept that Jon and Michael were taken for a reason and that even though Aaron Dunn took five gunshot wounds to the body, he survived. After Aaron Dunn was convicted of murder, we were given an eight week break before resuming the sentencing portion of the trial that would seal Aaron's fate.

Impending Judgment

It was now July 6th, 2010. Esmie picked me up around 8:15 a.m. After we greeted each other, we decided to pray for everyone involved as this trial was about to come to an end. Today, we found ourselves in fervent prayer for Aaron Dunn and his family. I realized God was taking me through the process of forgiveness and that the bitterness and resentment was slowly leaving my heart.

As I prayed, I reflected on what I had learned about his background and began to put together all the pieces of his life and see who Aaron Dunn really was.

I thought about how Dunn was born into a family of drug dealers and how they were readily accessible to him. I began to understand the neglected life he'd led; raised by a violent selfish father whose violent, hateful, selfish ways often left Aaron to fend for himself. Aaron was a time bomb just waiting for the perfect motivation to explode.

That is not to say Aaron was not entirely off the hook. We all have choices we have to make along life's path. Some of us have harder choices than others but ultimately we make our own choices. We can choose to serve God, desiring to make right choices or we can listen to the devil's promptings and make choices that not only hurt ourselves but everyone we come into contact with. So, even though I had sympathy for Aaron Dunn because of the family and life he was born into, I knew he could have chosen a different life for himself. He didn't have to follow the path of death and self-destruction.

My thoughts turned to Jon and how he was also reared with all the odds against him. He had no mother to nurture him and then the early death of his father and the neglect of his remaining family left Jon living on the hostile streets of Oakland, California. But unlike Aaron Dunn, Jon chose to do what was right and not let his environment, hurt, pain, and anger shape his life or his future successes. Although his promiscuous lifestyle and treatment of women was a result of his resentment towards his mother, Jon did not choose to vent his anger by indiscriminately killing women.

The Bible says in all your getting, get understanding.[24] When we gain understanding, we get to a place where events of life are put into proper perspective and then forgiveness can begin its process. God used the trial and the various testimonies to help me gain understanding about what motivated Aaron Dunn's actions that night four years ago. One powerful revelation came from all of this as I realized that even though Aaron Dunn didn't shoot me that night, harboring unforgiveness towards him could kill or paralyze me just as effectively as if he had. I knew I couldn't forgive him in and of myself; he had done far too much harm in my life for me to be able to do that. God did, however, expect me to be willing to forgive and acknowledge how wrong and detrimental harboring unforgiveness was to my health. What God did for me He will also do for you.

Matthew 6:14-15 gives us benefits of forgiveness and the consequences of unforgiveness.

For if ye forgive men their trespasses, your heavenly Father will also forgive you: But if ye forgive not men their trespasses, neither will your Father forgive your trespasses. (KJV)

---

[24] See Proverbs 4:7

Justice is Served

I hardly slept the night before the sentencing. I was rest-less and my mind just couldn't settle into a peaceful resolve. Finally, Aaron Norman Dunn would be sentenced for the crimes he committed four and a half years ago. I wished I could have gotten a good night's rest before such an impor-tant event, but instead the anxiety got the best of me. Knowing I needed strength for the coming day, I knelt down by my bed and thanked the LORD for allowing me to see another day but more importantly, for keeping me for such a time as this.

As I prepared for what would be my last day in court, I tried to think of what I might say in my statement before the judge but nothing solid would frame in my mind. I knew the media would be out in full force today because the death penalty was still a very rare thing. I wanted to make sure that what I said would be compelling and leave an impact on everyone in that courtroom including Aaron Dunn. I didn't want to read from a script, but wanted it to flow from the heart. I called Esmie and told her I didn't know what I was going to say and she imme-diately began to pray with me asking the LORD to open my mouth like He opened the mouth of Moses and put the words in it to speak.

A peace came over me knowing the Holy Spirit would use me and speak through me as I prepared for my final opportunity to articulate and express uninterrupted how Aaron Dunn's actions that night impacted and altered many lives forever, including his own.

I knew I was not the only one making a final statement today. In a few hours the judge would also hear Assistant Public Defender Amy Rogers and Co-defense Counsel Hayes Gable III asking the judge to keep Dunn alive based on a terrible upbringing and meth psychosis. Today, they would make their last plea to keep Aaron Norman Dunn from receiving a lethal injection as payment for his crimes.

When we arrived downtown, I dropped Mom and Tristan off at the handicap ramp right outside the Superior courthouse and called Ahmanal to inform her I was parking the car and would be there momentarily. In a very nurturing tone she assured me they wouldn't start without me but urged me to park quickly as the judge, the defendant, Scott and the Daly family had already arrived. Although we had often been delayed during the course of this trial, I knew that today we would be starting on time and the bailiff would be walking out any minute to summon the crowd inside.

Once inside the court building, I quickly moved through the metal detectors, grabbed my purse and scurried to catch up with my Mother and Tristan at the elevators. Arriving at the third floor waiting area I found the Daly family, the press, the attorneys, and even some of the jurors waiting to enter the courtroom. Their presence brought tears to my eyes as I realized how the members of the jury were impacted by this case.

After nine long days of deliberation to determine Aaron's level of guilt, they needed some sort of closure for the judgment they had pronounced on Aaron Dunn. Knowing it had been a tough decision for them, I went around and thanked and hugged them for being so professional and judicious in their civic duty. I wanted them to know how appreciative I was for their level of service and commitment to the process. Then I quickly walked over to the Daly family. We embraced each other as we always did and together we all stood and waited for the final call to enter the court room.

It wasn't long before the bailiff opened the doors to Department 20 and summoned the families in. The cameras were rolling and it seemed like all eyes were on us as we walked through the double doors and took our seats to await what we had been anticipating for weeks; the sentencing of Aaron Norman Dunn. I took my usual seat up front on the end while Mom, Esmie, Julie and Tristan sat to my left. The Daly family took their usual seats in the same order they sat throughout the trial. While we were settling in, I could clearly see Aaron Dunn sitting next to his attorneys, as he had every day of the trial. Then a barrage of journalist, camerapersons, photographers, news reporters, etc. scurried into the court room, this time taking their seats in the juror's box instead of to the right of us in the courtroom.

Surprised as they pointed their cameras and microphones right at us, I turned and looked at Mom and Ez in disbelief. Up to this point, cameras had not been permitted inside the court room. My heart sank as I realized they would be capturing every word I said and watching every move I made as this highly publicized case would conclude today. I desperately wanted to be a good ambassador for Christ and for my late husband. In a wave of fear, I asked Michelle (my stand-in) advocate for Ahmanal to get the attention of Scott Triplett so I could let him know I wanted to give my impact statement last, after Michael Daly's brother, but Scott shook his head no and told me I was the only one speaking before the judge. He whispered that he would be reading the other family's statements and then they would conclude with my impact statement. Gripped with fear, I clutched Esmie's hand and we prayed asking the Lord to give me the words to speak.

Judge Orders Death

Assistant Public Defender Amy Rogers and co-defense Counsel Hayes Gable III asked the judge to use his discretion to grant Dunn mercy based on the arguments they posed at trial. He suffered from meth psychosis, they said, and wasn't in his right mind because of the breakup of his marriage and the loss of his daughter. His heroin-addicted father and uncaring mother made his life a very dysfunctional one. So, in other words, he was not to blame for what he did.

The judge agreed to the difficult circumstances of Dunn's life but said they did not come close to excusing what Dunn did on a spring evening a little more than four years ago on Laguna Boulevard in Elk Grove.

"I further find that these killings involved great violence and displayed a high degree of cruelty, viciousness and callous disregard for the human life," Judge Sweet said. "These were random acts of violence perpetrated against complete strangers who became victims literally because they happened to be where they were when they were. The murders, the attempted murders, the manner of their commission and their impact on the survivors and family members are so horrendous that it warrants death instead of life without parole," Judge Sweet concluded.

Now, on Tuesday, July 6th, 2010, Sacramento Superior Court Judge Michael W. Sweet told the defendant, in a loud clear precise voice, "It is the judgment and sentence of this court that you, Aaron Norman Dunn, should be put to death within the walls of San Quentin in the manner prescribed by law upon the date to be fixed by this court in the warrant of execution."

Judge Sweet's imposition of death carried an anticlimactic feel. Taken from a report by Andy Furillo, Sacramento Bee

After Judge Sweet read his statement, Scott Triplett read a letter from the first victim's sister, Dianne McGarry. Her written statement to the defendant said, "Aaron Dunn, you have brought these consequences upon yourself with the actions you chose on March 25, 2006. You are truly a cold, ruthless killer and have expressed no remorse or offered any apologies." After Scott read the letter, the judge ordered a recess and we went on a 30 minute break.

I was relieved the judge allowed a break before my statement as this extra time gave me an opportunity to gather my thoughts and give my niece Ameerah time to get to the court house before reconvening for the second half. I went into the Ladies restroom and was fixing my hair when I bumped into Lynsey Paulo, a reporter for KCRA channel 3. She deeply touched my heart when she said she would be praying for me as I gave my impact statement. It was just what I needed to hear and affirmed that God had a divine purpose for this day and it wouldn't be me speaking but Him.

After she left, I took a deep breath, said a quick prayer and walked back to department 20 where many people, including the press, were waiting to reconvene. Ameerah suddenly bolted off the elevator, afraid she had missed everything. I told her God had answered her prayers as we were on a short recess and I was next. She exhaled and gasped a sigh of relief as we anxiously waited for the bailiff to resume the proceedings.

All Rise

Back inside we sat and waited for the judge's entrance. As I panned the court room, I noticed every seat was full. I counted five sheriff deputies among them. Their presence reminded me that we were dealing with a cold blooded murderer, a man too dangerous to be released back into society ever again.

Anchored with chains to his seat, Aaron sat there still looking unremorseful and unmoved by all that was going on around him. Unlike during the trial when Dunn was dressed in slacks and a button down shirt, wearing his jail pants and white striped button down shirt he looked like a hardened criminal.

My heart was pounding as Judge Sweet again entered the court room. I felt all eyes were on me as I clutched Esmie's hand on my left. On my right, clutching my other hand, was alternate Advocate Michelle (my sister in Christ). I held on for dear life as my mind raced trying to frame what I was going to say. At this point I knew it wasn't about me, it was about Christ and Aaron Norman Dunn. Finally, the moment I had been awaiting for. Judgment day had arrived.

"Mrs. Johnson," the judge said, "would you please stand."

As I slowly rose to deliver my Impact Statement to the judge, media and a packed out court room, Esmie and my advocate stood with me, one on each side. Esmie put her arm around me as I looked at the judge. He gave me an encouraging smile as the court room became totally silent waiting to hear what I had to say. I was generally comfortable with public speaking, but this was nothing like one of my many speaking engagements; this was the sentencing of Aaron Norman Dunn charged with murdering my husband. Where should I start, I thought? Suddenly, the presence of the Lord came over me and I knew many silent prayers were going up for me. As my confidence was restored and the nervousness subsided, I launched into my statement.

I began by thanking the judge, the prosecution and the jurors for their diligence, empathy and professionalism during the trial. Then I referred to the July 4th holiday we had just celebrated which represented freedom, independence and family.

"This 4th of July," I told the judge, "I could still sense the void in my life caused by the absence of my husband. Jon loved all the holidays. Our last 4th of July together Jon bought a huge box of fireworks and dazzled the kids with them."

I nearly choked as I remembered how my dear friend's daughter had been particularly impacted by Jon's absence as she remembered that July 4th when Jon had lit her fireworks and had been so kind and caring towards her.

As I began to dialogue to the judge about Jon's upbringing, Aaron swiveled around in my direction to hear what I had to say. Surprised by his interest, I continued to address the judge but soon shifted my focus toward Aaron. As I spoke, he looked me dead in the eyes and listened intently while I told him he wasn't the only one who grew up with great challenges and family dysfunctions. I passionately expressed how my husband had grown up dirt poor in Arkansas and how after he lost his father at a young age, he had to raise money to move to Oakland, CA, where he was raised around pimps, prostitutes, and drug dealers. Esmie whispered in my ear reminding me of Jon's estranged Mother, so I went on to say how his mother had abandoned Jon, never giving him any love or support and creating a damaging void in his life.

Though Jon began life at a disadvantage, he chose not to let it destroy and ruin his life.

Jon chose to go to school and try to make something out of his life in spite of his rough beginnings. I told Dunn that all the media people in the court room were Jon's colleagues. Then I told Dunn I was a spiritual person who serves a God who forgives.

"Aaron Dunn" I said, looking him dead in the eye, "I have forgiven you for what you have done."

Dunn shocked those of us that could see him when he replied, "Thank you."

I was amazed by what God had put in my mouth to say. What a compassionate, loving caring God He is. He is merciful and gracious even to those who do the greatest wrong. When I heard the response from Aaron Dunn, I knew the Holy Spirit was working in that court room and had moved on Dunn's heart.

I explained to Aaron that my forgiving him did not mean I condoned what he did that night, and then I told him a second time, "I forgive you."

Dunn responded a second time with, "Thank you."

God had orchestrated the order of this day so that only I would speak to the court and to Aaron Dunn. I knew my step-children and Jon's sisters had also wanted to speak, but they did not show up in court that day. I had thought Michael Daly's brother would speak but God wanted me and only me to speak on this day. The experience was so surreal. I closed my statement by telling Aaron Dunn that he would either die in a prison cell of old age or by lethal injection. Either way, I exhorted him to realize God had given him an opportunity this day to give his life to Christ. If he chose to give his life to Christ and serve the living God instead of Satan before he died, God would forgive him and grant him eternal life in heaven as well. Sure that I had said all that God had wanted me to say, I took my seat. I couldn't believe the amazing strength and courage God had given me to say those things to the man that had murdered my husband and turned my world upside down.

I sat and listened as the judge concluded the proceedings and dismissed the court. I watched as Aaron Dunn was swiftly taken away in chains. I saw him nod to the TV cameras on his way out. In just a matter of days he would be moved to his new residence joining the 705 other inmates awaiting execution on death row in San Quentin, CA.

As the doors of the court room were flung open, I was amazed at how quickly the media had exited the court room and reassembled themselves outside. Just minutes earlier they were in the juror's box and now they were in the hall anxiously waiting to get interviews.

As I came out, Lynsey from Channel 3 asked the first question concerning Dunn's response to my statement. I told her that although I was surprised by the defendant's response, I assured her and the rest of the press that Aaron Norman Dunn did respond favorable to my remarks. As they asked more questions, I let them know that I wanted God to be glorified throughout the entire ordeal.

As I have reflected on this experience I can testify that I have seen my favorite Bible promise fulfilled.

And we know that all things work together for good to those who love God, to those who are the called according to His purpose. For whom He foreknew, He also predestined to be conformed to the image of His Son, that He might be the firstborn among many brethren. Moreover, whom He predestined, these He also called; whom He called, these He also justified; and whom He justified, these He also glorified. (Romans 8:28-30)

Reflections

Aaron Dunn wanted so much to be his daughter's father that he was willing to go to any lengths to accomplish it. Aaron was hurt as a result of his upbringing and had a history of making wrong decisions and choices. He chose to follow the dictates of his corrupted heart and life's unfair situations. As evidenced by the tattoo of the grim reaper on his body and the possession of a Satanic Bible, it was obvious to whom his loyalties where given. On that night of March 25th, 2006, fueled by Methamphetamines, Dunn set out on a mission which was commanded by none other than the Devil himself. With his soul made one with Satan, he set out as the angel of death or as his tattoo implied, as the Grim Reaper.

Thinking what he was about to do would free him of all the emotional pain he had endured for years, he drove to Elk

Grove as a servant on a task for his evil master. Precious lives were taken that night and a sense of accomplishment and victory was felt by Dunn as he raised his hands and shouted a victory cheer as each gun blast found its mark. An entire neighborhood was terrified as the angel of death passed over that night.

Neighborhoods went on high alert as families feared to go out to dinner with friends and loved ones. People lost trust in one another and nervously looked over their shoulders wondering about the people they passed on the street. You could feel the uneasiness everywhere you went; whether it was pumping gas at the local gas station or standing in line at the supermarket. Just below the surface of everyone's thinking lurked the fear that another hurting person might explode with rage and wreak havoc on another unsuspecting neighborhood.

All that Aaron did to try and keep his family together destroyed not only his chances to raise his own child but brought destruction and death to two other families leaving them without a husband and a father. Now another man would raise his child.

The Bible tells us, there is a way that seems right to a man but the end leads to death and destruction.[25]

---

[25] See Proverbs 14:12

A Letter to Aaron Dunn

Aaron Dunn, I want you to know that Satan, your boss, turned and did a number on you. That's the way the Grim Reaper operates. He draws you in with lies and deception acting like a loyal friend. Once he captures your will, he influences your decision making and makes you His own. You then become his slave, addicted by the promise of more drugs and alcohol which keeps you coming back for more. You serve a Master who doesn't care if you live or die as long as you live for him and die with him. He can make you wealthy and famous as he has done with many of the Hollywood stars. But then he keeps their souls tucked away in his safety deposit box until he is through with them. When they have done his evil deed, he kills them with drug overdoses, suicide, sickness or some other hideous misfortune.

He didn't make you rich, Aaron, but he made you famous, from a negative standpoint. Though he kept you poor, you didn't sell him your soul, you just gave it to him and then he used you to hurt and destroy the lives of so many others. When you completed your assignment and went to him to get your return, he laughed at you and said he had nothing to give you, never did and never would. He took back his dark cloak, the hoody you wore that night, and left you for dead in a pool of blood on the roadside. That's the way the Devil oper-

ates; that's the way he shows his hatred for all of God's creation. When you become a Satanist, you become a Zombie, a living dead working for a ruthless Master. He chews you up and spits you out and says, "Next." Now you sit on death row awaiting the day of your execution. The grim reaper has come to reap YOU. It was not the jury who sentenced you to death, it was the Devil himself. He cannot create so he uses what God has already created to carry out his acts of cruelty, hatred and death. You wore the dark robe of death to carry out all his evil attacks.

I challenge you, Aaron Dunn, to stand and take off that dark robe of evil and exchange it for a white, spotless robe of righteousness that Christ so desperately wants to give to you. You can receive forgiveness if you would confess to God and ask Him to forgive you with a sincere heart. You can exchange your evil master for the true King of kings and Lord of all lords. Death row can become an opportunity for you to move from death to life. It can become life's row where you can experience God's mercy and step into the joy of the Lord forevermore.

A death sentence, like a terminal illness, gives you the opportunity to make some serious decisions and right choices. You can choose to live eternally or die eternally. The choice is yours. It is my prayer that today you would choose life and live forever with Christ Jesus in the kingdom of heaven, where

He has gone to prepare a place for those who accept His free gift of salvation. I pray that you will accept that free gift and receive God's mercy.

Conclusion

I'm Still Standing

Those who sow in tears shall reap in joy. (Psalm 126:5)

For the victims who have lost a loved one, whether it's due to a violent crime, divorce, abandonment, betrayal of a spouse, friend or family member, I believe healing comes in many forms and degrees depending on the circumstances and the person's personal walk with the Lord. No two people experience loss the same way and our coping mechanisms will differ as well. No one can say how long it will take, but what I do know is that to be restored and made whole is a choice.

I can tell you from experience that it takes hard work to push through the many seemingly insurmountable obstacles caused by the tragic loss of a loved one. It doesn't just happen by chance. Once my feet were planted firmly on solid ground again, I found my way out of the dark pit and into the marvelous light and I'm still standing. Four and a half years later, I have emerged from this life altering experience stronger, wiser and more in love with Jesus Christ! When I was walking around weak, wounded and confused, Satan rode my back like a mink coat trying to get me to destroy myself.

Right after Jon's death I was attacked on all fronts. I found out my husband was leading a double life causing me to have to deal with another woman who claimed to be his wife. Then I found out my husband had five children beside the two I knew about. Then I found out money had been taken out of my bank account just days after the murder to pay off a judgment against Jon. I had to fight with Diana to get the victim's support I was entitled to as Jon's true wife but *I am still standing.*

My identity was stolen by a close family member. Then a fraudulent loan was placed on my home by a trusted friend who said she was just trying to help me refinance. I later found out she made over $32k on the loan and my home went into foreclosure due to the type of loan she sold me. An internet war on Elk Grove On-Line was waged against my character and the legitimacy of my marriage to Jon by my sister-in-law, my step-children and their mother while certain residents of Elk Grove gossiped about my personal life. One of my board members tried to usurp my authority though I was and still am the CEO of the Jon Johnson Assist One Foundation. My house was broken into while I attended a hearing regarding the man who murdered my husband, but *I am still standing.*

I had many people talk about the strength I displayed as I walked through the grieving process. Many said they didn't know how they would have held up if they had found themselves in the same circumstances. If I had not been grounded in the Lord I know I would have dropped out of the race long before I reached the finish line. I could have turned to destructive behaviors and adopted a life of bar-hopping, clubbing and endless parties to drown out the pain, fear and loneliness that permeated my life, but *I am still standing.*

I could have turned to alcohol and drugs.

I could have committed or attempted suicide.

I could have become angry and bitter at the world blaming everybody for my misfortune.

I could have played the victim role and allowed myself to stay paralyzed by depression.

I could have fled my home town right after it happened to escape the memories.

I could have run away and never faced my fears.

I could have jumped in and out of relationships looking for love in all the wrong places.

I could have turned on a loving, merciful God blaming Him for my loss.

I could have become an emotional eater and destroyed my body using food as a coping mechanism to stop the pain, but I didn't do any of the above and *I'm still standing.*

Now I understand what people mean when they say, "what doesn't kill you will make you stronger." Experiencing any one of these attacks could send one into a downward spiral of self-destruction but even though I faced one hit after another, I held my head up while enduring the shame. God gave me strength to keep standing through it all.

So, I would say to you as I conclude this book, regardless of what you may be going through, don't let it break you. You may be forced to bend some against the initial onset but every moment you stand firm you'll find yourself becoming stronger. The tears may flow and you may find yourself standing alone but stand firm until the wind stops blowing. Stand until the hurricane blows over and the earthquake stops! Stand until the blizzard ends and the flood waters recede!

Finally, my brethren, be strong in the Lord, and in the power of His might. Put on the whole armour of God, that ye may be able to stand against the wiles of the devil. For we wrestle not against flesh and blood, but against principalities, against powers, against the rulers of the darkness of this world, against spiritual wickedness in high places.

Wherefore take unto you the whole armour of God, that ye may be able to withstand in the evil day, and having done all, to stand. (Ephesians 6:10-13)

The great gospel artist, Donny McClurkin, so powerfully says, "after you done all you can, you just stand!" *I am still standing!*

May the love of God and the Peace of Salvation be with you all now and forever more.

Blessed be the name of God forever and ever, for wisdom and might are His. And He changes the times and the seasons; He removes kings and raises up kings; He gives wisdom to the wise and knowledge to those who have understanding. He reveals deep and secret things; He knows what is in the darkness, and light dwells with Him. "I thank You and praise You, O God of my fathers; You have given me wisdom and might, and have now made known to me what we asked of You. (Daniel 2:20-23)

For Karen's calendar of events, speaking engagements, book signings or blog web site postings, go to: www. coveredandkept.com or e-mail: karenj@coveredandkept.com

Jon Johnson Assist
One Foundation

The Jon Johnson Assist One Foundation is a 501 (c) 3 nonprofit organization that seeks to bring an intense awareness of the plight of the many abused and abandoned children that are caught up in the foster care system. It assists children in finding loving adoptive families through the creation of cutting-edge informative documentaries, hard-hitting public service announcements and ***call-to-action*** media campaigns.

The goal of JJAOF is to speak up for these "lost" children and let their voices be heard through the sharing of their unique stories, hopes and dreams in a well thought out concise video. As the late Jon Johnson once said, "there are no unwanted children just unfound families."

To that end we will:

- Form collaborative partnerships with foster family/adoption agencies
- Produce hard hitting Public Service Announcements, documentaries and media campaigns
- Partner with media giants to air programs and to aid JJAOF in the dissemination of compelling messages to the community
- Proactively pursue positive connections between loving qualified families and children who are yearning to find a loving home
- Provide education to the community about this systemic issue
- Network children from foster family agencies with mentors to provide hands-on encouragement and real life coaching and spiritual guidance especially to the children who aging out of the system

- Provide Jon Johnson Assist One Scholarship Awards in communications specifically earmarked for foster children

You can make a difference! Your gift can help the Jon Johnson Assist One foundation meet our lofty goals to keep these displaced children out of the penal system, off the streets, off drugs and out of the morgues-**one child at a time**!

I want to take this opportunity to thank my current board members, Coach Gary Henson, Doug Hill, Ronnie Cobb and Jackie Hunt and all our past board members for supporting me and helping Jon's vision for the Assist One Foundation continue even after Jon's untimely death. Each of you hold a very special place near and dear in my heart and have helped to make this powerful tool effective in the lives of so many children.

http://jjassistone.org

About the Author

Karen R. Johnson is a fun loving, high energy, God centered woman who enjoys nature and helping people live life healthfully. Karen, graduated from Long Beach State University where she obtained her Bachelor of Arts degree in Radio, Television and Film. She worked in the cable television industry for five years before changing careers.

She is a Certified Personal Fitness Trainer and Group Instructor and has over 25 years of practical group exercise experience and 10 years of personal fitness training experience. Karen's motto is "fitness is a way of life" so she founded "Try 7 Fitness for Heaven." Her life's mission is to make a difference by teaching health reform through seminars and health consultations, covering such topics as disease prevention, causes and cures. She has managed to pursue the two things she enjoys most in life; fitness and public speaking and is a passionate inspirational speaker.

Karen is also the President and Chairwoman of the Jon Johnson Assist One Foundation and is determined to make a difference in the lives of children by bringing awareness about the plight of children awaiting adoption, and the need for health reform for our children. She currently resides in Elk Grove, California with her son, Tristan Gardner, who is a full-time student at Sacramento State University pursuing a Bachelor of Science degree in Criminal Justice.

Additional Thanks

Mom, you were the motivation behind me hanging in there and I know you really wanted this story to be told to help other women who might be experiencing some of the similar things I went through during my marriage to Jon. I want to thank you for your willingness to recount my earlier years growing up and allow our lives to be shared with the readers. Your willingness to be a part of this process by allowing me to read countless pages of the manuscript to you late at night and early in the morning over these past years has been a blessing. Your guidance through this process has been wonderful. I want to thank you for loving me unconditionally as you have always been in my corner even when we didn't agree. I love you! You are an amazing mom and woman.

To my dear sister, Patricia: I salute you for all that you have done for me over the years and your suggestions on marketing and management of this project. Though you are only two years older, you have been like a second mother to me especially when I really needed guidance in my earlier years of development. You are a great listener, open and honest with your communication and I love that about you. You have always been in my corner with my best interest in mind. I could have never had a sister better than you. You are a shining star; full of light, love and wisdom. I love you very much.

To my dear sister Cherryl who also stood in for me when I was weak, confused and disoriented. I thank you for your wise counsel when others were assassinating my character. You assured me I had done nothing wrong, reminded me I came from a strong family and suggested I hold my head up. Your words of courage and strength spoke volumes to me and helped me to grieve with dignity. I am forever grateful and love you very much.

To my dear brother Ronnie, I am so thankful to have a brother that is so caring and willing to help out whenever needed, never complaining or criticizing. Though you are a man of few words, your actions reveal your deep love and care that is rare to find in a man and a brother. Thank you, I love you very much.

To my precious twin sister Kathie, I know whenever I hurt you hurt; therefore, I know it was extremely difficult for you to walk through this experience with me as you were challenged with the issues of life at that time as well. But I want to let you know I am in your corner and I am so proud of your decision to make positive changes in your life.

To Ronnie Cobb, who believed in me and the importance of this story being written: Your encouraging words ignited the spark that challenged me to write one page a day until the book was finished.

I owe a special thanks to Angel Thomas, an angel sent from above for such a time as this. I appreciate you putting your life on hold to read "Covered & Kept" with an open heart and a prayerful spirit. I appreciate how you gave reading and editing a top priority during a time when your life was really crazy due to moving and opening your new office. Thank you for delving right in and reading it non-stop for seven hours so I could meet my deadline.

I would also like to thank Anthony White, for reading the manuscript, offering words of encouragement but more importantly for reading with a critical eye making suggestions and constructive criticism during the editing process. I thank you for being so selfless, kind and thoughtful.

To my long time dear friend Allen Wayne Warren, I want to thank you for being a man of your word standing by my side every step of the way during the grieving process. When others were no where to be found you stood in the gap. Thank you for your friendship and a listening ear, for supporting the Jon Johnson Assist One Foundation by sitting on the board and with your acts of love, kindness and support.

A very special thanks to my sister in Christ and dear friend, Felicia Byrd, for being by my side right after the tragedy, during the trial and for being a loyal and trusted friend while asking nothing in return. You are a woman after God's heart, always ready and willing to help from being a contributor, to reading the manuscript, and offering suggestions all along the way. I love you like a sister.

Esmie, you have been a real trooper. You have been with me for the good times and the bad times. I just want to extend a very special thanks to you for your love and support from the time we first met, during my marriage to Jon and right after the murder, to your dedication during the court trial, for picking me up, paying for parking, and buying me lunch when I had no money. I thank you for your insightful guidance to write this Christ-centered book that I hope to share with the world. You allowed me to vent my feelings while writing and editing, not judging but nurturing me through this emotion filled, tedious process. Your countless hours of hard work have helped me capture what was in my heart adding clarity and authenticity to my life experiences. You helped me communicate what I believe God wants us to say to the readers in these last days.

To Pastor Arthur Branner, beloved brother in Christ, I want to thank you for officiating at my wedding and also at Jon's funeral. Each represents a very pivotal point in my life journey and I am so blessed you have been with me during the highs and lows of my life. Your brotherly love, wise counsel, prayers and mediation through the many trials has been a life raft in the storm and I am forever grateful.

I also want to acknowledge my niece Ameerah, and nephew Andrew, for your prayers and standing in the gap for me right after the tragedy, my many nephews, and Pastor Ivan Williams for your loving support and encouragement. To my Capitol City Church family, my adopted St. Paul family, close friends and those who prayed and supported me in my deepest, darkest hours, I love you for standing in the gap. Each of you has touched my life in a very special way that words alone cannot express. Thank You!

I would also like to give a special thanks to my editors. I am forever grateful for your gentle guidance and willingness to work with me in moving this project forward by faith. Each of you were very professional and non-judgmental in assisting in anyway you could to help bring this book project to life. Thanks!!

Editors:
- Cheryl Moore
- Pam McLaughlin
- Dr. Larry Keefauver